CINEMA AS THERAPY

Loss is an inescapable reality of life, and individuals need to develop a capacity to grieve in order to mature and live life to the full. Yet most western movie audiences live in cultures that do not value this necessary process and filmgoers finding themselves deeply moved by a particular film are often left wondering why. In *Cinema as Therapy*, John Izod and Joanna Dovalis set out to fill a gap in work on the conjunction of grief, therapy and cinema.

Looking at films including *Million Dollar Baby*, *The Son's Room*, *Birth* and *The Tree of Life*, *Cinema as Therapy* offers an understanding of how deeply emotional life can be stirred at the movies. Izod and Dovalis note that cinema is a medium that engages people in a virtual dialogue with their own and their culture's unconscious, more deeply than is commonly thought. By analysing the meaning of each film and the root cause of the particular losses featured, the authors demonstrate how our experiences in the movie theatre create an opportunity to prepare psychologically for the inevitable losses we must all eventually face. In recognising that the movie theatre shares symbolic features with both the church and the therapy room, the reader sees how it becomes a sacred space where people can encounter the archetypal and ease personal suffering through laughter or tears, without inhibition or fear, to reach a deeper understanding of themselves.

Cinema as Therapy will be essential reading for therapists, students and academics working in film studies and looking to engage with psychological studies in depth as well as filmgoers who want to explore their relationship with the screen. The book includes a glossary of Jungian and Freudian terms, which enhances the clarity of the text and the understanding of the reader.

John Izod is Emeritus Professor of screen analysis at the University of Stirling. He has published several books, including *Screen, Culture, Psyche: A Post-Jungian Approach to Working with the Audience* (Routledge).

Joanna Dovalis is a marriage and family therapist with a doctorate in clinical psychology, specialising in grief work. She works in private practice in southern California, USA.

CINEMA AS THERAPY

Grief and transformational film

John Izod and Joanna Dovalis

Routledge
Taylor & Francis Group

LONDON AND NEW YORK

First published 2015
by Routledge
27 Church Road, Hove, East Sussex, BN3 2FA

and by Routledge
711 Third Avenue, New York, NY 10017

Routledge is an imprint of the Taylor & Francis Group, an informa business

British Library Cataloguing in Publication Data
A catalogue record for this book is available from the British Library

Library of Congress Cataloging in Publication Data
Izod, John, 1940–
Cinema as therapy : grief and transformational film / John Izod and Joanna Dovalis.
pages cm
Includes bibliographical references and index.
1. Loss (Psychology) in motion pictures. 2. Grief in motion pictures.
3. Bereavement–Psychological aspects. I. Dovalis, Joanna. II. Title.
PN1995.9.L59I95 2015
791.43'653–dc23
2014030158

ISBN: 978-0-415-71867-7 (hbk)
ISBN: 978-0-415-71868-4 (pbk)
ISBN: 978-1-315-73158-2 (ebk)

Typeset in Bembo
by Cenveo Publisher Services

Printed and bound in Great Britain by
TJ International Ltd, Padstow, Cornwall

CONTENTS

ACKNOWLEDGEMENTS

We gratefully recognise the generous advice we received from Jana Branch, Isabelle Gourdin-Sangouard, Katharina Lindner, Nadin Mai, Kathleen Morison and George Rosch.

Earlier versions of certain chapters were published previously. We acknowledge with thanks their editors' permission to republish them here. '*Birth*: Eternal Grieving of the Spotless Mind' in *Jung and Film II: The Return* ed. Christopher Hauke and Luke Hockley (London: Routledge, July 2011) 66–91. '*Tsotsi*', *Spring* 76 (Fall 2006) 2, 317–24. '*Million Dollar Baby*: Boxing Grief', *Kinema* 24 (Fall 2005) 5–22. 'Grieving, Therapy, Cinema and Kieslowski's *Trois Couleurs: Bleu*', *The San Francisco Jung Institute Library Journal* 25, 3 (Summer 2006) 49–73. 'Grieving, Therapy, Cinema and Kieslowski's *Trois Couleurs: Blanc*', *Jung Journal*, 2, 3 (Summer 2008) 39–57. 'Grieving, Therapy, Cinema and Kieslowski's *Trois Couleurs: Rouge*', *Jung Journal*, 2, 4, (Fall 2008) 70–94. 'Physician, Heal Thyself: *The Son's Room*', *Kinema* 37 (Spring 2012) 5–20.

1

INTRODUCTION

Cinema is pre-eminently the medium that engages people in a virtual dialogue with their own and their culture's unconscious, more deeply than is commonly taken for granted. The movie theatre shares symbolic features with both the church and the therapy room: all are sacred spaces where people can encounter the archetypal and ease personal suffering, in the case of the cinema whether through laughter or tears, without inhibition or fear. Yet bizarrely, there is a dearth of writing from a psychological perspective on the conjunction of grief, therapy and cinema. The present authors propose to occupy that gap.

We focus on grief for several reasons. Inescapable in life, it frequently comprises the core element of feature films, both popular and artistic. This is not accidental. Individuals need to develop the capacity to grieve in order to mature fully. Yet most Western movie audiences live in cultures that do not teach people how to engage in this necessary process. Personal growth becomes stunted, choices limited by what has been left behind. For that reason, depth therapists find that much of their work becomes devoted to clients' unresolved grief.

Archetypal symbols penetrate the emotions at a deep level and give the cinema its power to bypass the conscious state and go into the unconscious. Immersion in film viewing distracts the ego so that it disengages from its usual function as the primary filter of awareness. In fact the ego is busy anchoring itself in and assembling the story from the film's plot (the stream of shocks provided by images, dialogue and sounds). Meanwhile, the unconscious, stimulated by symbols in the film, releases archetypal energies in the spectator's psyche. Through their involvement in this process, spectators are freed from their usual inhibitions, which allows them to connect to their emotional lives. In identifying certain characters or familiar situations with aspects of their own lives, they project disowned parts of the self onto the screen. That enables them to receive what the screen presents them with as it reflects their own projections back at them. Cinema is thus, as we shall see, an important agent for the stimulation of inward growth and the process of individuation. It has the capacity to provide viewers with a transformative intellectual and psychic experience in which self-discovery can occur.

The large screen functions in this manner as a psychological mirror of images and sounds that simultaneously partake of and invest in the two realities, the inner and outer lives that occupy healthy people. Within the affect-charged psychological realm that cinema sustains, self-reflection may occur and the meaningfulness of the experience evolve. In the darkened auditorium, the threshold of consciousness is lowered, opening the way to an encounter behind the curtain of the phenomenal world. When the boundary between the seen and the unseen is loosened, spectators may, as we have said, be drawn into a realm populated by images that interact with and reflect aspects of their *personal* psyche. Ultimately it can facilitate growth, transformation, and a maturing of the individual's total personality.

However, film theatres are designed to foster shared experience and become, as the auditorium lights go down, a *temenos* or sacred enclosure. They create the social and cultural conditions necessary to shared remembering of forgotten or misplaced memories. As a liminal space or container, the cinema functions as the centring source of such shared images. This helps intensify the emotional experiences that films can provoke and assists their digestion. As a medium of images (both visual and aural), cinema is able to bring us back to our own and the culture's psychological depths. Thus spectators may also be afforded *transpersonal* experiences which sometimes allow them to encounter the numinous (Dovalis, 2003: 2–4).

We should mention that we believe it difficult to experience films with intense emotional engagement anywhere other than the cinema. Being in an environment that is not prone to interruption produces a more creative relationship, sinking one into the depths of the film (or the relationship with the therapist) and ultimately the inner life. For our part, we see a resemblance between the inner life experiences of the client going to therapy and those of the cinemagoer.

Entry into the subtle imaginal realm that cinema can illuminate presupposes a willingness to explore the unknown in a way at once creative and new. Working in this realm distinguishes depth psychology from other psychologies. The work is shaped by the belief that transformation is virtually impossible unless urged by strong affect. Knowledge alone does not suffice to promote change: real understanding is acquired through the synthesis and digestion of the feelings that accompany cognition. Psychological shifts seldom occur other than when affect meets the assimilation of new insights (Dovalis, 2003: 5). Furthermore, as Marie-Louise von Franz wrote, 'this psychic growth cannot be brought about by a conscious effort of will power, but happens involuntarily and naturally...' (1964: 161).

In the cinema spectators are more open to being moved emotionally than in their daily lives. In the movie theatre they do not need to defend themselves against other unwanted emotions such as the shameful feeling of exposure that they might have to contend with when revealing themselves in a real relationship. Thus, film allows viewers more freely to surrender themselves to their present feelings (Dovalis, 2003: 5). Indeed, it seems that audiences have an appetite for the kinds of stimulus that may put them in the way of psychic change. John Beebe has observed that cinema and psychoanalysis have grown up concurrently, close siblings nurtured on a common zeitgeist, and sharing a common drive to explore and realise the psyche (1996: 579).

> As Jung was radically optimistic about the healing possibilities of the self, so audiences seem to approach films, like Dorothy and her friends off to see the Wizard, with the expectation of a miracle, an extraordinary effect upon one's state of mind. Often enough this hope is disappointed, and yet there are films which induce an unexpected new consciousness in many who view them... [This] may be why film viewing and criticism have become such important activities within our culture: in addition to wanting to be entertained, the mass audience is in constant pursuit, as if on a religious quest, of the transformative film.
>
> *(Beebe, 1996: 582)*

The goal of transformation is individuation, the process of psychic growth that occurs independently of the ego's will. Phyllis Kenevan has discerned three ways in which, when it happens, a person's individuation may proceed. It may occur unconsciously, or it may progress through self-motivated, conscious reflection; alternatively guidance from a trained analyst may lead the growth of self-awareness (1999: 14). For our part, we endorse Beebe's opinion that another way should be identified since films can function as an active mirroring guide with potential therapeutic value for spectators. That appears to be the case, whether or not those spectators who experience one or a number of films as such a stimulus, consciously realise the therapeutic effect they have had. Our intention is to augment their consciousness of that effect.

For their part, depth psychotherapists recognise the unavoidable condition of human suffering as potentially serving transformation. Suffering that has been metabolised and integrated holds the possibility of consciously expediting a person's individuation if he or she is psychologically and spiritually prepared. The process of grieving, no less than other forms of anguish, can spur individuation. Greg Mogenson says, 'the more precisely we imagine our losses, the more psychological we become' (1992: xi–xii).

> From the imaginal point of view, the end of life is not the end of soul. The images continue. Deep inside the grief of the bereaved, the dead are at work, making themselves into religion and culture, imagining themselves into soul.
>
> *(Mogenson, 1992: xi)*

The imaginal, then, can dislodge the suffering in grief from its intolerable state frozen in the personality and the body, into a psychological space that is deeply connected to the Self (in the sense of the unified psyche). As we shall discover in our analysis of *Three Colours: Blue*, grieving, when actively dealt so that it works a transformation in the mourner's personality, is intensely creative (Mogenson, 1992: xii). Like any other creative process it is by no means exclusively rational and in order to engage the psyche must conjure up curiosity and openness. That, as we have mentioned, is something that films can sponsor most effectively. We wrote our book to facilitate this self-reflective process – both for our readers and ourselves.

We first put together a list of feature films designed to illustrate aspects of grieving, and did this in the initial stages of considering what the themes of the book should be. At that point we reckoned that what might result from analysing these films could be a wry treatise on how to prepare for death. However, feature films are not first and foremost educational tracts but stories and mythmaking. They rarely seek to propagate a thesis although some may offer 'what if' speculations. So we decided, rather than look in feature films for some form of allegorical guide to psychoanalysis, it better suited our purpose to think of grief in the context of fictional characters' responses to the suffering it brings – whether they resist or embrace what chance or fate delivers.

The fate of fictional characters was not our only consideration. Our choice of films is also in part explained by Terrence Malick's observation that certain films

> can enable small changes of heart, changes that mean the same thing: to live better and to love more. And even an old movie in poor and beaten condition … can give us that. What else is there to ask for?
>
> *(Malick, 1979)*

From the psychoanalytic perspective, as we have seen, Beebe developed the complementary observations that 'there are films which induce an unexpected new consciousness in many who view them' and that 'in addition to wanting to be entertained, the mass audience is in constant pursuit, as if on a religious quest, of the transformative film' (1996: 582). The phrase 'transformative film' is worth re-emphasising because, although much of our attention will be given to characters undergoing emotional conflicts encountered in the narrative arc, we soon realised that we needed to widen our focus. In most of the films we have selected, therefore, their aesthetic beauty, not only storylines but images, the play of colour and light, the subtleties of sound effects and music, all combine to create associations in viewers' minds of the transformative kind that Beebe writes about. We were not concerned only, therefore, with emotions felt by characters, but also with those communicated to the audience at large, and to ourselves in particular. We chose only films that excited and stayed with us long after the screening, both of us aware that subjective, emotional engagement is a prerequisite for making Jungian readings.

The intellectual core of this study derives from a Jungian base because of its vast conceptual frame which, in relation to our work here, encompasses symbolism, the archetypes, myth, the religious function of the psyche, synchronicity, Self, spirit, and soul. Jung's work is thus teleological. Freud's more reductive psychoanalytic theory gives us a deep understanding of the characters' psychological organisation. In seeking authorities on coping with loss, we found Greg Mogenson's concept of the imaginal realm in the mourning process grounded the way we think about grieving. We also examine grief through Elisabeth Kübler-Ross's work, which describes a series of stages that many clinicians have observed: denial, anger, bargaining and negotiation, depression and finally acceptance. A further source is John Bowlby's focus on the internal processes of grieving, which include a three-phase progress that, citing him, 'begins with anger and anxiety, proceeds through pain and despair and if fortune smiles, ends with hope' (1961: 330). Murray Stein writes authoritatively about liminality and, because so many of our characters move through transitional phases, our debt to him is evident throughout, reaching its culmination in *The Tree of Life*.

We found that some films, because of their specific content, called for the application of particular theories to assist in their psychological interpretation. For example, in *Trois Couleurs: Blanc*, D. W. Winnicott's writing on transitional objects illuminated the analysis of the lead characters and their cultures. Two analysts Aldo Carotenuto (a Jungian) and Stephen Mitchell (Freudian) help us understand the themes of love and suffering in *Spring, Summer, Autumn, Winter … and Spring*. Paradoxically, for a film that features a leading character who will never have heard of therapy, *Morvern Callar* required the attention of three authorities. Edward Edinger provided an allegory for the evolution of soul from chaos to wholeness in his work on alchemy. Rose-Emily Rothenberg led us to find and understand the orphan, while Michael Meade elaborates the themes of fate and destiny that we employed in identifying the ways they play out in Morvern's life. Because of its extraordinary impact, *The Tree of Life* incited us to develop our methodology significantly: Jennifer Barker's work on embodiment in the cinema was fundamental. Murray Stein furnished understanding of the mid-life journey and the interplay between feminine and masculine consciousness. Finally, Paul Bishop's scholarly insights into Jung's *Answer to Job* were invaluable, enabling us to close out our reading of that film.

We have organised our working relationship to draw on our respective areas of expertise. Dovalis, a psychotherapist, uses Freudian and Jungian theory in her writing and private practice. Izod, who teaches film studies at the University of Stirling, brings to the project his interest in living myth. They have been writing together for some years, mutually celebrating that what they produce together neither could achieve without the other.

We conceived this book with both a general and a professional readership in mind. We said at the start that grieving is an inescapable reality of life. From that point of reference, it follows that many filmgoers (like ourselves) will find themselves deeply moved by a particular film and be left wondering why. Our book has an informal educational goal in offering such people an understanding of how deeply the emotional life can be stirred at the movies. Thus, the book's potential value extends beyond the ten films studied here.

For film studies departments our work encourages students to engage with the psychological reading of films in depth. It is intended to function as an interdisciplinary bridge – not only to link the two areas of study, but, as we shall claim, for its worth in personal development as well. Meanwhile for psychotherapists and clients, the book may provide a guide that may further explain and augment their experiences of grieving in the cinema. Most importantly, for filmgoers, students, therapists and their clients alike, it creates an opportunity to prepare psychologically for the inevitable losses we must all eventually face. For the deeply engaged reader, our analyses of the films are intended to generate a container for past grief and a template that might help hold future suffering.

Beyond our personal engagement with them, we selected films that enabled us to explore certain kinds of responses to grief by the main characters. The different forms of anguish that grip them call forth (just as when clients present in the therapy room) different theoretical positions. We have divided the book into three parts. In the first, through *Birth*, *Tsotsi*, and *Million Dollar Baby* we examine characters coming from very different societies with radically different lives and personal histories. They share nevertheless a common trait in being locked into particular patterns of grieving caused by devastating and undigested loss. All of them remain stuck, unable to move forward with their lives no matter what social or personal conventions govern their attitudes and rule their day-to-day behaviour.

Anna, the rich and beautiful woman at the centre of *Birth*, is the epitome of this condition. Partly because equally self-absorbed family members and friends surround her, she has not succeeded in accepting the loss of her husband after ten years of widowhood. A decade after her husband's sudden death, still in denial, Anna has not learnt that loss is an event that 'requires that some part of the individual be left behind and grieved before the process of transition and rebuilding can occur' (Humphrey and Zimpfer, 1996: 1).

As we have said, Elisabeth Kübler-Ross describes five stages of mourning. Anna locks herself in the first stage, denial. In the South African film *Tsotsi*, a gang leader uses a potent mix of poverty and rage to repress unacknowledged grief. The slum environment of desperate unemployment is his spur to plunder the *nouveau riche* elite as if their possessions were his by right. This violent thief – not long out of adolescence – exhibits the early symptoms of Kübler-Ross's grieving process, namely denial (which happened so long ago he has forgotten it) and the anger in which he has got stuck. In fact, he behaves like an infant suffering developmental arrest who believes himself entitled to whatever he wants. Only when he discovers the feminine (a thematic motif we shall uncover repeatedly in later chapters) does he begin to develop toward acceptance of responsibility for what he has done and who he is.

Frankie Dunn, the bruised boxing trainer in *Million Dollar Baby*, is a middle-aged man immersed in an all-male culture. Cut off socially from women and psychologically from the feminine, he exists in a milieu where displaying, or even feeling grief is acceptable only when someone dies. His business is contracting because, since suffering painful earlier losses his mindset (focusing on self-protection rather than attack) is unsuited to the aggressive sport he teaches. Eventually, however, a new and devastating loss causes him to progress step by step through Kübler-Ross's entire cycle, guided by people whom he can no longer ignore. Each of the three characters, Anna, Tsotsi and Frankie, illustrates another aspect of the grieving process as a cycle. Not only must grieving be undergone and understood for the cycle to be completed, but losses accumulate throughout life. If an earlier traumatic event is not consciously experienced, a later loss will trigger issues left unresolved.

The transformational potential of the three films that we discuss in Part 1 is mainly attained through the spectator's engagement with the leading characters. However, the structural organisation across a film's narrative of a character's cathartic development is not the only way of communicating to an audience the sense that a film can change one's perspective on life, tried and tested though that method is. Indeed, arguably, it may be precisely because the dramatic life-journey of a hero is so commonplace a device in the organising of pleasure-giving screen stories that it may actually be less effective in bringing about that impact with spectators than other methods.

In *Million Dollar Baby*, Frankie has, aside from his love of the sport, another near secret delight: he reads the poetry of W. B. Yeats. Toward the close of his story he recites 'The Lake Isle of Innisfree', which evokes an idea of paradise that can be reached in the peace of 'the deep heart's core'. Frankie's readiness to embrace his own transformation is thus signalled in part through his love of a tranquil poetry: it's a reminder of the obvious, that the arts move audiences.

Jung emphasised that wholeness is not so much a matter of achieving perfection as completion. This thought acts as an effective epigraph for our account of the treatment of grief in Kieslowski's *Three Colours Trilogy*, films which form the basis of the book's second part. The very aesthetics of these films imbue them with transformational energy. Through them we examine the means and processes by which six characters deal with their suffering by moving beyond idealisation and entering into relation with their shadow. Their progress enables them, after recovering from painful loss, to enter into what they hope will become real, loving relationships that achieve a sense of wholeness.

We open *Trois Couleurs: Bleu* with an account indebted to Murray Stein of the necessity for an individual going through a process of psychological change to create a transitional frame of mind – which Stein terms a liminal space. Julie, the film's leading character, gradually (and reluctantly) is drawn into this transitional space where her old identity gradually erodes as her new one emerges. By the very fact of changing, she resembles Anna only in being a grieving widow of striking beauty. We show with Mogenson's help how Julie's creativity enables her to make use of that liminal space to complete her grieving. In fact, *Blue* works not only through the engagement of the lead character in the creation of music, but directly through the film when that music is heard.

Trois Couleurs: Blanc is the second film in the trilogy. Its main character, Karol, a man of pallid personality, has regressed into dependency after marrying Dominique and moving with her from his Polish home. There his complacency is the social norm, whereas in Paris (her home) the challenging milieu creates psychic pressure which he fails to adapt to. As a consequence of his emerging dependency, we were persuaded to give primacy in this chapter to D. W. Winnicott's theories. Karol is a plain example of an individual who 'may be successful in the world, but success based in the false self leads to an intensification of the sense of emptiness and despair' (Winnicott in Abram, 1996: 84). People who protect their true self in this way disrupt their intimate relationships, making it impossible for others to connect with them. This is the condition of Karol's marriage and the predicament he has to resolve.

In *Trois Couleurs: Rouge*, which concludes the trilogy, the stage on which the characters perform is vast, as it was with *Blue* and *White*. The intimate lives of four individuals (like those of Julie, Karol and Dominique) play out against the backdrop of the social and psychological collective. Here, the iconography of commercial advertising is eye-catchingly strapped across the screen. It raises the question of beauty and its role in orienting psyche and culture. Beauty in advertising is seen to betray by perverting the deeper truth of desire which it suborns to commercial profitability. In their personal lives, all four characters in *Red* experience the trauma of betrayal. It is their initial reactions and later the meaning they assign to betrayal that distinguish Auguste, Karin, the Judge and Valentine from each other. *Red* shows how complicated it can be to create a loving relationship, and how blind chance can powerfully intervene. This is key: the synchronicities that occur weave their fates and, when the conclusion of the trilogy unites all three stories, links them with great numbers of people.

Four films make up the final part, namely *The Son's Room* followed by *Spring, Summer, Autumn, Winter ... and Spring*, *Morvern Callar* and finally *The Tree of Life*. None of them can be read without recognising that either psychological or spiritual experience must be taken on in the process of healing profound loss. But only two of these films reveal how the psychological and the spiritual may be brought into relation in the mourning process.

In *The Son's Room*, the principal characters – a bereaved family – suffer numbing grief. Although they eventually recover a sense of connection with life, none is drawn toward exploring the consolations of either organised religion or personal spirituality. For them, the hierarchical dogmas and the authority of a priesthood that does not connect with the emotional crises suffered by the bereaved renders the Catholic Church at best irrelevant and at worst inimical to personal healing. The archetypal realm stands outside the family's ambit and, keeping faith with its characters, *The Son's Room* does not engage with it either.

In the three remaining films the main characters transcend personal suffering. Passing through the final stage of grieving, which is acceptance, they enter into a state of wholeness and make contact with the numinous. In the Korean film *Spring, Summer, Autumn, Winter ... and Spring*, that connection is made as the fruit of a deliberate, rigorously disciplined struggle for spiritual enlightenment. The film centres on the lives of two monks in a Buddhist temple – a Master and his younger successor. We focus not only on how their devotions endow them with spirituality, but also on how the Master's limited understanding of the nature of the psychological life makes him a poor guide to the Young Monk when ordinary human passions waylay the latter. With the help of Carotenuto and Mitchell we develop a psychological understanding of the characters. That in turn allows us to distinguish how the film demonstrates some of the similarities and differences between Buddhist philosophy and Jungian theory.

Morvern Callar, a simple and affectionate supermarket worker in her early twenties, has lived with her lover, a writer, for some time. Nothing could have prepared her for returning home at the end of her shift to find her boyfriend lying dead by his own hand beside their Christmas tree. She is traumatised to the degree that she cannot tell anyone, even her girlfriend, and is incapable of asking for help. Directed by the orphan archetype, she is alone in her inner world, knows nothing of therapy, and has no links to any church or social support. Thanks to the instinctual side of the archetype that she neither denies nor refuses, she finds her own way. Her passion for the music she once shared with the dead man leads her in a creative mourning process that is not based on rationality. It takes her from horror and isolation to a new psychological birth. She is her own alchemist, purifying the dross and refining it to newly made gold. Responding to the film's subtle creation of Morvern's inner world in our writing, we found guidance in Rothenberg's depiction of orphan psychology (2001), Edinger's synthesis of alchemy and the individuation journey (1985), and Meade's mythologising the shift from fate to destiny (2010). Above all, *Morvern Callar* exemplifies the union of the psychological and spiritual life.

Chapter 11 starts the analysis of *The Tree of Life* by extending the methodological remarks offered above. We found it necessary to develop our working practice, in particular by bringing into play concepts of embodiment proposed by Barker and others. Their work enabled us to reflect on spectators' responses to this film as well as our own experiences.

In the final chapter, *The Tree of Life* presents spectators with a mystery. On first viewing that appears to be a consequence of the way plot points are hidden. A second viewing allows spectators to clarify their understanding of the plot, but the mysteries remain since they are based at a deeper level than what happens to whom, where and when. Nevertheless, the lives of a young family with three sons growing up in the 1950s are readily discerned. With the help of Stein's *Solar Conscience/ Lunar Conscience* (1993), we gain a psychological understanding of the family's dynamics and the interplay between the feminine and the masculine consciousness. Beneath that, the film's beautiful images and music create a liminal field exciting the unconscious as they draw us into nothing less than a twenty-first century myth of the Universe's creation and evolution.

PART 1

Encountering phases of grief

2

BIRTH (2004)

Eternal grieving of the spotless mind

Most summary plotlines of *Birth* state that Anna, a 35-year-old woman widowed for ten years, is on the point of remarrying when a boy comes to her apartment and announces that he is her former husband. In line with this précis, discussions among writers who have taken Jonathan Glazer's film as seriously as it merits tend to have given primacy of focus to Nicole Kidman's Anna. In privileging this character they are responding to cues latent in the text (some obvious, others less so). To mention the most obvious, the emotionally wracking predicament that afflicts the lissom widow is an inevitable source of narrative interest when a leading film star is playing that protagonist.

David Lowery remarks of Anna's grieving,

> If you look at this as the story of a woman who comes to believe her husband has been reincarnated, you are only seeing half of the film; you're missing the story of a woman realizing just how much she loved her husband, and how damaged her loss has left her.
>
> *(Lowery, 2004)*

We contend, however, that the boy's story has equal thematic weight with Anna's. Not that the mystery surrounding the claims of 10-year-old Sean to be Anna's dead husband has been ignored. On the contrary, it has been considered extensively because the narrative thrust bears on the plausibility or otherwise of his claim. However, the intense experience that the boy undergoes has been insufficiently understood. Questions that have been largely disregarded include why a child should make such a claim in the first place; why (resolutely defying the outrage of his elders) he should stick with it courageously; and why he should then suddenly give it up.

The first words (heard in darkness before light hits the screen) are a lecturer repudiating the idea of reincarnation: 'I'm a man of science. I just don't believe that mumbo-jumbo.' This is Anna's husband Sean (Michael Desautels), who has framed his response in a mock scenario the irony of which echoes through the film.

> Let me say this: If I lost my wife and the next day a little bird landed on my windowsill, looked me right in the eye and in plain English said, 'Sean, it's me, Anna: I'm back.' What can I say? I guess I'd believe her. Or I'd want to... I'd be stuck with the bird!

The opening shot establishes a register at odds with Sean's complacent sarcasm. As he jogs through the wintry gloaming of Manhattan's Central Park, the Steadicam glides after him, not at eye level but about twenty feet above the snow-covered path. The shot continues without a cut for a long minute and a half while the man moves forward resolutely. At the screen's periphery, dim lights, vehicles and apartments bear witness to the city's life, but at such a distance that the runner is isolated by the snowfields around him, the absence of other people in the park and the camera's vicarious eye. That unblinking gaze insists on the actuality of what it shows while simultaneously abstracting it from reality via the gliding over-head view of the runner's back. But the black-clad and hooded man, a shadow figure if ever there was one, is brutishly anchored to the earth as he labours onward. The effect of trailing him is like attempting flight that cannot quite break free from Earth. The aesthetics carry this tension. As Darren Hughes notes, it is barely colour photography at all, but predominantly blacks, greys and browns (2006). On the sound track, Alexandre Desplat's Prelude propels movement. Flutes and bells sparkle sweetly over jabs of brass like metronomes that insist on time's passage, while sombre, spreading strings mark out the symphonic scale of what is to come.

Like other commentators (for example, Hughes, Ibid.; Chaw, 2004 whom the opening shot reminds of the labyrinth sequence in *The Shining*; and Lowery, 2004) we notice resemblances to Kubrick's work. These are particularly marked in the establishment of a register comparable to *Eyes Wide Shut*. As Izod has written else-where, both films offer a take on the New York world that they project which embraces both expressionist fantasy and observable reality. Shimmying between the rational and the fantastic, neither film locks into either mode to the exclusion of the other (2006: 52).

Tension between contraries becomes explicit when the title *Birth* is superim-posed on the second shot as Sean runs toward an underpass. Reaching it (silhou-etted to stress his isolation), he staggers, collapses and dies. The short tunnel has, reasonably enough, been likened to both womb and tomb (Cozzalio, 2006). In evoking the birth canal it provides an image of a transitional space creating move-ment from one reality to another. However, the final shot of this sequence pulls back to reveal that Sean has fallen beneath a bridge. It makes an obvious emblem for connection; and in retrospect we can see that thematically Sean could not have crossed over since he has given up on maintaining emotional connection. More immediately, the bridge underscores the thematic relevance of the next shot (explicitly connecting contraries) in which a baby is born. Death before birth. Glazer conjoins the opposing termini of life on earth in an order that reverses orthodox secular understanding. The more familiar conventions show the individual as a singular physical being existing from birth to death. The physical birth of Young Sean will be followed ten years later by his psychological birth. Immediately, however, the connection between Sean's death and the birth of a child can be read in two opposing ways – either as mere coincidence or as implying that this birth (like all others?) is rebirth. Throughout the film spectators are drawn to oscillate between sceptical and mystical positions; but the opening setup brings to mind *2001: A Space Odyssey*, which concludes triumphantly with the death of the astronaut Dave and his rebirth as the star child.

The plot proper commences ten years later with a simple sequence that gathers significance as events unfold. Once again we are in a snow-covered landscape, but this time in a cemetery. Anna, isolated in the dreary waste by a long static take, weeps beside Sean's grave. Watching for her return from a car some distance away, Joseph (Danny Huston) is distracted by laughter from a funeral where mourners are amused by a shared recollection of the deceased. Only when we know Anna better can we realise that she would not have countenanced levity at Sean's interment – her unresolved loss the focus of blackest grief.

Anna takes her leave of Sean, trudges back to the car, takes a deep breath, looks at Joseph meaningfully and says 'OK' – nothing else. The reflected branches of winter trees frame the couple through the driver's window – a chill omen. Later we realise she has chosen this moment in the graveyard to accept Joseph's proposal of marriage. It is bizarre, to say the least, that she decides to do this at the very moment she takes final leave of her late husband. Is her grieving incomplete?

The engagement party is thrown in the plush Manhattan apartment where Anna has always lived with her mother, Eleanor (Lauren Bacall). Decorously serviced by hired caterers, it is one of those nervy affairs where everyone seems to be tiptoeing on eggshells. Joseph, lit cruelly to make his facial features gross, relates a self-congratulatory account of courting his hesitant fiancée – but she is nowhere in sight. Down in the lobby meanwhile an anxious woman makes her husband go up while she delays. Director of photography Harris Savides first establishes with this character a style of lighting actors' faces that prevails throughout much of the film. Little if any light reflects from the eyes, and what there is steeps the sockets in brown shadows that harmonise dully with the *mise-en-scène*. There's a subtle allusion in this to the living dead of horror films. If the old cliché holds true that in cinema the eyes are windows of the soul, then the psyches of the protagonists in *Birth* are veiled to the point of morbidity.

The anxious woman Clara (Anne Heche) reaches a decision, crosses the street into Central Park and scrabbles among leaves and dirt where she buries her gift. Then she buys an expensive replacement and goes up to the party. In the interim, her husband Clifford (Peter Stormare) has found Anna and affectionately congratulates her while apologising for the length of time since they last saw each other. We are left to wonder why there has been so long a break between people obviously fond of each other. Their ease evaporates as soon as Joseph comes to be introduced. He smoothly rids himself of a guest who belongs to Anna's past by inviting Clifford to 'enjoy the facilities'.

In the lobby ten floors below, a boy of ten has been quietly observing the comings and goings. Next morning, in a less affluent quarter of the city, this same lad Sean (Cameron Bright) sits on his bed. His thoughts occupy him so completely that he does not respond when one of his friends calls him out.[1]

The child is barely established before we cut back to more celebrations in the Manhattan apartment – another winter evening, another meticulously organised and stolid event, a family affair in honour of Eleanor's birthday. The matriarch has both her daughters and their men living in the apartment. Not only Anna and Joseph but the heavily pregnant Laura (Alison Elliott) and her husband Bob (Arliss Howard) are at the table. However, the carefully buffed polish of these lives is about to be disturbed by the boy Sean, who arrives uninvited behind late guests – a synchronistic surprise that will deliver them new experience to counterbalance their one-sidedness.

His entry coincides with the lights being doused as Anna walks through the flat carrying a birthday cake crowned by a forest of candles. Unseen in the dark, the boy follows her. Until the electric lights are switched on again, he seems no more material than a ghost, while the candle-lit Anna looks like an emanation of his imagining. Are they in the presence of the divine child archetype, the seedling symbol of future hopes and life's potential (Hopcke, 1989: 107)?

The sense that mystery is invading this home of moneyed blandness is further enriched by other factors. Kidman's 'extraordinary stillness' in the role of Anna has been likened to Maria Falconetti's evocation of Jeanne d'Arc in Carl Dreyer's 1928 film (Chaw, 2004). Cameron Bright invests the same quality in his playing of young Sean. Both actors have razor haircuts that recall Falconetti's role. These striking resemblances and the hypnotic fascination that develops between boy and woman entice us to wonder how deep the connections run. Are both characters, like Jeanne, immolated by passions that they cannot extinguish?

When the lights come on, Sean disrupts the party by asking to speak in private to Anna. She first humours him, as those adults do in whom the presence of children encourages whimsy; but when he announces with certainty that he is her late husband, Sean, she bundles him out of the apartment. Her reactions first conflate hilarity and unease, but in the following days the unease intensifies when Sean sends her a note telling her not to marry Joseph. Her family resorts to mockery, which fails to conceal disquiet. In part their anxiety is aroused by the intrusion into their polished lives, in part, we guess, by concern for Anna's hard-won emotional recovery. More, Sean has chafed the persona of every member of this regimented family. Behind the polite masks of New York's upper crust, the boy's persistence excites discordant emotions of which they have no understanding.

Joseph shows the strain first when, denting his suave mask, he intervenes absurdly, like an alpha male pricked by jealousy. The boy has incurred his annoyance by personating the dead husband who has long been both his sole and soul rival.

Ignoring Anna's wishes, he obliges the child to take him to his father (Ted Levine) who happens to be in the building giving music tuition to a client.[2] The adults corner the child and insist he stays away from Anna, but over and over again, Sean says he cannot. The adults use no physical force, but the concerted effect is brutal, culminating when Anna bends down, locks eyes with him and tells him not to bother her again. With that the elegant couple, who are late for a formal event, stride off briskly; but as Anna departs she turns and sees the boy collapse (doubly mordant in echoing her husband's death).

Instantly the shuddering buzz of a hundred rasping strings overwhelms Anna's being, while the clomping of murderous goblin hoofs (pizzicato basses) evacuates her sense of time and place. This, the Prelude to Act 1 of Wagner's *Die Walküre*, takes over the soundtrack while Anna, no longer aware of her surroundings, is hauled by her fiancé into the opera house. As they enter the auditorium, the camera zooms from a wide shot of the stalls into a tight close-up on Anna's face. Having clambered into her seat, she sits transfixed for endless shocked minutes. As the shot runs, the framing (from slightly above eye level) combines with the increased flattening created by an extreme telephoto register to broaden the image of Kidman's face. She looks not unlike an agitated child on the precipitous edge of tears. The shock of Sean's collapse has reopened her wound, leaving her helpless before the dawning conviction that the boy is her late husband reborn.

Kidman's extraordinary performance, augmented by Glazer and his crew into a great cinematic moment, leaves no room for doubt that a powerful mystery is being played out. She encounters the numinous in this episode – an experience charged with sacred terror. Although she has yearned and longed for Sean, nothing, understandably, has prepared her for that desire's obscure fulfilment. Although the film will show us other, mundane aspects of Anna's personality, the force of this apperception never wholly leaves her, nor those members of the audience affected by it.

The drama that Wagner's Prelude anticipates is relevant for two reasons appreciated by Robert Cumbow.

> Siegmund's arrival at Hunding's home ends up breaking up the marriage of Hunding and his wife Sieglinde, as the boy Sean almost does with Anna and Joseph's engagement. Second, Siegmund not only steals Sieglinde from Hunding, but beds her, even though she is his long lost sister – thus consummating a 'forbidden' love, like Anna's love for the 10-year-old boy who might be her long-lost husband.
>
> *(Cumbow, 2006)*

What does Anna's trauma reveal about her state of mind, interpreted in Jungian terms? Based on the premise that the completion of individuation cannot be done alone, but in relationship, we consider Anna to be in the phase known to alchemists as the lesser *coniunctio*. Edward Edinger describes the greater *coniunctio* as 'produced by a final union of the purified opposites, and, because it combines the opposites, it mitigates and rectifies all one-sidedness' (1985: 215). Marriage has thus tradition-ally provided an apt symbol of the completion of individuation. However,

> the union of opposites that have been imperfectly separated characterizes the nature of the lesser *coniunctio*. The product is a contaminated mixture that must be subjected to further procedures. The product of the lesser *coniunctio* is pictured as killed, maimed, or fragmented.
>
> *(Edinger, 1985: 212)*

To illustrate this the dangerous aspect of the lesser *coniunctio*, Edinger cites alchem-ical texts originally collated by Jung that refer to the out-of-kilter marriage of a widowed mother with her son.

> But this marriage, which was begun with the expression of great joyfulness, ended in the bitterness of mourning... For when the son sleeps with the mother, she kills him with the stroke of a viper.
>
> *(Ibid.)*

The concept of imperfectly separated opposites that characterises the lesser *coniunctio* fits not only Anna and Sean's marriage, but also Anna's relationship to Joseph and her fractured state of mind after her commitment to remarry. It also assists our understanding of the boy's attraction to her, where we are in the richly ambivalent territory of the Oedipal complex. Edinger again: 'for the alchemist, the mother was the *prima materia* and brought about healing and rejuvenation as well as death... The immature son-ego is eclipsed and threatened with destruction when it naively embraces the maternal unconscious' (1985: 212) – just so, Sean collapses. However, Edinger continues, 'such an eclipse can be inseminating and rejuvenating' (ibid.). Thus the image of the *coniunctio* refers to a phase of the trans-formation process, in which death can precede rebirth (1985: 214). When Sean enters into relationship with Anna he initiates a synchronistic event that has the potential to result in their mutual healing.

Like all new beginnings, Anna's engagement to Joseph brings with it not only the potential for joy (though it scarcely touches these two) but also vulnerability, which may spur a potential to regress. If the regression is consciously reflected upon, it may provide an opportunity for further growth. However, while Anna and Joseph's future marriage may be the immediate cause for each of their forthcoming regressions, it will not necessarily prove to be the root explanation.

The striking boy's advent may, as hinted earlier, signal activation of the child as a powerful archetypal image. It can either look back at the past of the person to whom it appears or forward to the future. As a retrospective figure, it represents emotions and unconscious drives that have been excluded or repressed as a neces-sary precondition to growing into adulthood. This occurs when the individual's development is constrained by the drive to enhance and specialise consciousness, a process that Jung found characteristic of Western cultures (1951: §276). Conversely, when the archetypal image of the child looks toward the future, it does so by representing nascent drives forming in the unconscious that are likely in time to enter and alter the individual's conscious. Jung remarks –

> Our experience of the psychology of the individual… shows that the 'child' paves the way for a future change of personality. In the individuation process, it anticipates the figure that comes from the synthesis of conscious and unconscious elements in the personality. It is therefore a symbol which unites the opposites; a mediator, bringer of healing, that is, one who makes whole.
>
> *(Ibid.: §278)*

The child can therefore signal a change in personality before it occurs, presenting to the conscious mind as it does the early intimations of rebirth.

This early in *Birth* the spectator lacks sufficient insight into Anna's psyche to adopt with confidence any of these readings. Nor can we tell by focusing on Sean. One consequence of the driven, internalised power with which Kidman endows the crucial scene at the opera is that although the boy's collapse jolts us through his overpowering grief, we cannot yet empathise with his suffering as with Anna because we cut away from him after he falls. The scene that follows the opera gives us a first, barely audible clue to his state of being. As his father puts him to bed,[3] the continuing pianissimo clomp of Wagner's bass line undermines any illusion that he has reached safety. The worried man tells his wife, 'He says that he's somebody else and he believes that he is.' The parents are not alone in failing to understand the boy's state of mind. That remains obscure, the mystery that protagonists and audience alike are drawn to solve.

Nevertheless it is plain that a radical change has come over Sean. When his mother (Cara Seymour) comes into his bedroom to comfort him with their good-night ritual, the boy refuses to be his old self: 'I'm not your stupid son anymore.' His behaviour next day confirms that he no longer fits his old world but is experiencing a second birth of the psyche. He ducks out of school and leaves a phone message for Anna to meet him in Central Park – she will know where to go. As Anna enters the park, unsteady on court shoes in the slush, a synthesised pulse like an anxious heartbeat draws a tense wire that dissolves momentarily into Wagner before she nears the fatal underpass. The point of view is identical to the end of her late husband's run; and echoes of Desplat's score for that scene (underlined by the heartbeat) emphasise the significance of the bridge. As Anna and the boy Sean meet, a runner clatters through the underpass – a moment of synchronicity too striking for the spectator to miss, hinting that the boy and his namesake are connected.

Recovered from the shock he suffered the previous evening, the self-assured Sean asks Anna to arrange for her brother-in-law Bob (a doctor) to test him. His certainty shakes Anna and she retreats abruptly with an aggressive-defensive put down: 'You're just a little boy!' She wants to stop him getting any closer for fear not only that he might prove to be what she most desires, but also because (as the unfolding plot eventually confirms) she resists the stirrings of an awareness that his quasi-magical, synchronistic advent signals the coming of almost irresistible changes in the way she sees, thinks and lives.

Although Anna has survived the loss of her husband, it appears she has learned nothing from the experience and thus has undergone no further maturing of the self. Following the truth requires courage: the boy's persistence means that she will find it tough to dodge the truth on which he insists, that the horizontal move in her life to Joseph will not bring her the safety and security she seeks. The truth that will eventually be revealed is at present literally concealed underground. As Stephen Mitchell puts it 'Our conscious experience is merely the tip of an immense iceberg of unconscious mental processes that really shape, unbeknownst to us, silently, impenetrably, and inexorably, our motives, our values and our actions' (1993: 22). If ignored, rather than serve development of the self, the unconscious holds the potential to destroy. For Anna and the boy, the synchronicity of their meeting leaves neither of them real choice, since they cannot turn away from what has come powerfully from the unconscious.

In her turmoil Anna tells Joseph about the child's persistence. This second challenge from his rival rankles Joseph who escalates hostilities and has Bob put the boy to the test. The interview is recorded and in playback Sean's astonishing knowledge and confidence transfix Anna's family.[4] Nor does the boy baulk at turning the tables, questioning Bob about his married life and recalling that Laura had not been thought able to bear a child.

Sean's answers reveal significant details about Anna's late husband. He and Anna had married thirty times in thirty days at thirty churches. This saturated, fairy-tale quality colours Anna's romantic memories of her husband. But what can such obsessive behaviour mean in terms of their late relationship? Romance had fuelled their marriage, adding a quality of intensity and excitement to being alive and dreams of their future. But romance lives in newness, mystery, even danger, and may disappear with familiarity. Its intensity gives a false sense of a truly intimate connection that this couple had confused with a connection of depth. From this vantage point Sean's death can be seen as an emblem of romantic love that dies because nothing more real anchors it. It may, as with the boy, excite the idealisation of an adolescent. Yet idealisation is, by definition, illusory. Rather, there are signs of addiction in the multiple weddings, an addiction like any other acting either as a counterfeit high or a container for undigested suffering and grief.

Emotionally, the blissful state of desire is what propels couples to bond in order to initiate a secure attachment – but it is not of itself sufficient to maintain and develop that bond. Anna has found a place where she can feel the spiritual high of the union she seeks in marriage without the hard work of becoming a psychological being. Her idealisation (bathed in illusion rather than a real relationship based on a depth of connection where both people are emerging) inhibits the necessary ego-self axis from developing as part of the individuation process. One of the most painful attributes of marriage is the eventual, unavoidable revealing of both partners' shadows. The shadow may give the relationship its spark but often couples avoid it by attempting to manage the negative emotions it generates (in which case the marriage may last, if firmly invested in comfort, but will not thrive). If the shadow is not consciously dealt with, the intensity of connection from the initial spark may die. One outcome can be that, as we eventually find out of Anna's late husband, the partners will look for it elsewhere. As each partner in an individuated marriage attempts over the long haul to understand and relate to their shadow by increasing their capacity to hold the emotional tension it provokes, they further integrate the unrelated parts of themselves, healing each other in the process and their own psychological splits. In Anna and Sean's *idealised* marriage (going to thirty churches in thirty days) they achieved no such understanding. Looking back at Sean's fatal collapse as he lumbered through fields of ice, we find the image that lets us see where the relationship became frozen.

Continuing the interview with Bob, the boy Sean inadvertently alludes to the poisonous undercurrent beneath Anna's heady romance, although he cannot understand the implications of his words. He mentions that, as her husband, he and Anna had lived with Eleanor because he was seldom home. Finally the lad takes control of the interview: 'Look, you can think whatever you want… It doesn't matter. I'm Sean. I love Anna and nothing's going to change that. Nothing. That's forever.' The challenge to Anna's family in general and Joseph in particular is now too direct to be ignored. They summon the boy to stay over at Eleanor's apartment so that Anna can disabuse him of his delusion by proving her intent to marry Joseph. On arrival he moves round the apartment like a Pied Piper reversing the old tale, followed every step by the fascinated adults. He promptly lays claim to his old desk and identifies a visitor whose name he does not know as 'the one that told Anna there wasn't a Santa Claus'.

Cross-questioning the boy gets Joseph nowhere but he cannot stop scratching the jealous itch in his ego. Late at night he goes downstairs in the dark to gaze at the boy asleep on the couch and mutters, 'You don't have me fooled.' Plainly Joseph's saturnine anger puts him into identification with the boy as, driven by irresistible emotions, he (no less than the sleeping child) drifts in semi-conscious realms. Although, with the exception of certain horror film cycles, the image of the archetypal child rarely figures as an adult's shadow, Sean does take on this role in relation to Joseph. The man lacks soul, while the boy has it in abundance. This is a key relationship not only for what it signals about Joseph but also the family into which he is marrying.

Anna is intending to tie her life to a man with a materialist disposition as bankable as her parental family and her late husband Sean, but lacking the scientist's inquiring mind. Joseph fits well in Eleanor's family because none of them has a curious, self-reflective nature. Sheltered in moneyed security whose realism is so insistently grotesque that it lays bare the fantasies on which it is built, their wealth encourages the delusion that the pragmatic empiricism of their professional and social lives endows them with a complete, all round understanding of life, notwithstanding their total neglect of the internal world. Their concrete minds lack the curiosity and imagination that accompany the inner child, both being qualities that act as guides to individuation. These adults are as emotionally dead as the deceased Sean.

This holds true for Anna as well as the others. She is obsessive but not inquisitive – with an obsession so powerful that the boy/man rapidly becomes the carrier of her animus projections to the extent that he almost (but never wholly) seems her invention. That she projects her animus onto a child may be, as mentioned earlier (whatever the merit of his claim to be her late husband), the first sign of impending rebirth that connection with the archetype of the divine child often foretells. Alternatively, as now seems increasingly likely, it may imply earlier narcissistic wounds that have yet to be worked through.

Indeed, the disturbance caused by the boy intensifies in Anna a complex of which she had no prior awareness. It erupts when she calls on her late husband's old friend Clifford to open her confused heart. With emotion battling reason, unable to make sense of her conflicted passions, she rambles on about her feelings for the two Seans, her suffering, her fears and her wishes – simultaneously knowing the child is not her dead husband yet aching for him to be – in sum, struggling to discover what is real. Eventually she manages to stammer that she needs help. She wants Clifford to intervene and stop her falling in love with Sean again. That she cannot see the absurdity of this request reveals her narcissistic choice of mate.[5]

As further evidence for the activation of a complex, the entire monologue concerns herself except when she describes Joseph as having *not* grown insecure over the boy. Since she could not be more mistaken about this in that only Joseph's suave manners mask his anxiety, it raises the thought that Anna represses painful matters that she cannot fail to notice. In her fiancé's case the truth would force her to recognise that his devotion is not an all-encompassing shelter from the doubts and conflicts that come with all relationships. If this is a repeating pattern, she may have denied herself hurtful reflection on her husband's frequent absences from home by repressing the painful awareness that the marriage was not what she thought it was. The psychic energy needed to sustain that repression would add to her relentless grief for a perfect mate ten years after his death. As in all relationships, a constant calibration between closeness and distance – between what feels so suffocating it may threaten loss of self, and what feels too far away stimulating a fear of abandonment – is a challenging undertaking. If an early relational trauma has been suffered, the ability to sustain an intact connection may become more complex, ending in disruptions such as excessive arguing or passive withdrawal. Anna's prolonged grieving indicates that something was amiss both during and prior to the marriage.

The next day, as agreed with the boy's mother, Anna meets Sean out of school; but rather than despatch him as planned with cold words, she takes him for ice cream and a carriage ride through Central Park – and discusses their mutual attraction! Following her appeal for help to Clifford, these actions can be seen as another aspect of a deep-rooted psychological pattern. Anna needs the men close to her to take responsibility for what she is unconscious of, her own shadow. She wants Clifford to stop her from falling in love. That only makes sense when we see her projecting her demons onto him. In summoning Clifford for help, she has unconsciously picked the very person who cannot assist because his own blindness (soon to be revealed) makes him as unconscious as her. In her previous life her husband's role was to secure her in a hermetically sealed realm of perfect love (which his early death has sanctified), buttressing her world from the vagaries of human behaviour. Joseph is to replace her husband as a stable, middle-aged version of her former mate, forgiven his want of romance because he is wealthy and dignified enough to fill the absences in Anna's life. The boy's function in replacing Joseph as her reincarnated husband will be to reopen the tomb of impossibly perfect lost young love.

The date with ice cream and the carriage ride in the park are, as Cumbow (2006) mentions, a cliché of romantic movies rendered almost comic by the circumstances except that the familiar anxious pulse fades in again, mixed through the older Sean's music. Afternoon wears into evening and Anna watches her young beau – just a healthy boy in this – enjoying climbing frames and swings. Meanwhile Joseph stands like a jilted lover waiting for her in the window of a suitably grand apartment that Anna should be viewing with him as their future home. We zoom in long and slow with reflections of winter-dead trees once again darkening the glass. His self-absorbed face broadens just as Anna's did at the opera, revealing not the inner child he denies but the worn visage of a middle-aged man pushed near to breakdown. Joseph is caught in the Sol Niger, the darkening and depression of a man in the second half of life. Unable to regenerate himself because of a defect of heart, he projects his anima and thus cannot develop a feeling connection. Overly identified with male ego (which tends to overvalue power and material wealth) he nevertheless appears to feel something deep is missing.

Anna brings Sean back to Eleanor's apartment to hear the wedding music, arguing that it might persuade him to give up his fixation (another projection of her own obsession onto an animus figure). Joseph gets back from the aborted house hunting and is about to enter the bathroom when he hears the voices of Anna and the boy. The latter has stepped as casually as a husband into her tub. This image intricately restates the lesser *coniunctio* and recalls Jung's reading of 'Immersion in the Bath'. Here the alchemical King and Queen start their process of individuation by stepping into the incestuous relationship signifies the as yet imperfect differentiation of conscious and unconscious (1946: §453–6).

Had Joseph gone into the bathroom, he would have heard Anna once again asking Sean to leave; but, rather than face his suspicions, he turns away. Evasion racks up his tension with his shadow piquing him horribly.

Soon the entire household is lined up in the drawing room to hear the pretentious nonsense commanded for the wedding.

> It appears to be a chamber music recital, but what they are playing is soon revealed to be a rather silly version of the Bridal March from Wagner's *Lohengrin* that we know as 'Here Comes the Bride,' and we realize that this is another pre-wedding function. But notice that just as a performance of Wagner's *Die Walküre* became the centerpiece of the film's Act One, so this little mini-concert of another Wagnerian piece becomes the pivotal moment of Act Two.
>
> *(Cumbow, 2006)*

All the family (except the haunted Anna) are gratified by the music's confirmation of their good taste. Although opera goers, they appear blithely unaware of its ominous associations in marking the moment when the newly wed Elsa violates the sole condition her husband Lohengrin has attached to the marriage. By asking who he is as they enter the bridal chamber, she destroys the marriage, precipitates his return to the kingdom of his father and her own death. The scenario plays (if only Anna were aware of it) like an ironic epitaph on what she had left undone in her first marriage by failing to ask her husband who he was. Had she the feminine psychic energy to initiate the necessary inquiry that she ducked, the death of delusion could have led to her rebirth. As it is, through neurotic repetition she risks replaying the whole self-defeating cycle once again.

Meanwhile the boy again disrupts the calm and goads Joseph by kicking his chair even after his rival orders him to stop. In a setup borrowed from Kubrick's *Barry Lyndon* (Hughes, 2006; Cumbow, 2006), Joseph's rage erupts as volcanically as Barry's. He lashes out at the infuriating boy – the only time he does anything from deep-rooted passion. As when Barry runs amuck and his peers restrain him from slaughtering young Bullingdon, some of the men present hold Joseph back. He denounces the boy: 'He has no clue how to make something happen!' Yet his very outrage proves him wrong and what really exercises him is maintaining his dignity: 'I'm the one that should be respected, but obviously not...' Then he goes after the boy again and spanks him hard before the adults can haul him off. When finally secured, this scion of Manhattan's finest roars like a humiliated baby, 'He kicked my chair!' But it is the shadow child who has succeeded in ripping open his public persona to reveal Joseph's infantile rage. A child must feel possession over his love object to experience a secure attachment, but Joseph, with his repressed id let free, has exposed his latent insecurities. The false self feigns arrogant security.

Anna gazes appalled at her fiancé's ungovernable anger, confronted with the vortex in his personality she had failed to notice. The other adults (a further echo of Kubrick's scene) are at least as shocked by Joseph's violation of social decorum as by his attacking a child. So when Eleanor watches him moving out of the apartment, far from rebuking him, she promises to bring Anna round. Eleanor knows a good marital prospect when she sees one and has no intention of letting her daughter lose this prosperous bachelor even though his usually impeccable manners have slipped just this once.

At the climax of the brouhaha Sean had grabbed his coat and run out, the cue for a grieving music that recalls the moments of sorrow after battle in war movies. Anna follows the boy to the snowy street where they kiss tenderly – as simultaneously both child with woman, and lovers. The scene returns to the apartment above and time passes. The sombre music continues with bass notes melded through synthesiser to produce a sound not unlike distant foghorns. Eventually Clifford arrives, searches through empty rooms (the brown gloom and slow editing never more evident) before discovering Anna in the kitchen. He has come, as asked, to save her from Sean. But before they can talk, the boy materialises and embraces him affectionately as a long lost friend. Although Clifford does his best gently to assure Anna that the lad is not her late husband, she will not be deflected from her conviction (all the more resolute after the kiss) that she has found him reincarnated. Her inflated mood shows that she has been touched by a numinous presence; she has no intention of giving up either the child or the troubled ecstasy he brings her.

Only when Eleanor sternly threatens to inform Sean's mother and the police does Anna reluctantly rouse the boy (whom she had previously installed in her bed at an hour suited to a 10-year-old) and take him back to his parents in a taxicab. During the ride she begins to fantasise how they might be together. Anna is now caught in the grips of her complex, exhibiting the twin intensities of urgency and compulsion. Her perspective has shifted dangerously: for her the boy is no longer *like* her dead mate, he *is* him. A psychic boundary has been crossed between inner reality and external reality. It seems that if young Sean is to reveal himself as a symbol of renewal, that moment cannot be long delayed.

It quickly becomes clear that matters cannot be reduced to a simple issue of whether the boy either is or isn't the dead man. Although the boy obviously loves Anna, something else is competing for his attention: the memory of an episode in Eleanor's apartment. While everyone else was occupied he had let Clara in. She had immediately instructed the boy to help wash her dirty hands (as if washing her shadow). To Sean it had seemed an odd command that he obeyed politely but without enthusiasm. Clara's order does not surprise, however, when we recognise that children are often left holding what adults are unconscious of (Clara is soon revealed as blinded by sexual greed).[6] Now, some hours later, the boy recalls the engagement party. In flashback he remembers observing Clara's hesitation and following her into Central Park where he watched her bury the parcel. Clara, who has heard Anna rave about the boy's uncanny knowledge, has now revisited the spot to confirm certain suspicions and has silently shown the boy that she knows. We realise that Sean must have dug it up and that Clara is now mutely confronting him. Retrieval of this package can be read as analogous to the discovery of what lies buried in the unconscious – a gift of wisdom that must be laid bare to consciousness. The ego needs the guidance and direction from the unconscious to lead a meaningful life – paving the psychic road between ego and Self.

With his secret uncovered, the boy takes the package to Clara's apartment. It contains Anna's love letters to her husband; but Clara shocks him by disclosing that the dead man had been her lover. He had given his wife's letters unopened to Clara to prove how much he loved her. So brutal a twist to infidelity proves that his subjective experience of the marriage differed greatly from Anna's. It suggests a significant loss of connection between the couple had ended in Sean's emotional withdrawal and his unrealistic hope to find enduring love with yet another idealised mate. He seems in the affair to have attempted to revive the lost spark of which we wrote earlier – an impossible endeavour without psychological growth so that his death signals the dead end he had reached.

The revelation that the boy has read Anna's love letters appears at first thought to implode the intricate web of mystery surrounding him. It seems that almost all his knowledge must have come from the letters, though he may have discovered other details about the family in equally accountable ways. For example, he may have found out where Anna's husband died – something the letters could not have revealed – by chatting to his friend the janitor. Further reflection, however, shows that the boy's conduct cannot be accounted for solely by causal explanations. They do not explain many factors, not least the deep currents of emotion he feels and cannot fully control. First, no one has put him up to making his extraordinary claim. Second, he does not have a scam in mind. Third, the coincidence of his name and the dead man's may have triggered his interest, but the source of his fascination with Anna lies in the letters' expression of love; for, fourth, he certainly loves Anna. How else to explain his much remarked, unblinking solemnity, his collapse and the sacrifice that he will soon make? Fifth, how can we rationally explain that he recognises his forebear's desk? Or, sixth, that he can identify the woman whose name he does not know who told Anna there is no Santa Claus? The answer may lie in his intuition.

Intuition can play a supreme role in individuation. It is experienced as if it delivers something knowable that mysteriously comes from a place beyond our conscious knowing. In that, it differs from instinct, which is a function of the corporeal senses. Intuition has a feminine quality not to be confused with gender. But Anna, caught in her gender role as a result of her one-sidedness, literalises the feminine whereas the child's symbolic androgyny could serve as her guide toward integration of the masculine and feminine – as when the alchemical King and Queen bathing together in symbolic incest start the process of bringing masculine and feminine, conscious and unconscious, into balance in the greater *coniunctio* (see Jung, 1946: §453–6).

Sooner or later, every avenue of inquiry opens on the boy's soul. The temporal link between his physical birth and the death of Sean the man opens the idea of reincarnation. Having said which, Clara's objection cannot be ignored that if he had been her lover reincarnated he would have come to her: in fact the boy is unmoved by her. However, reincarnation can be considered symbolically as ancestry's invisible pull, linking individuals to both the personal and collective unconscious; and it seems thus that the boy has knowledge of past life.[7]

Clara cannot deny (indeed it arouses her jealousy) that Anna's letters have stirred great love in the boy. He has identified with Anna's need for a perfect loving relationship, and that has enriched his confidence to move from boyhood to young adolescence. It has endowed him with the certainty of his soul's connection to an imago of psychic love – the source of all human love that embodies the higher form of the archetype of relatedness. However, what he reads as the intense love between wife and husband at its most sacred and incandescent is knowledge that he can only receive as an innocent. The letters bring about his second birth.

Inevitably the boy and Anna seek different objects, his goal being a variant of what Erich Neumann terms uroboric incest (1954: 17). Her love letters initiate him into the mystical uroboric union of male and female for which his soul yearns. Renouncing his birth mother, he dissolves the primary union he had shared with her as an infant. Nevertheless, the new symbolic union with Anna that his soul embraces cannot be permanent. She becomes the deeply felt archetypal projection necessary to his development – part mother (providing ice cream treats), and part lover (romantic dates and the warmth of an enveloping pre-sexual eroticism). By definition, a symbolic union with what the mother imago represents (even in its variant form of Anna as mother/lover) cannot be a state of the psyche that endures if the child is to mature healthily and differentiate into its own individuated self (see Neumann, ibid.).

Consumed by her own galling wants, Clara sees nothing of this. She admits to Sean that she had intended to vent hatred on her rival by making the evidence of her dead lover's betrayal an engagement present for Anna – but in the event, she could not go through with it. Ironically, if Anna had known the truth it might have shattered her hypnotic grieving and allowed her to move on (Cumbow, 2006). Be that as it may, Clara tells the boy that had he come to her first she would have explored the possibility of rediscovering her lover in him. Ten years after his death, she is no less in thrall to the memory of Sean than Anna, with the difference that Clara has not been touched by the boy's numinous glow. Greedily she struggles with him and grabs the letters back.

Pounding kettledrums that recall the older Sean's fatal collapse accompany the boy as he flees into the park in crisis. He climbs high into a leafless tree and remains there into the winter night. When the police find him dazed and muddy hours later (he must have slipped from his perch) they can neither grasp what he says nor catch hold of him. 'I thought I was Sean but I found out he was in love with another woman. So I can't be him because I'm in love with Anna.' As he runs off into the dark we, unlike the bewildered cops, realise that he has discovered something significant about himself. It is not the latest adult attack that has made him distraught, but discovering Clara's affair.

The boy runs to Anna's apartment where the maid puts him in the bath – a hint here of baptism cleansing the shadow to initiate rebirth. Anna comes home and goes in to him with a 'plan' (both ludicrous and dangerous) that they should run away, wait until the boy reaches twenty-one, and then get married.[8] This adolescent fantasy meets his pre-adolescent heart's desire, but he has to refuse. For although the mud still sticks to him, he now knows what has sullied him. Other children might have gone home to their parents with the police, but Sean speaks with more maturity than a child of his years or indeed Anna: 'I'm not Sean – because I love you.' He protects her by keeping secret both her husband's betrayal and the disparity between the man and her image of him. Securing an adult's delusion is a tough role for a child, but he does this heroically and at no small cost, personifying the wisdom gained on the postmodern hero's journey. Anna brands him a liar, shakes him yet again with the fierce, self-centred emotions that he has found in all the adults outside his own family – and is lost to him as the woman he loves. When her anger gives way to tears ('You certainly had me fooled – I thought you were my dead husband'), self-pity stops her remembering that the boy had believed it too.

Despite the shock of Clara's revelation, it has had a developmental impact on the boy. Having to face 'his own' betrayal of Anna, he has suffered a rude awakening from the uroboric condition in which he had been sheltering. It brings about his third birth, a transformation of the psyche that now becomes further differentiated in a form suited to a 10-year-old. Neumann describes the developmental stage through which the boy is moving.

> Detachment from the uroboros means being born and descending into the lower world of reality, full of dangers and discomforts.
>
> *(1954: 39)*

And again,

> Detachment from the uroboros, entry into the world, and the encounter with the universal principle of opposites are the essential tasks of human and individual development. The process of coming to terms with the objects of the outer and inner worlds, of adapting to the collective life of mankind both within and without, governs with varying degrees of intensity the life of every individual.
>
> *(Ibid.: 35)*

We see the boy only twice more. Cleaned up after his bath, he sits with Eleanor by the front door, waiting for his mother to collect him – Anna presumably being too distraught to sit with them. Out of nowhere Eleanor says, 'I never liked Sean.' What has drawn this declaration? Here is just one of the interwoven currents of life among Eleanor's family and friends that could have been scripted by Henry James. Bacall – once a beauty with face no less expressive than Kidman – plays Eleanor as a steely matriarch who has always exercised power over her entire family with the exception only of the older Sean. The boy has both reminded her of that and put her command over Anna at risk. So, her power having survived intact, she now finds no further reason to suppress disapproval of both man and boy. Old enough to be Sean's grandmother, Eleanor could have played the role of wise old woman as head of her family, but she does not. Instead she rules, in place of sagacious advice having only sardonic put downs to offer, as when she first sets eyes on Laura's newborn daughter: 'Maybe that's Sean.'

Eleanor's lack of emotional engagement with either Laura or the infant is striking. Her coldness has left her children suffering from a lack of the mother's nurture. Indulgent and dutiful parenting is not nurturing. Anna's neediness and inability to work through her grief for her husband's death originated in her childhood feelings of emotional abandonment. So Eleanor holds for her daughter the archetypal image of the Devouring Mother deriving from negative experience of parental caring. In Anna's later life it explains a power relationship in marriage with parental overtones in which she subordinates as the younger partner. Eleanor's merging way of connecting is narcissistic in nature, leaving no room for another mind to safely develop needs and wants different from hers. If separation does not take place, the matriarch, so necessary, cherishing and nurturing during infancy, turns in the dawning light of consciousness to an imagined figure of darkness and destruction as she prevents the emerging ego of the child from differentiating itself from the unconscious and establishing itself in its own right (Neumann, 1954: 39–47).

Jung concluded from his case studies that,

> It is not possible to live too long amid infantile surroundings, or in the bosom of the family, without endangering one's psychic health. Life calls us forth to independence, and anyone who does not heed this call because of childish laziness or timidity is threatened with neurosis. And once this has broken out, it becomes an increasingly valid reason for running away from life and remaining forever in the morally poisonous atmosphere of infancy.
>
> *(Jung, 1956: §461)*

He also saw that a woman who has remained bound to the mother typically lives through fantasies of a hero figure. A man who enters upon a relationship with such a woman 'will at once be made identical with her animus-hero and relentlessly set up as the ideal figure…' (Ibid.: §465).

This has been Anna's fate, still playing itself out in her thirties; and just as her own fate contrasts with young Sean's, so too the suffocating propriety of Eleanor's family differs from the homely kindliness that prevails in the boy's home. His 'good enough' parents remain constant in support of their son and, once they have perceived the authenticity of his experience, never gainsay it. By thus making space for him to follow the demands that his own developing psyche places on him, they hold secure the family base to which he now returns.

As we have discovered, things are different in Anna's circle where repression and betrayal are commonplace. Anna has never admitted to herself the thought that Sean might have had a lover. However, as Hughes suggests, the religious intensity of her grieving may hint that she senses something unthinkable and represses it (2006). Another instance of repression is glimpsed when Bob, though a medical doctor, is embarrassed when the boy refers to Laura's supposed infertility. What unknown story lies behind that flicker of discomfort? For their part, Clifford and Clara behave awkwardly when in Anna's company. It seems probable that Clifford has found out about his wife's affair with Sean and the knowledge lies injuriously between them. In the negative aspect of her personality Clara is an embittered manipulator: witness firstly her wangling an invitation to Anna's party to take revenge on her lover's wife, and secondly her attempt to control a 10-year-old boy. However, when plunged into the dreadful predicament of a mistress whose lover has died, she would have found herself trapped in her secret without the socially acceptable right to mourn. It would be in character if, unable to contain her suffering alone, she had vented her gall on her own husband.

We see repression enacted as soon as the boy is out of the picture, when Anna goes to Joseph in his office (as her mother has counselled). Bristling with the majesty of a man unjustly injured, her fiancé ushers her into his boardroom and hears her out impassively. As Jung wrote of Joseph's type fifty years before the film was made –

> The man finds himself cast in an attractive role: he has the privilege of putting up with the familiar feminine foibles with real superiority, and yet with forbearance, like a true knight. (Fortunately, he remains ignorant of the fact that these deficiencies consist largely of his own projections.)
>
> *(Jung, 1954a: §169)*

Unable to take responsibility, Anna declares (three times in all and not without tears) that she cannot be held accountable for what happened with the boy: there was no way she could have behaved any differently. Then she says (three times over) that she wants to be with Joseph and adds that she wants to be married, to have a good life, be happy and find peace. Although she does breathe an apology, her words only address her own wants – nothing about how she feels or what she might do, no inquiry about how he feels or what he might want, nothing about what they could share. After a pause to make the point that he is in control, Joseph responds 'OK' (echoing her acceptance speech in the graveyard). She kneels and kisses his hand in fawning gratitude; and in this dreadful manner the deal (a negotiation ensuring Anna's perpetual subordination) is sealed. Where there is no potential for growth, depression cannot be far away – the kiss of death.

The wedding, a stylish affair, takes place in May and at the family's seaside villa (just as Eleanor wanted). While the guests enjoy champagne in the garden, a photographer puts Anna through the interminable poses required of a bride. As he does so her mind pulls away from the moment and immerses her in a letter received from Sean. Long quiet chords for violins abstract us sadly from the celebrations while in voice-over the boy apologises courteously for having upset the family and making Anna sad. He tells about his life resuming with help from family and experts and reports that the spell has been lifted. As he speaks, we cut away to him sitting for the school photographer, now indeed a cheerful, ordinary boy. Nevertheless, this moment of synchronicity implies some form of continuing connection between him and Anna – a connection impossible for her to ignore.

The boy is free, but his final words, 'I guess I'll see you in another lifetime,' hold Anna in the spell's grip. The quiet strings surge as the world of this wealthy young woman – accustomed to wanting and getting, or at least getting the illusion of having what she wants – is ripped to shreds. We cut to hand-held shots at the beach where she staggers between sea and sand, rejecting both, crazed, unable to commit to death or life, belonging neither to the oceanic womb of the unconscious nor to the security of consciousness and the land. When Joseph finds her on this brink and embraces her protectively, she pulls back toward the waves, unable to respond to him, her beautiful face distorted into a silent Munchian scream (*cf.* Chaw, 2004). Finally dragged by her new husband out of what seems an eternity of grief, she reluctantly gives way to him. Joseph gently leads his catatonic bride along the misty margins – their future together well outside the range of prediction. We can say, however, that although Anna may yearn for the beloved spiritual experience, and once again hope to find in marriage a feeling of completion in the greater *coniunctio* for which she sought ten years earlier, she has not made the necessary developmental shift to inhabit its psycho-emotional space.

All that said, this may not be the film's only verdict on Anna, because it has not quite finished – at least not for those who watch the credits roll. The sound of waves slowly fades, replaced (just as the title *Birth* hits the screen) by a trite tune that violates shockingly the register of all that has gone before. 'Tonight you belong to me' laments the loss of a lover who is now with someone new. It was recorded by sisters Patience and Prudence McIntyre aged 11 and 14 whose rendition projects an unmistakeably coy, prepubescent sexuality. It became a top five North American hit in 1956 ('Ronnie', 2003). Fifty years later, however, changes in society's attitudes toward child sexuality augmented by the tune's location, tucked into an ignored crevice at the end of the film, give it a raw impact. Its sudden intrusion, coupled with the harsh break of register, indicates an irruption from the deep unconscious, that 'chthonic portion of the psyche' (Jung, 1927/1931: §53). As we have seen, the intense, warded focus of Anna's mind (not to mention her family's defensive empiricism) has been so profoundly one-sided as to repress unwanted contents deep into the unconscious. However, the more energetically such contents are repressed, the more vigorously they are apt to erupt back into consciousness. This is equally the case for individuals or collectives. When repressed contents erupt, they exert a force that counters or complements the bias of the conscious position. Therein lies the function of 'Tonight You Belong To Me'. Its sentiments are wholly at odds with the empirical circumstances, with Joseph and Anna now wed, but precisely in tune with what may be presumed to be going on in the unconscious. But whose unconscious? Anna's or Sean's (the boy, the man?) or somewhere their souls touch? Since we are dealing with the unconscious, we cannot know.

In the world of the well-socialised people who surround Anna (and who cele-brate in Eleanor's hedged garden what they consider to be her return to the shelter of marriage), her fixation on Sean can be classified as neurotic and infantile. We interpreted her mindset in this frame, finding its roots in the impositions of a dom-ineering mother and an absent father. The reading is legitimate but limited to what Jung termed the reductive analytical programmes of Freud and Adler – the former focussed on the sources of trauma to be found in childhood, the latter on the ego's urge to power (Jung, 1943: §44–55). Differentiating his approach to psychoanalysis from theirs, Jung argued that neurotic symptoms 'are not simply the effects of long-past causes, whether "infantile sexuality" or the infantile urge to power', they may also be goal oriented, being 'attempts at a new synthesis in life' albeit they have, as symptoms of psychological distress, yet to succeed (Ibid.: §67).

The difference between grieving and mourning is well illustrated by Anna. In effect, she is stuck. She grieves to the end of the film and beyond, but she does not mourn. That would involve a process, a moving forward, and an accommodation with the imaginal world and memories of her first husband. In actuality, the advent of the boy intensifies her grief to the point where only an impossible union with him could resolve it. She seems therefore to fall into the type of people 'who have the whole meaning of their life, their true significance, in the unconscious, while in the conscious mind is nothing but inveiglement and error' (Ibid.: §68). We are drawn by Jung's observation to consider the soul once again: whether Anna is not trans-fixed by her craving for that other union, the soul's perfection. Such a union may be impossible in this life, but the appetite for it is inextinguishable where an individual like Anna is in the grip of an ecstatic passion. Through the recorded ages the intensity of ardent lovers' feelings for their beloved has seemed to them to have the quality of a sacred passion that can bring them to knowledge of the divine. Contemplation on the beloved person (like Dante's longing for Beatrice) generates a wonder so concentrated that it draws the mind of the lover beyond mere physical attraction to penetrate the confusions of his or her emotional upheaval and attain a sense of being touched by the numinous. 'Sean', the doubled image of a godlike man-boy, who in Anna's mind has taken on the dimensions of the perfect masculine, is so powerful a presence that it ought to lead her to birth in the spiritual realm. Sadly no such release into the light appears likely because her conscious mind (despite the pressures to the contrary that 'Sean' exerts on it) remains powerfully dependent on empirical materialism.

A truly beautiful woman, Anna's soul (notwithstanding her infantile tendencies) is rendered hauntingly lovely in its anguish by Desplat's music. His themes, with their suggestion of otherworldly energy, augment her beauty and make her into an unwitting symbol for what she has the potential to be – in the particular Jungian sense in which symbols are forward-looking and constructive and compensate for one-sided, conscious bias (Fredericksen, 2001: 34–5). Her search for soul almost draws her into fulfilment and knowledge of herself, regardless of the cost – but not quite. She turns back at the sea's margin, unable to commit to total immolation.

Birth offers a radical alternative to the familiar perspective on protagonists in which they are understood each to have a psyche, albeit injured to one degree or another. Obviously the film presents such a point of view, but in parallel it plays with another hypothesis compatible with some Eastern religions, namely that on the contrary the psyche has the characters. This belief is related to the postulate that Jung called the *unus mundus* wherein the physical and psychic worlds are both held within the one cosmos (1954b: §769). In a universe in which psyche overarches the physical, the boy's written farewell to Anna, mentioning that they may meet in another life, would be more than a self-deprecating and courteous closing line. Rather it would invoke with sincerity the wished-for prospect of reincarnation. In such a world Sean's karma would require that during his present life he give up Anna because as an unfaithful husband in his previous incarnation he had not earned the right to reclaim that role. He would also have to work out his earlier denial of reincarnation. For her part, Anna too would have karmic work to do. Before she could meet Sean on equal terms, she would need to find the courage to face her intuitions and follow where they lead her without hiding in repression's bolthole.

In the final analysis, *Birth* (perhaps playing to its presumed liberal-minded audience) commits to neither epistemological perspective but lets them both stand.

To judge by blog reviews posted by audience members, the resultant conflict between opposed worldviews (to which the filmmakers cannily offer no resolution) is one of its distinctive attractions. Playing with so many linked oppositions, *Birth* challenges the audience no less than its protagonists to think – better, to feel their way through – issues relating to the development of the psyche and rebirth while in its very being reaffirming the value of fantasy in securing the psyche's integration.

Notes

1 Although he is 10, his bedroom is still decorated to suit a 6-year old, possibly inferring some developmental arrest.
2 Which explains why the friendly janitor allows the boy into the lobby.
3 Cumbow notes that the music tutor cannot afford black tie and opera (2006).
4 Another moment of synchronicity seems to invoke the supernatural and thereby authenticate young Sean's claims: a black cat runs between him and Bob during their interview.
5 As Anna's chosen love object, her husband had been purely ideal, typical of an interrupted adolescence where the necessary phase of de-idealising the parents has not occurred to make it possible to separate from them and become a fully actualised person (see Laplanche and Pontalis, 1973: 258–259).
6 Consciousness of the inner child can help direct emotion to transform relationships.
7 'Our ancestors move along with us, in underground rivers and springs too deep for chaos to reach' (Lamb, 2008).
8 Among many details that link *Birth* with *Eyes Wide Shut* is the way Nicole Kidman makes both Anna and Alice Harford coyly bleat the word 'married' like a spoilt girl.

3

TSOTSI (2005)

To move from *Birth* and its representation of pompously extravagant Manhattan lives to *Tsotsi*'s evocation of harsh poverty in Soweto is to traverse in the imagination a wide gulf. The principal figure in the South African film, unaware that grief has him in its grip, is no less blocked in his development than Anna. The lead character on whom *Tsotsi* focuses is a gangster, but although his and Anna's social circumstances could hardly be more different, their inner psychological worlds are similar. Poverty of this kind is not held back by wealth.

The film presents the gangster's deeds in a moral framework, showing violent, organised theft to be his method of escaping the depths of Sowetan poverty that threaten to engulf him. In what follows, we reflect on the way that post-apartheid societal and cultural pressures have shaped the character's individual psychology and we thereby seek to complement *Tsotsi*'s representation of township life. We also argue that the ravages of apartheid's aftermath have almost wholly blocked access to traditional methods of tapping into the collective unconscious. The male characters possess no knowledge of such resources or their benefits.

The origins of Soweto are harsh. Its full name, South-Western Townships, was decreed by white officialdom. It recalls the apartheid era in South Africa when white authorities felt no need to conceal under the thinnest of administrative masks the cruel racial division of humanity enacted for the benefit of whites only. Soweto was an overcrowded place zoned for blacks. With some houses originally built by the government soon surrounded by miles of shacks, it was sited near to the Rand gold mines. To this day some men work there. However, in the twenty years before the release of *Tsotsi*, employment in the mines fell from over 450,000 to 130,000 (many being migrant workers from neighbouring territories) (Mogotsi, 2005: 15–16). Meanwhile in the 2001 census, Soweto reported some 900,000 residents. These figures confirm the fact that the township has always been used as a labour sink. In the apartheid era its people were needed by the white economy to fulfil service and menial posts. Banned from living among their apartheid masters, they had no alternative but to travel northeast to Johannesburg in search of jobs.

The legacy of apartheid, though that pernicious ideology fell with the ending of white domination in the 1990s, still casts a long shadow over South African society – nowhere more excruciatingly than in its economic structures – witness Soweto. Even to this day, the greater number of those Sowetans who are employed (and 60 per cent are not) find work as domestic help in white suburbs or work in services or factories in Johannesburg and its environs (see the 'City of Johannesburg' website). One aspect of that legacy (notwithstanding the comparative wealth and decent housing enjoyed by an elite minority) is the grinding poverty of most of its inhabitants. Mass penury weighs heavily on the whole population not only because of the desperate neediness of most but also through rampant crime. Gangsters have for decades been endemic, so common that they became known in township slang as *tsotsi* – said to be a corruption of the term 'zoot-suit' in reference to the young men's fashionable clothes that as long ago as the 1950s they wore as a menacing sign of power and prosperity (see 'Sophiatown').

Not only does South Africa suffer from an appalling murder rate, one of the worst in the world, but the contrast between wealth and poverty is as extreme as anywhere else. Typically, no matter where they dwell, the significant minority who are affluent find it necessary to defend themselves from the attacks of organised bandits and common thieves by employing guards or carrying small arms. They also find it necessary to defend their luxurious villas with fortified fences and alarm systems. To the cost of their mortgage repayments, they must add unrelieved anxiety over their safety.

This, then, sketches the social backdrop to Gavin Hood and Athol Fugard's screenplay. As the only semi-educated member of the gang tells his leader, Tsotsi (Presley Chweneyagae), his is not a real name (but our anti-hero refuses to admit to any other). It makes him as much a social type as an individual. His story focuses on both societal and cultural inequity; but as Tsotsi feels stirrings in his soul, it also follows his journey out of self-blindness to the point where he recognises that becoming a human being with moral dignity is a feasible and worthy goal.

The story begins with the shaking of dice. Tsotsi's gang relax in a shebeen, biding time before their next raid. The exuberant music track 'Mdlwembe' that accompanies the gaming captures a triumphant African paradox – the vigour and passion of its people in the face of their lives' dire circumstances. The ivories fall on four and five. 'Eleven!' someone shouts. We have just begun to wonder what are the rules of this high-spirited game when Boston (Mothusi Magano) whose nickname is Teacher-Boy, corrects the addition. The game is not unfamiliar and the men are burdened with another of poverty's misfortunes, want of education. Right from the start, then, fate is seen to be implicit in the rolling of dice.

Their game done, the boys strut down an impoverished street under a threatening sepia-toned sky that has caught in the sun's dying light the red dust stirred by the township's passing multitudes. The gang take a train into the city. South Africa as a nation is riven by internal borders, and although the adamantine racial divides of apartheid have in some measure softened, vast differentials of income and wealth still separate people. So the train journey carries Tsotsi and his mates across an invisible borderline between the out of work and the employed. They arrive in central Jo'burg in time to leech on the evening rush of working men and women commuting home.

In the terminal concourse Tsotsi scopes the crowds and spots a complacent businessman purchasing from a vendor's stall a colourful scarf to take home to his woman. The contrast between the exuberantly coloured fabrics (not to mention the intimate affection) that the well-to-do can afford and the dull russets and browns of the township catches the spectator's attention. So too does this momentary intimation of femininity – the first we have seen, and soon to be obliterated. The gang ignore these fripperies that they cannot afford and focus piercingly on their intended prey. They follow him onto a crowded train, surround him with silent skill and lift his wallet. Warning the target not to protest the theft, one of the gang pokes a sharpened steel instrument against his chest. But when the victim strains to contain his outrage, Butcher (Zenzo Ngqobe), true to his nickname, needlessly slips the rod between his ribs, killing him instantly.

The intimacy of the murder brings to mind its opposite, namely the love enjoyed by the businessman who will never return to his woman, and which is so strikingly absent from the brutal lives of these boys. We are left with a powerful image of the four struggling to support the slain man's dead weight as they conceal the crime by keeping him standing until the train empties – an eloquent metaphor for their own internal emotional deadness. Then Boston vomits, unable to contain the hideous experience.

The men return to the shebeen where beer unlocks the dark thoughts that they have brought home with them. Tsotsi mocks Boston for throwing up. The latter responds defiantly by asking the gang leader to tell his real name. Then he tries to draw in the other guys – seeking to teach them moral knowledge they need urgently– by asking if they know what decency is. One replies that it is making a decent wage. Boston, now searching inchoately to find his centre and bring it back to life, tells them it's about the self-respect that he has lost. He smashes his bottle and scores his own arm until the blood runs. 'When we dropped that man,' he says, 'it felt like this inside.' At this, rage flares in Tsotsi's eyes, but Boston will not give over interrogating him about his family and feelings. The insistent questions cross an internal border and thrust toward opening out the leader's (and his own) obscure inner being. Plainly feeling this an intolerable intrusion upon his unknown inner territory, Tsotsi responds in the only way he knows, with extreme violence. He jumps Boston and beats him savagely, leaving his face pulped with one ruined eye. Without pausing, Tsotsi races out into the night where the dark (like his traumatised mind) is pierced by thunder and lightning. Something awakens inside – flashback to a memory of running as a young boy. But what made him run then, and what has it to do with the anger that is driving him now?

In the pouring rain Tsotsi loses all sense of time and place, inadvertently leaving his own territory once again. Shaking with cold or fear, he picks his way under a hectic sky that mirrors his bursting emotions. As he walks through a suburb of immense prosperity, another flashback hits him: rows of children living in a stack of cement pipes, with his childhood self dwelling among them. While in memory he stares at his former survival shelter, in raw contrast the present finds him gazing at the costly and pleasant home of well-paid professional people. As he muses, a car drives up to the gate. The woman driver (Nambitha Mpumlwana) gets out and, her remote control having failed, calls for someone inside to open the security gate. Before they can react, Tsotsi seizes the moment, holds her off at gunpoint and jumps into the driver's seat. In panic, the woman opens the passenger door. Tsotsi reacts automatically, shoots her and speeds away, his habitual pattern of fleeing from crisis now becoming apparent.

He has not gone far before a baby starts to cry from the back seat and Tsotsi looks behind him instinctively. Lacking driving skills, he lets the car go off the road and crash. Although he gets out unhurt and starts to walk away, this time it does not prove so easy to escape. The baby's cries escalate and something about the intensity of the noise calls him back. He finds a grocery bag and places the baby inside. Already, the African rain clouds have disappeared as fast as they came, leaving a full moon lighting the manic wasteland that divides the rich folks' mansions from the poor hovels way below. Tsotsi, shopping bag in hand, makes his uneven way across this empty no man's land. He seems, like some underworld pilgrim compelled to hellish business, to know its dark crevices well. The moon, however, is a powerful presence pulling the other way. It invokes the lunar, maternal archetype at what seems a most unlikely moment when the infant has just been snatched from its mother. Likewise the moon, redolent with ancient associations, encourages us to feel the illumining of the scene by the unconscious. Certainly no one could be less in conscious control of his actions than the panic-driven Tsotsi. Apropos, Richard Tarnas remarks that the feminine dimension comes to light whenever a re-birth is about to occur. He adds that the significance of the birth to come is in direct relationship to the degree of suffering that precedes it (2006). Tsotsi's relationship with this motherless child will lead us into the themes this film sets out to explore.

When he wakes in the morning, Tsotsi has an unpleasant introduction to his new parenting role. We can see that he does not have to share his single room with others, and that he possesses some high quality audio equipment, which he has no doubt stolen. Both facts mark his success as a gangster. But this morning the place stinks of baby. He has little idea what to do and his confusion has a comic as well as a dangerous edge. First he operates clumsily with a switchblade to cut off the messy diaper. Meanwhile, as the baby's yelling crescendos, Tsotsi feels exposed and blares his music system so no one can hear the crying. Sweetness momentarily surfaces in his nature when he dances to soothe the baby. To substitute for a diaper he uses the only material he can lay hands on, a newspaper. It makes a bizarre swaddling, all the more so in displaying a fragment of headline saying 'MOTHER'. The equally bizarre new 'mother' finds a can of condensed milk and does his best to pour it into the child's mouth. Although it makes another fine sticky mess, Tsotsi's eyes turn soft while feeding. The baby's powerless neediness has indeed ignited his own maternal instincts. It is the first hint that empathy with the infant's demands may have brought him briefly into contact with the hidden parts of himself – both baby and feminine.

Lest we forget the bigger picture and grow sentimental, we cut away to the baby's true mother, Pumla Dube, who is struggling for life on a hospital respirator. Nor does Tsotsi enjoy peace for long. One of the gang, loyal but slow-witted Die Aap (Kenneth Nkosi), comes to get Tsotsi's instructions for that night's action now that Boston is out of things. To hide the baby, Tsotsi keeps the surprised man at the door, pretending that his own sick gut has caused the vicious stench within. He is by no means free to reveal any hint of a softer side: it would merely make him vulnerable in the company he keeps. So he agrees to do another job and meet Die Aap (The Ape) and Butcher at the central station.

Prominently placed on the terminal building, a vast billboard carries a message that refers to the medical crisis devastating sub-Saharan Africa: 'WE ALL ARE AFFECTED BY AIDS.' Tsotsi, having crossed the border back into the territory where the gang hunts, is intent and hyped up for the next piece of action. He surely does not see the message, and the underlying idea that the fate of individuals is linked to their whole society certainly would not impress him. However, his untried presumption that every man acts only for himself is immediately tested. As he comes into the concourse, he trips over Morris (Jerry Mofokeng) a decrepit beggar with a glass eye, who has set his wheelchair where passersby cannot miss him. Although this man has lost his legs in a mining accident (and obviously has not been awarded compensation), the gangster quickly turns hostile. Surfing the dark waves of terror that he rides so familiarly, the young thug harasses the old man until the latter pisses himself. Yet, despite his defencelessness, Morris shocks his tormentor by admitting the humiliation, defiantly accepting his fear and facing it. Expecting first to be robbed and then, when Tsotsi pursues him into a squalid underpass, to be killed, he begins to throw stones at the youth. Despite his dreadful physical condition, the ex-miner is a man endowed with the kind of decency and courage for which Teacher-Boy Boston was grieving. Unexpectedly, rather than shoot the old man (although he has his gun in hand) Tsotsi picks up the lid of a trashcan and defends himself.

Tsotsi's passive posture creates a space (disguised by his continuing show of anger) in which the two men begin tentatively to explore each other. Tsotsi asks Morris why he wants to live like a dog. The old man responds simply that he likes to feel the sun on his hands. In this setting, trapped by night, an ugly city underpass and his disability, Morris's desire to be touched by the warmth of the sun – the archetypal image that stands in complementary relation to the moon – sits well with his self knowledge. It also complements Tsotsi's unconscious yearning to be in a meaningful human relationship. However, not only vulnerability but also a willingness to let go of the need to be in control is required for this level of integration. Tsotsi, by no means ready for that, closes off the relationship that has begun to develop by telling Morris to pick up his money – and then he walks away.

This time, however, Tsotsi is not absconding in his usual manner. Instead, rather than meet up with Butcher and Aap, he leaves Jo'burg on foot, walking along the railroad track under a smoky brown sky. He once again enters a borderline area on the threshold of his unconscious, but this time it seems closer to the light than before. Wrye remarks that a psychological threshold –

> may be understood as a particular kind of narrative space, which requires [of the individual entering it] a new logic and perspective beyond conventional orders of causality, sequence and selection. A threshold is a particular, often ephemeral, set of consciousness, in which the limits of familiar sameness and reputed difference are extended and enriched by holding simultaneously in mind a glimpse of other and self... The new way is... transitional in the sense of promoting change.
>
> *(Wrye, 2002)*

Murray Stein augments this in describing such liminal space as a cultural and psychological field in the imagination located interstitially between conscious and unconscious. Such a liminal state may predominate during periods of change in an individual's life cycle and link the old and new fixed identities between which the person is in transit (1980). As we shall discover in greater detail (see Chapter 5), it holds the potential to nurture an imaginal environment in which redemption from grief may be found.

Back home, Tsotsi finds the baby howling in the brown shopping bag that he has left under his bed. The infant has ants all over his face, drawn by the sticky condensed milk that still plasters his mouth. Tsotsi gently swipes the insects away, but recognises that he cannot meet the baby's needs. So he has to find a way to take care of this child whose eyes hauntingly mirror his own gaze. Next morning he looks around outside his shack and notices among the women and children waiting in line to draw water a young mother dressed in golden fabric with her baby wrapped to her back in the traditional manner. This is Miriam (Terry Pheto). The rich colour of her costume allied to her strikingly beautiful physical presence immediately offer her to spectators' eyes as a radiant cynosure of motherhood and the feminine – her image an icon of everything that the gangster lacks.

With his baby concealed in its bag, Tsotsi follows the young woman to her door. There he pulls his gun, making Miriam drop her full pail. The image of the spilled water becomes an eloquent emblem of how the life-giving feminine may be overturned by an overly aggressive masculine presence. That is mirrored in Tsotsi's conduct as he pushes Miriam indoors and, confident of the pistol's authority, instructs her to feed his baby. In fact, he now behaves like an infant suffering developmental arrest who believes himself entitled to whatever he wants. But then, when he sits and watches her breastfeed, hearing the baby's satisfied gulps, his eyes soften. To hide this weakness, he wanders around her home, so different (not just in its cleanliness) from his own.

In painful contrast to this curious domestic scene, Pumla, the baby's true mother, still lies in hospital bereft and crippled, though now breathing unaided. Her husband John Dube has had to take on the role of carer (not wholly unlike Tsotsi) as he directs the search for their stolen child.

Back in Miriam's room, Tsotsi swings between different states of mind, further evidence of his being caught in liminal space. Mobiles hanging from the ceiling arouse his curiosity; but when Miriam speaks of the emotions they evoke in her, he gazes at her like a curious child who doesn't understand. Tsotsi has had to learn to disown emotional experiences. In his life survival has been paramount and dreaded vulnerability must be avoided at all costs – yet for a moment he falls asleep, seduced by the security that the young mother radiates. Then he jerks awake again in order to maintain the vigilance of his ego: it is psychologically too dangerous for him to regress. But when Miriam washes the baby, talking to it melodiously, the comfort in watching her actions hypnotises him into another waking daydream. As the intense energy that he focuses on keeping control of consciousness diminishes, another painful childhood memory flashes back on him – his own mother turning her sick face toward him. Once again he jerks back into brutal survival mode. This time, gripped by fear, he leaves with the baby in its bag, warning Miriam that if she tells anyone he will kill her.

Reckoned together, Tsotsi's encounters with the baby, the crippled man, and Miriam the healthy mother are synchronistic events that call him to engage with the injured masculine, the maternal-feminine and the child archetypes. The inexpressible, magical quality that these chance meetings have in breaking the deeply inscribed routine patterns of his social and psychological life, provide him with an opportunity to correct his one-sided attitude. As we shall show in more detail in Chapter 7, synchronicities tend to appear at times of crisis or births and deaths. Sometimes they may be understood as signs that the universe can convey numinous messages. In Tsotsi's present circumstances they do not reach that wide or deep but furnish him with liminal space to dissolve the intense suffering he holds in his unconscious and thereby support his growth.

Tsotsi walks home under a blue sky. For the first time, instead of hiding the baby under the bed, he sets him comfortably on top against a pillow on which the sun shines luminously through the window. For the first time too we are conscious of the sun exerting its influence obscured by neither smoke nor dust, just as brilliant as the moon had been two nights earlier. As solar and lunar energy (masculine and feminine) move back into balance, it is worth recalling that the baby brings to mind the numinous offspring of such a union, the Divine Child. The latter can be interpreted as 'a symbol of future hopes, the seedling, the potentiality of life, newness…' (Hopcke, 1992: 107). Tsotsi's baby signals that potential in him, even though he has not yet realised it consciously. Appositely, according to Jung, the Divine Child as an archetypal image brings light and points to the conquest of the dark, yet its birth is troubled. 'Abandonment, exposure, danger, etc. are all elaborations of the "child's" insignificant beginnings and of its mysterious and miraculous birth' (1951: §285). It is easy to perceive that, psychologically speaking, there are two babies on Tsotsi's bed.

Tsotsi now remembers his sick mother calling him to her bedside to hold her hand. His mind releases the core, repressed trauma of his young life. In a dreadful substitute for the primal scene, his drunken father enters the family's shack, yelling at him to keep away from his mother lest he catch her sickness. Thus, Tsotsi has learnt from his parents that while the adult male commands without countenancing contradiction, the female wastes away. These are the core roles that have moulded his attitudes. As his father's voice pursues him we hear for the first time the boy's name, David. He runs away into the wasteland and finds refuge from his father's endless shouting in the stack of concrete drainage pipes alongside other homeless children. By extending our gaze beyond his own life to reveal countless other kids suffering the same misery, the film shows us that the collective experience of mother loss has significantly shaped the national culture and the morality by which great numbers of its people live. We can now read Tsotsi's as a story about a child whom AIDS has made motherless. Nor does that diminish the significant imbalance between the father and mother, the masculine and feminine since, according to many journalists' accounts, the rapid spread of the disease through Southern Africa owes much to men's promiscuity and unwillingness to use condoms. At the core this is an attachment problem: these men have no regard for the other in relationships.

The latest flashback experienced by Tsotsi is a further symptom that the psychological movement between conscious and unconscious states has opened up a space for him to begin grieving over his loss. Mourning, as Greg Mogenson suggests, is an intensely creative process: 'Much of what we mistake for psychopathology is unconscious mourning' (1992: xiv). Tsotsi now has an opportunity to create a healing emotional environment in the liminal space occupied by the interplay of horrible, memory-driven daydreams. Here he may begin to shift his suffering from the painfully concrete repetition within which he has been locked, to a place of movement and ultimately redemption. Within this psychological realm, a new meaningful experience may occur.

Back in present time, Tsotsi's grieving over his past advances when he takes the baby across the wasteland to see the abandoned children who still live in the concrete pipes. He has returned to his original place of mourning to touch not only his personal loss but also his cultural history. The image of rows of pipes (cold wombs containing hungry, motherless children, and destined to carry sewage) captures a collective pain. Freud described civilisation as a failed mourning process and this profound image is a testament to that insight. Yet there is wisdom to be found in this desolate place too: one of the children asks Tsotsi if the baby's mother died. Tsotsi tells him that one of the pipes used to be his and the boy understands that Tsotsi wants the baby to see his old home.

Anxious because the baby has been crying hard, Tsotsi returns to Miriam so she can feed him. Again the warmth of the young woman's generosity softens Tsotsi. She soon draws him out of his familiar defensive ground (it could hardly be called a comfort zone), and although it would be impossible for her to miss the type of youth he is, her words to him are kind. But then she tells him that her husband was murdered coming home from work. The information that the other man was a victim of tsotsi crime has to impact him in complex ways. No matter whether another gang, his own, or at worst he himself killed her man, his guilt by association cannot be dodged. Adding to the confusion this discovery causes Tsotsi, her acceptance of sorrow further bewilders him even as it expands his awareness of the potential depth of human dignity. Meanwhile, her vision as an artist stretches his comprehension of people's practical and spiritual potential. Amazed that she can sell for good money the mobiles that to him are nothing but pieces of junk and broken glass, he learns there are ways of earning a living, and mental ways of being which he knows nothing about. As Miriam speaks of enjoying the colour and light in her mobiles, a prism of light glows like hope on Tsotsi's face. It is a pigment in the broader emotional spectrum that she knows well but he has never felt.

Miriam asks Tsotsi to leave the baby in her care and Tsotsi accepts. In complete identification with the infant he gives him his own name and reminds her that the baby is his. By vicariously participating in 'David's' experience with a warm and healthy mother, Tsotsi begins to submit to the feminine and heal. This becomes obvious when he goes to the sick Teacher-Boy Boston (the sight in one of whose eyes has been damaged by the beating he took under Tsotsi's fists) and brings him back to his own place to take care of him. As they reconcile, Boston admits he was not able to sit his final teacher-training exam and Tsotsi offers to pay for it.

After nightfall, Tsotsi and the remainder of his gang return to the suburbs and look at baby David's house. Why, of all possible targets, have they chosen this place? Die Aap and Butcher know nothing of its significance to Tsotsi, and they have come to steal. For their leader, however, the house has significance as David's home. Perhaps he wants to know more about 'his' infant; perhaps his growing awareness of others has made him feel a need to connect to the parents.

A silver Mercedes drives through the gate and the boys sneak in behind it. They hold the home owner, John Dube (Rapulana Seiphemo), at gunpoint and tie him up. But finding themselves in the plush home of a corporate executive, these young men have only uncertain ideas what to look for. The most focused is Butcher who loots the master bedroom searching for valuables; and Aap, detailed to guard the owner, gorges on the abundant food and wine in the dining area. Meanwhile Tsotsi enters David's nursery, an infant's happy cornucopia of stuffed animals and toys. His face lights up as he takes it all in. Downstairs, the owner distracts Aap, encouraging his greed by pointing out where the best food and drink can be found, and manages to reach the alarm button. When it goes off, Tsotsi delays just long enough to stuff a bag with toys, powdered milk and a bottle. Butcher, however, is swifter and already has John Dube in his sights, on the point of pulling the trigger. A gun goes off and blood splatters on Dube, but it is Butcher who drops dead, shot by Tsotsi. Aap remonstrates outraged, but Tsotsi vindicates himself: with Butcher, he says, it was always kill, kill, kill.

The two survivors escape in Dube's Mercedes and quickly sell it to a car-jacking syndicate. Agreeing with his henchman that the latest calamity has ended their relationship, Tsotsi walks away; but then he changes his mind, goes back and gives Aap half the cash from the car sale, an act of decency toward his loyal follower.

Since Tsotsi and Dube are rival fathers to baby 'David', and at the same time the young man (as the true David) has positioned himself in quasi-filial relation to his rival, he would have permitted a symbolic act of patricide had he allowed Butcher to slaughter the householder. But by instinctively gunning Butcher down, Tsotsi has killed off his rage against his own father. He has now gained sufficient psychological distance to see that, although hitherto he could only perceive his father's cruelty in keeping him away from the mother he desperately needed, his parent was trying to protect him. The memory of that scene contains profound loss; but Tsotsi is now able to grieve that loss for himself. By extension this film, in encouraging grieving in HIV/AIDS-ravaged and disinherited African communities, offers a starting point from which other people in similar communities might journey to find themselves. It also allows its audiences to see how a masculine culture (which is impoverished in so many ways and which also excludes the feminine) tries to allay its manifold hungers by gorging on anger. However, that male dominated community does so in vain, creating only a vortex where every act of emotionally baffled fury powers up the torque. A culture detached from the feminine remains homeless in body and soul, negating its capacity for interior agency.

Miriam further stimulates the young man's capability for active interior existence when he returns for baby David. She could not have failed to have suspicions about Tsotsi from the moment he held her at gunpoint; but by this time she has read a newspaper report and knows for certain that he kidnapped the baby. Nevertheless she does not treat him with revulsion but prepares a meal for him. She refuses the money he offers (declining the taint of theft), but gently guides him toward accepting that he must return 'David'. She even offers to take the great risk of delivering him to his parents on Tsotsi's behalf. Finally, when Tsotsi gathers the baby to leave (accepting moral responsibility for his own actions), she gives him hope. With traditional demure acceptance she allows him to see that he may visit her again after the child has been restored to its parents.

Discarding for the first time his gangster's leather jacket (the iconic tough skin that holsters both his pistol and his over-emphasised masculinity), Tsotsi dons a simple white shirt (a sign of his ordinary humanity) and returns to the central station. He stops by Morris the crippled beggar and gives him money by way of apology. Where once (no doubt rooted in fear that his own fate might prove no better), hatred governed Tsotsi's desire to dominate this poor man, the strength to accept the value of embracing a submissive, healing love has evolved in his psyche.

Tsotsi goes one last time to the Dubes' home. He sets baby David down at the gate, planning but unable to walk away. So he presses the call button and tells John that he has brought back his baby. Little David begins to cry at the very moment when escape would have been easy for Tsotsi. Instead of attempting to flee, he puts himself at risk and lifts the baby up to cradle it. The feminine in his psyche has developed to the degree that he cannot abandon the infant any more than the Madonna could have left the Divine Child. Inevitably, Tsotsi's delay gives the Dubes' new security guard time to notice him and call the police.[1] They arrive swiftly and hold Tsotsi in their gun sights; but it is the baby's parents who control the negotiations, telling the police to back off so that no one gets hurt. They act with great courage and dignity given that their child is in the line of fire. John Dube talks to Tsotsi without anger, remembering that *in extremis* the youth opted to save his life. From her wheelchair, his wife Pumla demands with authority that Tsotsi give over her child. John opens the gate and crosses the street to take the infant and place him in his wife's arms.

The street presents us with a last emblem for liminal space – away from which Tsotsi is now finally moving. Although he has in the past crossed temporarily to the other side as an invader, he has now committed himself to the far side from the Dube family, the side nearer the shacks of the poor from whom he has sprung. With the moon flying in the back of the dark sky, Tsotsi's image simultaneously connects him with his past and reveals him in new colours, his white shirt hinting at his readiness for redemption. He weeps as he obeys the police and raises his hands, simultaneously surrendering as Tsotsi and claiming back his true name, David. His tears confirm that in returning the baby he has not surrendered the divine child in himself: he is ready for rebirth and new growth.

As we have indicated, synchronicities serve to break the boundary between subject and object and a whole set of them preside over Tsotsi's change back to David. Connecting with his baby self enables him to mourn at last his personal history. Synchronicities also oblige him to face and accept the handicapped and injured. In presenting him with mirrored aspects of his wounded self, they help mature him: the blinded eyes of Morris and Boston ultimately teach David how to see differently and understand what decency is. In returning the baby (as it were, via Miriam) to Pumla, he himself vicariously returns to the all-inclusive feminine. By now he recognises that he bears a terrible responsibility for having hurt each of these people gravely: he may not yet know that in attacking them he further injured himself. He has also had a first glimpse of the potential latent for his psychological growth in Miriam's entering his life. She is the positive anima who encourages him to move forward. At the last moment of their time together his relationship with her has shifted from a fixation on the anima as a projection of the mother to the beginnings of perceiving her in another guise of the anima, a reflection of his own healing, his increased self love and self worth and therefore as a possible lover. Even at the early stages, his new relationship with the unconscious or *anima mundi* humanises Tsotsi, beginning to illuminate him.

Recall now that the movie opened with the throwing of dice. A long, seemingly universal cultural history connects the game with attempts to foresee fate. (We write in depth on fate and destiny in Chapter 10.) Fate, according to Jung, is a label for whatever remains locked in the unconscious. With this in mind, he warned that the survival of civilisation depends on humanity re-connecting to the unconscious. Only when (both as individuals and in our collectives) we regularly experience the energy that can surge uncontrollably from the deep unconscious can we develop the grounding that will enable us to cope with it. This, framed as a necessary compensation for Europeans' over-valuation of intellect, was a good prescription for twentieth-century Western humanity, and probably remains so. However, the social and cultural conditions in *Tsotsi's* Soweto require its adaptation – certainly for this story world and presumably for the actual township and beyond it much of the African continent. The film, in short, shows its characters' need to enhance consciousness in addition to opening themselves to deeper understanding of the urges that arise from the unconscious clamouring blindly for satisfaction.

We have drawn attention to scenes in which the moon appears, encouraging a reading of the young gangster's psychology which sets it against the ignored background of the feminine principle and the lunar unconscious. Whilst the sun is in the sky in many scenes, *Tsotsi* is remarkable, given its South African location, for how seldom the hard-edged, brilliant light of day bears down on its protagonists. As we have said, the sun invokes in its familiar Jungian aspect not only the masculine principle but also consciousness. Here dust (augmented by lens filters, on-set lighting and printing techniques) shrouds the characters in a reddish urban miasma. No need further to explicate how this atmosphere captures *Tsotsi's* obscure soul; but the murk falls on the entire Sowetan community.

Looking back we can see how that opening throw of the dice gave the game away: through it, the players could have addressed either the known or the unknown world. In fact they barely engaged with either. Boston as teacher picks up on the lads' bad arithmetic. Their lack of education plainly has contributed to a condition of injuriously under-as opposed to over-developed consciousness. Their indifference to the damage they wreak on others plainly provides further evidence of that. However, throwing the dice also has powerful associations with divination, analogous to throwing the bones. Since shamanic spiritual healing practices remain common to this day among African peoples, the false addition of four and five as eleven might have been read by the players as having mystical significance – but no such interpretation of these 'bones' occurs to them. It is an indication that, although the men in *Tsotsi* are largely governed by the unconscious, they have lost through desuetude the means of gaining access to the images, ideas and other emanations that surface from it. Where shamanic practices would have guided their grandparents, these young, savagely impoverished urban dwellers have lost that advantage. The absence of containing ritual in their lives is all too evident.

The only character with confident and controlled access to unconscious impulses that feed her emotions (and thence her conduct) is Miriam. In her life the arts have substituted divination. Her civility, moral dignity and stature as the giver of life have the authenticity to remind the audience that only when people become aware that emanations from the unconscious counterbalance what the conscious mind seizes on can they be reasonably sure of being able to find an understanding and deal with those intrusions. Just as making her mobiles has helped Miriam gain a deeper knowledge of self, so the moving sounds and images that make up *Tsotsi* have comparable power to help its Southern African audiences.

Note

1 Just as the Dubes' guard provides them with a new security, Tsotsi's path of individuation has now built in him an internal security that he did not have before. Prior to this journey he had a false self organised around defending against the internal terror caused by the trauma of losing his mother. By reconnecting to his wounded baby self he learned to hold himself psychologically and emotionally. Only when one can hold oneself does an individual stop projecting undigested experience onto others, which allows a real encounter with another.

4

MILLION DOLLAR BABY (2004)

As Ed Buscombe remarks in his review of *Million Dollar Baby*, it resembles most movies that feature boxing in that fighting is not its principal subject, but a metaphor for life (2005: 67–8). In this sub-genre, themes such as courage, loyalty, comradeship, endurance, betrayal, blind anger and one form or another of corrupt behaviour (both in and out of the ring) commonly occur. At various times the main protagonists in *Million Dollar Baby* show most of the virtues and vices just listed. These moral qualities provide, so to speak, the basic topography against which *Million Dollar Baby* is plotted. The film is distinctive, however, because while these moral issues are constantly in the background, it foregrounds two less familiar themes: firstly, the strange, counter-instinctive skills that the boxer must learn; and secondly, the repression and displacement of grief together with the necessity eventually to confront that pain.

In *Million Dollar Baby*, the boxing world is grubby and, for all but the stars, impoverished. The Hit Pit Gym owned by Frankie Dunn (Clint Eastwood) looks so run-down it bears out his remarks that nobody ever made money from operating a gym. The gym scenes' drab colours and dull, relatively low-key lighting match the short sequences in Frankie's house. This is the more striking in that the bright exterior of the domestic property is not distinguishable from others in the sun-washed streets of this tree-lined Los Angeles suburb. Seen from outside, it fits well with the whitewashed neighbourhood church where he attends Mass each day, quite different from the grubby industrial wasteland into which the gym is squeezed. Yet the interior of his house, far from being a welcoming home, has the bare functionality of an unloved bachelor pad to which its owner retreats only to sleep. Its drab, brown rooms signal the dulled state of its owner's psyche. Frankie drives a battered, dying car and could not now afford to purchase a property in this smart middle-class street; so we presume he bought it when his training programme was more successful. In fact, although Frankie is short of cash and looks as though he will go out of business if the gym does not recruit more boxers, he differs from Tsotsi in that poverty is not one of the root causes of his problems.

A figure even more impoverished than Frankie is his caretaker, Eddie Scrap-Iron Dupris (Morgan Freeman) who ekes out an existence only one step from Poverty Row. Living in a box room at the gym and seemingly dependent on his boss for handouts, his one luxury is the pay TV service on which he watches fights. Scrap's socks have holes in them – because, he says, he prefers not to take the money Frankie offers him lest he gamble it away. That could be true, or a sardonic invention to save Frankie's face; yet this is not an exploitative relationship. Each man depends heavily on the other and there are strong bonds between them. Wary friendship and mutual loyalty link them, and the strength of their relationship gives them the psychological and social support that Tsotsi lacks until he begins to trust Miriam.

As Frankie's good but under appreciated shadow, Scrap is not only a protagonist, but also the film's narrator and back-street philosopher. In this respect he resembles Red, the character whom Freeman played in *The Shawshank Redemption*. Although no older than Frankie except in the burden of self-knowledge, he functions as both the trainer's and the audience's wise old man. The sorry condition of Scrap's socks punningly implies his access to the [w]hole. In this respect he differs from Frankie who would never stoop to 'holy' footwear – rather, he looks for the holy in Church. Scrap talks about the nature of boxing as seen not by punters in the ringside seats but by the pugilists. It is a craft whose techniques demand so much in labour, energy and focus from trainees and trainers alike that it overwhelms every other preoccupation. The boxer must have heart, but that's far from the most important quality. The gym sports a sad example in Danger, a hapless street kid whose heart bursts with desire to escape nonentity and be a champion. But lacking both technical skills and the focus to acquire them, he is a danger to himself rather than others whenever he steps into the ring. He never gains in competence and is brutally hurt by the gym bully in a one-sided knock down to which Danger willingly if stupidly submits. This gangly youngster's naïve attraction to danger represents the compulsive need of someone who has been exposed to it in his earlier life. We shall discover that in this he and Frankie stand at opposite ends of a spectrum: the older man avoids risk, the younger recklessly hurls himself at it. Yet at the end of the story, Danger returns to the gym. It's an indication that to grow, people have to confront risk.

Danger cannot master the phenomenon that Scrap describes as the way everything goes backwards in the sport. Boxers, the older man says, have to be trained by endless repetition to act in patterns that run counter to what instinct tells them. Where instinct says go left, boxers must learn to go right. They push themselves beyond endurance, risking everything for a dream that nobody but them sees. The camera dwells on the wearying practice of these routines – whether they occupy the foreground or grind on in the background while the main protagonists are focusing on other matters.

As Laplanche and Pontalis remark in a passage that could have described the sport:

> At the level of concrete psychopathology, the compulsion to repeat is an ungovernable process originating in the unconscious. As a result of its action, the subject deliberately places himself in distressing situations, thereby repeating an old experience, but he does not recall this prototype; on the contrary, he has the strong impression that the situation is fully determined by the circumstances of the moment.
>
> *(Laplanche and Pontalis, 1973: 78)*

The idea of doing things backwards contains the kernel of a metaphor with a long reach. The early Greek imagination envisaged the past and the present as in front of us, which explains how we can see them. The future, however, is invisible and therefore behind us. Only a few wise men can see what is behind them; some of these, like the blind prophet Tiresias, have been given this privilege by the gods. The rest of us, though we have our eyes, are walking blindly backwards into the future (Knox, 1995). Sure enough, the half-blind Scrap is the only man who can foresee the future in *Million Dollar Baby*, the only man who is not walking backwards into his fate.

Frankie Dunn, unlike the usual battle-hardened trainers in most boxing movies, is (within tight limits of his own imposing) not an unreflective man. Yet the business of training in which he is involved quells in him no less than his fighters any emotion that cannot directly be used in the ring. This discipline serves particularly well in the repression of feelings of loss since every boxer (so Scrap's mantra goes) can lose one fight. It's just that he must then work all the harder and with even more steely determination in order to return and triumph in the ring.

Frankie attends Mass every day, partly, it seems, so that he can torment the priest with obdurate questions about the nature and mystery of the holy trinity. This sparring contest has been going on for a long time between Frankie (playing the blockhead he patently isn't) and the clergyman. Exasperated that Catholic doctrine should be so blatantly challenged, Father Horvak (Brian F. O'Byrne) briefly rids himself of his scourge by telling Frankie to stay away from Mass for a day or two, pray and write to his daughter, Katie. Frankie receives this instruction with a touch of insolence, which hints that he is lying to the priest in claiming to write every week. It turns out much later that this has been a fine piece of acting by Frankie to hide a truth that he cannot bear to contemplate. This makes it also, of course, a particularly subtle moment in an extraordinarily compact and understated performance by Eastwood himself. It is quite late in the film when we discover that Frankie does indeed mail his daughter regularly. The letters have for years been returned unopened, yet he continues trying to reach her. So he knows where she lives, but she refuses any contact with him. Frankie's heartache over the loss of Katie is the first key to an aspect of his personality that he tries hard to conceal. But repetition, when neurotically obsessive, becomes as addictive as danger and keeps a person locked in the past. This has occurred with Frankie repeatedly attempting to get in touch with the feminine which constantly rejects him.

Although his pain is so deep that he has gone to the priest, he cannot, as a man locked into a man's world, admit his weakness. He taunts the clergyman to hide his feelings. His jibes, centring on core doctrinal teachings of the Catholic Church, at first hearing suggest that Frankie must be confronting an issue of faith. But the priest is not fooled. He realises that Frankie, coming to Mass every day for twenty-three years, has been seeking help, not to find a spiritual home but because, unable to hold his own suffering, Frankie makes the church its container.

Bereavement counsellors Geraldine M. Humphrey and David G. Zimpfer could have had Frankie in mind when they observe that loss is not only an integral part of life but that losses accumulate as an individual goes through the transitions that the years bring (1996: 1). In addition to his missing daughter, Frankie's woman has been gone so long that she is never mentioned by Scrap and only fleetingly in Frankie's bedtime prayer, 'Lord, protect Katie. Annie too.' And these two missing members of his family by no means account for all his losses. Frankie dreads allowing the people with whom he is concerned to face their own challenges. The mantra he drills into his boxers has become a part of the psychology that governs his own life: 'The rule is to protect yourself at all times.' But when he protects people, he inhibits them from the potential of maturing into the full dignity of their selves. What is eventually revealed to be a pattern is first seen when he holds back a boxer whom he has been training for a long time, an excellent prospect for major success. Big Willie (Mike Colter) has reached the peak of his ability and is ready for a title fight. But Frankie insists on an endless series of preliminary bouts with unimpressive opponents. Reluctantly Willie leaves his camp for a manager who secures the world title fight swiftly – at which the big man triumphs. Willie has recognised Frankie's limitation; but in prioritising necessary loyalty to himself, the boxer has inflicted another loss on the trainer. As it happens the injury this causes will be of advantage to the latter in helping him move forward eventually, though not until after his next protégée gets into difficulty through Frankie's inhibition.

Not until much later does Scrap reveal the source of Frankie's obsessive need to control and protect his fighters. It stems from a loss twenty-three years earlier when Scrap himself was the man in the ring. Hired as his second for that night only, Frankie had wanted to throw in the towel because his man had already been badly hurt. However, only a manager could do this, and Scrap's manager was in a bar getting drunk. Scrap insisted he could turn the fight around and continued when the bell rang, a ruinous decision that cost him an eye and Frankie his peace of mind. Ever since, Frankie has employed and housed Scrap in the gym, unable to forgive himself (in a false fantasy of omnipotence) for an injury he had no means of preventing.

As Humphrey and Zimpfer show, the grieving process necessary after any major loss matters because, once lived through fully, it enables an individual to move forward into renewed life. Unfortunately British and North American social conventions have shaped the culture so evident in *Million Dollar Baby* where grief is legitimated only by death. This inhibits grieving for the many other kinds of loss – phenomena as diverse as separation and divorce, change of home, theft of precious possessions and the physical and mental changes that come with ageing. Here, in stark outline, is Frankie's predicament. It is always with him because, as Humphrey and Zimpfer insist, the grieving that follows loss cannot be the passive process many perceive it to be. It is not an affliction to get over as one gets over an unpleasant illness such as mumps or measles which cure in their own time. On the contrary, grieving must be undergone, with the pain suffered (not avoided in the way Frankie tries) and the whole process understood. The full recognition of loss must then be incorporated in the individual's life in order to permit adaptation to his or her changed circumstances (Ibid.: 1–2).

Losses are multiple in the sense that the experience of each loss is influenced by the previous ones that the individual has suffered (Ibid.: 1–2). Frankie has suffered losses that are linked and has not found a way to mourn them and move on. Despite the crippling impact on both his professional and personal life of what has been taken from him, he has found no means of adapting his expectations to meet the continuing emotional cost. By contrast, Scrap (who has taken responsibility for his own decision) has long ago worked through grieving for the loss of an eye and has adjusted to his injury in a way that Frankie never could.

The oppressive refusal to allow the people he cares for to take risks in the process of growing into full selfhood may have destroyed any relationship Frankie once had with his woman. It may well also have been the underlying cause of the rift from his daughter. Frankie imposes too much Law for anyone who wants to become his or her own person to live indefinitely within his orbit. The only exception is Scrap who has become wise through suffering serious injury and learning the healing power of acceptance. He alone among the male characters perceives that Frankie's insistence on his law requiring his trainees 'to protect yourself at all times' is driven ultimately by a need which he himself cannot recognise. It is the rule by which Frankie lives and permeates both his conscious and unconscious behaviour. Significantly, self-protection is one of the fundamental psychological themes that surface repeatedly in counselling. Keeping the barriers up – always protecting the self – is hard work. Furthermore, defending against the bad also locks out the good. Frankie will have to learn how to relinquish his insistence on protecting himself if, like anyone else who is frozen in pain, he is to adapt to the changes that circumstances impose on his life. Grief that is not lived through inhibits development of the self.

There is an absolute absence of the feminine in the tacky Hit Pit Gym until, determined to become a professional boxer, a youngish woman pushes her way in. No wives, girlfriends, or female trainees come through its doors, though other gyms do train women. Nor does any touch of Eros soften the pervasive Logos. Paradoxically, the dominance of Frankie's autocratic and masculine law may be a factor that actually attracts Maggie Fitzgerald (Hilary Swank), given that her circumstances mirror his. After her beloved father had sickened and died, her family had lost such balance as he had been able to maintain. No longer contained by the father, the others' dependency erupted and turned it into a hell-hole ruled by two monstrous and mean-minded women, her mother and sister. Usually a child primarily identifies with its same-sex parent and needs to be validated by the opposite-sex parent. Maggie, however, has identified with her father, the only healthy choice available to her. She can be compared with her sister who is identified with their mother. There is no spark of kindness in either the sister or mother, and their home offers Maggie no loving female exemplar on which to model herself. Their most pronounced quality is greed (the mother is grossly overweight). Narcissistic behaviour appropriate in a baby's appetite for its mother's milk, is pathological in adults. Indeed, the mother and sister are so undeveloped that psychologically they are babies. As Laplanche and Pontalis say, this primitive state, called primary narcissism is characterised by the total absence of any relationship to the outside world, and by a lack of differentiation between ego and id (1973: 256).

The only thing Maggie has been taught by the women in her family is that she is trash. Rather than sink into the mire, however, she uses grief for her dead father to create something new. Given her family history, it is no surprise that she wants to stay attached to a paternal figure. She is a father's daughter, something that makes her feel special. In her life only Logos has been shown to be dependable and professional boxing is her chosen way into that world. Therefore Maggie has made an emotional investment in being different. Loathing the cheating way her mother and sister live on bogus welfare claims and disgusted by dependency, Maggie waits on table in cafés and diners, eking out an existence on the margins. But after moving to LA from their trailer park in the Ozarks, she finds finances desperately hard. Reduced to eating leftovers from customers' plates and dossing in the meanest rooms, she scrapes together the cash needed for training. Paying fees months in advance gains her entry to the gym; but Frankie refuses point blank (time and again as the weeks pass) to have any part in training her. Symbolically he is rejecting the very feminine that he so much needs. Nevertheless, despite being brusquely dismissed by him – she is too old at thirty one… she has no hope of making it… she should go to one of the gyms nearby which do train 'girlies' – Maggie is undeterred. Since no rational explanation is offered for her choosing Frankie in the first place, nor for her persistence in the face of painful rebuffs, it is evident that an overwhelming intuition has led her to him.

Her persistence wins Scrap's sympathetic collusion first. He offers her a few training hints and by giving her minimal equipment and a thread of hope enables her to begin to wear Frankie down. Here we see an early indication that Scrap is a true, though wounded healer, fashioned after the type of the Ancient Greek Asklepios. By helping Maggie resist Frankie's attempts to eject her from the gym, he begins to reintroduce the feminine to the masculine. Scrap is the container of a wisdom (wisdom in the stink of the gym) that Frankie (who actively resists whatever advice the caretaker offers him) has yet to find for himself.

Eventually, however, Frankie's resistance is broken by the desperate need that underlies Maggie's dream of boxing glory. By assertively refusing to give up her dream she demonstrates masculine characteristics. When she shows him that this is the only way she can give her existence meaning, he concedes gruffly. Not that he abandons his personal armour. While reluctantly agreeing to take her on, he dictates a rigid set of conditions – in effect a one-sided, self-protective contract. She must do exactly what he tells her. She must not question anything he says. Furthermore, when he has trained her fully, she will have to find a manager for herself and then he will have no further contact with her. As usual, Frankie retains the Law firmly in his own hands and is repeating the pattern of exerting control to ward against loss. Sure enough, when eventually against all the odds Maggie does attain fight fitness, Frankie holds her back from major contests. In the meantime, however, she accepts his terms and devotes herself wholeheartedly to working up her craft. There is wisdom in the feminine: she knows intuitively what she needs.

A remark by Frankie hints at an unconscious readiness for change that he certainly would not have been able to admit to himself. He mutters that he probably keeps the gym going only because he loves the stink. In the context of Frankie's inner life, we can take this aside as a suggestion that his unconscious may be ready to ferment growth: our psychological life resides in the stink of the unconscious.

Maggie is a driven woman, and although Frankie's instructions amount to an attempt to control her, she has heart in plenty. In time personal feelings inevitably insinuate themselves into their professional relationship, however much Frankie resists them. For example, he cannot but admire the ferocious purity of her focus; and she in turn begins to flourish, nurtured by the sense of value gained from Frankie's minute attention to her training regimen. Their relationship deepens as the weeks pass and each gets glimpses behind the tough mask of the other. Frankie speaks briefly about the daughter with whom he no longer has any connection and mutters that Katie used to be athletic. Not hard to see that Maggie is the only person who could fill the hole in his heart; but it's not a role that she could claim in any overt way because his defences are too massively buttressed. So Maggie toils away as Frankie's trainee, observing the terms he lays down; but in fulfilling them she also gradually slips into the role of daughter. Her wry sense of humour begins to subvert the emotional detachment that he wishes to impose on the relationship through his dictatorial terms. However, wisecracks alone would never suffice to melt Frankie. It takes her combination of subaltern wit, toughness and aching need to begin to crack open his crusty facade. Neither of them could put this into words, and if someone like Scrap had spoken in these terms, they would have repudiated them. Nevertheless, Maggie in effect 'trains' Frankie's heart. She thaws his frozen grief just as he repairs her sorrow. Each becomes the other's family. The tortuous process through which they open each other out is the equivalent in their relationship of the boxer having to do everything backwards. And the development of feelings between them not only tests her strength but also starts to wear away his depression. Maggie eventually restores Eros to both Frankie's and her own life, introducing a sense of aliveness where depression had brought an emotional deadening.

Not that Frankie initially has any claim on her other than as trainer. And he gives up even that right (as he said he would) when he refuses to arrange a fight for her and pushes her toward a manager. However, for his own financial gain, that unscrupulous manager puts her in the ring with an opponent too strong for her. Maggie gets into serious difficulties. Goaded by Scrap, who sees that his old friend has betrayed his fighter by abandoning her, Frankie forces his way to ringside and takes command of the bout. His curt directions remedy Maggie's technique and sting her into the ruthlessness needed to redeem the fight. This is the first instance of the synergy of masculine and feminine arising from his responsiveness.

The episode marks the moment when Frankie begins to wrest a hard-won accommodation to the past traumas that have crippled his work and life. Loss is an event that 'requires that some part of the individual be left behind and grieved before the process of transition and rebuilding can occur' (Humphrey and Zimpfer: 1996: 1). Frankie has not only redeemed his betrayal of Maggie but also intuitively taken the first step toward recovery from the old losses in accepting the responsibility to manage her. In so doing he manages also his own grief rather than splitting it off. It is the first indication of his willingness (without being able to verbalise it) to change the ways to which he has become conditioned. Since the grieving process is a cycle that has to be worked through time and again, it is reasonable to anticipate that Frankie will have to experience more pain before the process is done (Ibid.). Nevertheless, the near disaster of that first major fight delivers more than a professional turning point for both Frankie and Maggie and marks the start of a mutually trusting personal relationship.

Frankie Dunn is no dullard. But nothing in what the audience has discovered about him prepares it for the incongruous use of his spare moments in the gym. Although he does not care to reveal it to anyone other than Scrap, he is teaching himself Gaelic and relishes the poetry of W. B. Yeats. He never explains why, but exercises his mind with repetitions that seem as tough and counter-intuitive in their own way as the boxers' physical routines. But here, rather than reinforce the old mental conditioning, he is developing new ways of thinking. Eastwood may well from the director's chair have had in mind doffing his cap to John Ford and John Huston. Both were Irish-American filmmakers with a well-known love of boxing and the old country. Certainly, *Million Dollar Baby* can be seen as an homage to Huston's *Fat City*, an equally keen evocation of the sport as a seedy business (French, 2005). But how do the literary interests of the character Eastwood plays fit his role? Frankie shows no ambition to visit the old country and perhaps has no more than a nostalgic passion for the ancestral home, in common with so many Irish Americans. So we cannot for a long time understand the resonances the language and poetry has for him.

In the meantime, buoyed by the knowledge and confidence she receives from him, Maggie seems suddenly to have become unstoppable. The synergistic effect of the masculine working in conjunction with the feminine makes itself felt constantly. Eastwood allows the audience to enjoy her successes as they mount up rapidly – her fans growing in noisy number, her opponents knocked over in the first round and her promotion to an altogether tougher league. Soon, partly from an unsuspected delight in showmanship and also to give Maggie her due, Frankie gives her a new name and the glamorous apparel of a championship contender. He has 'Mo Cuishla' embroidered on emerald shorts and her silk dressing gown, but declines to reveal its meaning before she becomes world champion. Rather than the blare of triumphant pop music that accompanies her opponents' parade to the ring, pipers escort Maggie's entry. She thrills to the panoply even though (like most of the audience) she has no idea what her new name, heraldic for Frankie, should mean to her.

As soon as she is earning good money, driven by winner's guilt, Maggie innocently overcompensates. She buys a house for her mother (Margo Martindale) so that she and Maggie's sister can move out of the trailer park. After winning a fight not too far from their home, she persuades Frankie to make a detour to surprise the women with the gift. But her mother (a woman so gross she must have stuffed her emptiness for decades) can only berate her daughter for the gift because she realises that owning a house will put at risk her ill-gotten welfare benefits. The sister, another welfare cheat, is so mean-spirited that she can only find fault with the new dwelling. And the mother repays Maggie's kindness by scorning her choice of sport as freakish. Envy devours both women. Maggie's unconscious attempt to heal her own wounded feminine has been a complete failure. She has mistakenly focused on her idealised internal imago of the woman who should have been formative in her personal development.

Back on the road, as they drive through the night, Maggie allows sorrow to well up. While their faces slide between darkness and visibility under passing streetlights, she tells Frankie that she has nobody but him. That day's experience of family has pushed her out of denial and into healthy grieving, recognising that she has been alone since her father died. Her words touch Frankie deeply because of his similar loss and he tells her that she has him. As Roger Ebert noticed, 'the rhythm of this lighting matches the tone and pacing of the words, as if the visuals are caressing the conversation' (2005). Like Tom Stern's chiaroscuro cinematography throughout, it complements the oscillating process of moving between darkness and light as they share their sense of loss of family. Maggie gives voice to emotional recollections of the father she loved and Frankie's gruff response speaks volumes about his empathy. The visit has been the second, necessary dramatic disaster Maggie and Frankie have shared. Whereas previously both father and daughter pairs were like different parts of the psyche that were not yet integrated (see Samuels, 1985: 30), this visit helps bond them as a new family and this time they both know it. Here are the beginnings of the new 'spiritual family', a new wholeness.

Now Maggie gives Frankie directions (reversing their roles in the first disaster) and guides him to Ira's diner, where her father used to enjoy the best homemade lemon pie in the world. The pursuit of perfection in this dish happens also to be Frankie's only sensual Grail – one of the few passions to which he can admit. At the risk of over-egging the pudding, notice that the lemon pie can be interpreted as soul – eating it is a metaphor for the process of recovering from grief. The bitterness has to be tasted, but after it, sweetness prevails. Having eaten, Frankie announces that he can now die and go to heaven. It is a quiet moment, but a celebration nonetheless.

Frankie now negotiates 50 per cent of a one million dollar purse for a title fight – the pinnacle of Maggie's career. However, the current champion does not wear the belt for her unaided pugilistic skills alone, but because she will do anything to win. She cold-bloodedly sets out to destroy Maggie with foul punches – another indication of the wounded feminine. Frankie, who has never done so before, orders his girl to use her only defence and respond in kind. Having weakened the champion with a succession of blows to the kidneys, Maggie floors her. In the bedlam that follows, our hero is already celebrating when the hired man acting as her second (Scrap having declined to join the team) puts the stool into the ring prematurely and on its side (mistakes which Frankie never makes). The downed champion rises from the canvas and takes a vicious swing at her opponent who has turned away to share success with her fans. The blow knocks Maggie over and her neck breaks over a leg of the stool.

Several people bear responsibility for the injury that leaves Maggie a quadriplegic dependent on machinery for every breath. The champion, Frankie and Maggie herself head the list for breaking the sport's laws. Scrap (for staying away) and the hired second for his ineptitude also share in the blame. However, Scrap in his narration shows no interest in attributing blame. Indeed, a dispassionate look at what passed in the ring reveals that, in addition to rule-breaking and incompetence, happenstance played a part in maiming Maggie. She also forgot to 'protect herself' after knocking down her opponent – a failure she admits to her trainer after recovering consciousness. However, had the bout been conducted according to the rules, she would have had no need to do so at that moment because the referee had already stopped the contest. When the rules of sport are abandoned, something akin to warfare breaks out. Frankie's decision to break the rules is an indication he has allowed himself to move beyond the rigid psychological position of rules and laws toward a fuller personal integrity. In psychological terms, in the immediacy of the crisis, Frankie has moved to save the feminine, his anima. His violation of the rules is driven by an appropriate regression from socially accepted mores to honour the stronger need to save Maggie – a moment that represents an awakening of his soul. The contestants in this bout have gone *backwards* to an elemental atavism in the attempt to gain victory. In psychoanalytical terms that implies transcendence, a topic to which we must return.

There is a curious obliquity in the presentation of the fight's ending since the spectator is left uncertain until much later whether Maggie has been judged to have won or lost. The point is that the championship no longer matters to either her or Frankie. They have other, more important concerns. That the protagonists have entered a new psychological as well as dramaturgical realm is signalled by the bloodless blue of the hospital sequences. Frankie initially responds to the maiming of his girl with rage that verges on hysteria. He tries to load his guilt into Scrap, transparently seeking to relieve his own sense of culpability. Then he directs his anger at Maggie's doctors, insisting their diagnosis that nothing can be done for her is wrong. This is classic behaviour on the part of grieving family members and shows their inability to hold the suffering. Faced with bad news about someone they love, they often experience anger directed at medical staff, a denial that may take the form of shopping around for different opinions, as Frankie does (Kübler-Ross, 1969: 149). In his shock he projects the complete failure of his own omnipotence onto the doctors. This is all the evidence we need that by repeating and intensifying what had previously happened to Scrap, Maggie's injury threatens to immure Frankie once again in the emotional ice from which he has only lately emerged. It is a time fraught for him with the risk of regressing and losing all that he had gained.

It is Maggie who once again saves Frankie from himself. She never complains about what has happened. Nor does she lose her fighting spirit or her sense of justice. Both animate what turn out to be her final dealings with her birth family. Despite Frankie's many phone calls, the rag-tag brigade shows no interest in visiting her, and the weeks pass. Eventually, after Maggie has been brought by ambulance back to LA, they do make the journey from the Ozarks. But having checked into a hotel, they devote their time to amusing themselves in Southern California's theme parks, re-emphasising their childishness. When finally they do call at the hospital, they bring along a lawyer and it soon becomes plain that their only interest is in persuading the incapacitated young woman to sign her money over. She is nothing but an object to them. Frankie's outrage is almost beyond containment, but Maggie insists on dealing with the family without his support. She commands full authority and no longer needs him to protect her because she now contains the internal resources to deal with them. His reluctant acknowledgement of her demand marks new trust of the feminine.

Indifferent to the injury that has left Maggie unable to move her limbs, the family wheedle for her cash. Showing no compunction, her hideous mother clumsily slots a pen between Maggie's teeth and urges her to sign the legal papers. Her relatives' narcissistic dependency on her is complete, but Maggie now no longer feels responsible for them. Fired to cold anger, she dispatches them with the one threat she knows will hit hard. Her mother having failed to sign the deeds for the house (because she would have had to give up her illegal welfare claims), the property still belongs to Maggie. She tells the family that she will sell it if they ever pester her again. As Scrap says, commenting on an earlier incident, Maggie always did like to knock out her opponents in the first round.

Thus, where it remains within her power, Maggie focuses her anger purposefully, without trying to remedy the irreparable. Far from being consumed by regret, she celebrates having been up there with the greats, telling Frankie that with her success and the enthusiasm of her fans 'I got it all — unless they keep taking it away from me.' Her anger is directed not at the past but against a future in which, as her body deteriorates and she loses a leg to gangrene, she can see how, blow by surgical blow, her vitality will be leached from her. She determines to refuse a half-life that negates everything she has achieved: the prospect of being cooped in her own rotting carcass sustained indefinitely by a respiratory machine is for Maggie a horror worse than death.

No human experience is more apt to induce narcissism than an individual's personal pain and suffering. This is obvious when comparing Maggie with her odious family. She is far from narcissistic, harbouring neither self-pity nor anger, focused instead on moving forward. Whereas in the past she, like Frankie, has had to grieve for a broken attachment, now she must seek non-attachment in order to achieve transcendence. Kübler-Ross wrote (in a passage that could have described

Maggie's achievement) that the process of dying, all the suffering, allows the patient who learns to accept it to temper the iron and gives her the opportunity to grow (1995: 35). In this process, a secure personal attachment allows sufficient space for each party to be what he or she is and to let go when the need arises. Maggie actually embraces a final opportunity for growth by seeking to bring on her own death in the face of inevitable physical decline. She no longer needs the body to individuate but can do so by surrendering to experience.

A parallel process of growth can be achieved by someone who loves a dying person. The more that preparatory grieving can be expressed beforehand, the less unbearable the death when it occurs (Kübler-Ross, 1969: 149–50). Frankie does not know this beforehand but arguably finds it out after giving Maggie the terrible help she asks for. Psychological preparation creates a larger container to bear the eventual suffering. Having said this, his easement does not come without extreme pain.

Maggie asks him to make the supreme sacrifice – to release her from living death. He is unable at first to let her go. Such is the extremity of her soul, however, that after he denies her she attempts suicide by biting off her tongue (doing it again after the medics stitch it back on). Her act has monstrous, even outrageous qualities, but makes her the wounded healer of herself. Commands proceed from the tongue, so her violent act mutely communicates to Frankie that if he won't respond to her, she has nothing more to say to him. She as the feminine, the soul, retains complete control.

Thus she confronts Frankie with a dreadful predicament, all the more conflicted by the bond that ties him as loving father to his maimed daughter. Not only is Maggie's body still dying by inches, but the nursing staff have injected a strong sedative, thereby robbing her of control. They mean to prevent her trying suicide again; but by succumbing to the moral and legal pressures to which all medical staff are exposed and attempting to preserve life at all costs, they have expunged the freedom of her soul. The moral and spiritual agony that her suffering causes Frankie drive him back to Father Horvak. The priest advises him, 'If you do this thing, you'll be lost somewhere so deep you will never find yourself.' This edict is a key indicator of the priest's limitations and explains why he has never been able to guide the trainer. He is a man of the Church and as such is directed by dogma. In fact, his relationship with Frankie can be compared with Maggie's mother to her daughter. Neither 'parent' is interested in change. Both are ill-equipped to go into the depths, and although Father Horvak has Frankie's interests at heart, he is not a soul-directed man and his anathema turns out to be mistaken.

Maggie's desperate attempt at annihilation and the guidance that Scrap offers persuade Frankie. The wise old man tells the trainer that Maggie is ready for death, having achieved her life's ambition, something more than most people do. It is what the other man needs. He returns to Maggie's hospital room in the dead of night with his medical kit. Only now does he tell her that her Gaelic *nom de guerre* Mo Cuishla means 'My darling, my blood'. These words anoint Maggie with the ritual blessings of a rite of passage. They show that he has earned the right of parenthood to his daughter. No sooner has he given her his blessing than he performs the ultimate sacrificial act of love and administers a massive overdose of adrenalin to end the existence of his beloved child.

The focus of the story now shifts to Scrap who has followed Frankie to the hospital, secretly observing his final moments with Maggie. It turns out that Scrap has been motivated by the trainer's courage to tell the story to Frankie's long-lost daughter Katie. By tenderly explaining her father to her, Scrap once again brings the masculine to the feminine and attempts to make things whole.

Scrap concludes his account by reporting that Frankie never returned to the gym and all-male experience. The consequences of what *in extremis* he did to end Maggie's life have forced him to flee. Now a fugitive from the law (an intriguing reversal of roles for the old Law giver), moving on has brought to an end the longest phase of his life. The boxing milieu and everything which that framed for him has been left behind. Taken together with the pain of Maggie's end, the transformation of his existence amounts to a kind of death. Yet there is regenerative compensation for his loss. When Scrap brings his account to a close, he allows us to conjecture that Frankie may have returned to Ira's country diner. Through its misted windows a man who could be Frankie can be seen at the counter eating the café's homemade lemon pie. Whether Frankie has in truth gone back there or not, the reprise of the shot with its suggestion of tranquillity and peace is psychologically right and complements his gracious act of compassion and kindness – it has indeed gained him a taste of heaven on earth. The implication confirms the hint given earlier when Frankie read Yeats's 'The Lake Isle of Innisfree' to the hospitalised Maggie.

Frankie's enthusiasm for Irish culture is not of itself sufficient to account for the significance of his quiet but emotional reading.

> I will arise and go now, and go to Innisfree,
> And a small cabin build there, of clay and wattles made:
> Nine bean-rows will I have there, a hive for the honey-bee,
> And live alone in the bee-loud glade.
>
> And I shall have some peace there, for peace comes dropping slow,
> Dropping from the veils of the morning to where the cricket sings;
> There midnight's all a glimmer, and noon a purple glow,
> And evening full of the linnet's wings.
>
> I will arise and go now, for always night and day
> I hear lake water lapping with low sounds by the shore;
> While I stand on the roadway, or on the pavements grey,
> I hear it in the deep heart's core.
>
> *(Yeats, 1893: 12–13)*

The lake isle is an image familiar to Americans: Yeats recalled that his poem owed something to Thoreau's *Walden* (Ibid.: 196). Both writers gave the paradise motif a post-romantic twist so that it voiced the search for peace attained through a life in which body, mind and soul harmonise with each other and the natural environment. Both encouraged meditation on the potential for deepening human experience in an enriching, quasi-religious manner through the marriage of the imagination's universe with sensory apprehension of the physical world.

Jung's observation that when archetypal images surface in the psyche they compensate the dominant state of consciousness is relevant in that poetry like Yeats's resembles the arcane language of the soul, a courtship of the anima. Although we have never been told why Frankie is learning the archaic language in which 'The Lake Isle' was originally written, his attraction to the poetry rises from a part of him that connects with unconscious energies. These energies are now pushing him forward into his future. It is not too difficult to see Frankie as a man who has been standing 'on the roadway, or on the pavements grey' holding an image of a paradise, than which none can be more archetypal 'in the deep heart's core'. The contrast could not be more sharply drawn between the contorted life of the boxer doing everything backwards (what Scrap describes as an unnatural dream) and Yeats's vision of the soul's peace.

By the end of the film, Maggie, who has become the million-dollar baby, has also achieved her dream. Dreams, whether lived out or held as an image, have significant value in opening the path toward transcendence. Dreams instil hope and are the foundation of faith in the search to find what we are missing. Joseph L. Henderson describes transcendent symbolism, which may indeed manifest in certain big dreams, as connected with periods of transition in a person's life by pointing to his or her need for liberation from a state of being that is too immature, too fixed or final. He adds that transcendent symbols concern the individual's 'release from – or transcendence of – any confining pattern of existence, as he [or she] moves toward a superior or more mature stage in his [or her] development' (1964: 146). It then becomes clear that the function of suffering and sacrifice in Maggie's and Frankie's lives has served its obscure purpose.

At the end of her life, although Maggie has physically regressed into a defenceless and dependent baby, she is not an infant at all but a rich innocent in her life and psyche.

PART 2
Transitions to wholeness

5

TROIS COULEURS

Bleu (1993)

We mentioned in discussing *Tsotsi* (Chapter 3) that a principal factor linking psychotherapy, grieving and that film's principal character is the liminal space of the imagination within which his concern with loss is activated. Murray Stein describes liminal space as a cultural-psychological interstitial field that predominates during periods of change in an individual's life cycle. It links the old and new fixed identities between which the person is in transit (1980: 21). Such a liminal state holds the potential to nurture an imaginal environment in which redemption from grief may be found. In part this is effective in the cinema because it creates a powerful dialectic between what it projects mechanically (sound and image) and what is perceived (emotionally charged darkness and light). As a modern technological and imaginal space that has an extraordinary capacity to articulate the imagination, cinema creates a psychic borderline area – a field with both the means and space to entice the psyche into discovering new life. The familiar physical world dissolves, engendering sensitivity to the realm of the imagination. Spectators become immersed in the viewing, drawn further in by the archetypal images that films typically present. Krzysztof Kieslowski's *Blue* provides us with an excellent demonstration of liminality experienced both by the lead character and the audience.

On the surface, Kieslowski's output as a director was diverse. In the 1970s he made documentaries, focusing on Polish political and social life under Communist rule. Later he concentrated on feature films that took the lives of plausibly characterised individuals as their subjects. In his own mind, however, it is apparent that, even as it evolved, his work was all of a piece in its central concern. As he said in interviews toward the end of his life, 'the inner life – unlike public life – is the only thing that interests me' (1999: 162). However, as he had observed on an earlier occasion,

> The inner life of a human being... is the hardest thing to film. Even though I know that it can't be filmed however hard I try, the simple fact is that I'm

> taking this direction to get as close to this as my skill allows... The goal is to capture what lies within us, but there's no way of filming it. You can only get nearer to it.
>
> *(Kieslowski, 1993: 194)*

In his films, the inner life is intensely dynamic, revealing (to quote Janina Falkowska) 'strong emotions that seem about to burst through the surface of the elegantly composed images' (1999: 137). Furthermore, although the emotions themselves are easily recognised, their causes, meanings and implications (for both the narratives and the aesthetics that frame them) are by no means always simple to understand. They can, indeed, be mysterious.

> Within the framework of the film, ... these mysteries often involve very small things or things that are inexplicable... They are often very tiny, insignificant things. But I think that there is a point at which all these trifling matters, all these little mysteries, come together like droplets of mercury to form a larger question about the meaning of life, about our presence here... I think it has very clear existential connotations – that it is purely and simply the mystery we actually face every day. The mystery of life, of death, of what follows death, what preceded life: the general mystery of our presence in the world at this particular time, in this particular social, political, personal and familial context, and any other context you might think of.
>
> *(Falkowska, 1999: 167)*

Although Kieslowski insisted that his films had no religious connotations, he would have had in mind Poland's dominant Catholicism. When religion is considered as an aspect of the quest for inner understanding, however, it cannot be denied that his films engage with the numinous.

One other recurrent thematic feature of Kieslowski's films must be remarked on, namely the impact of chance on his characters' lives. The significance of the topic is obvious in that he made a film entitled *Blind Chance*. Completed in 1981, it was banned in Poland by the Communist authorities of that era (for reasons that the storyline makes obvious) and not released until 1986. Yvonne Ng reports that it develops three versions of one man's life, each of which opens with the hero running to catch a train. In the first Witek, a medical student, gets on the train, meets a Communist, and is inspired by him to join the Party. In the second version, Witek misses the train and is arrested for scuffling with railway staff. Once in jail, he meets a member of the Opposition, becomes an activist on the other side of the political divide and thereafter is baptised as a Catholic. As the third version of his life commences, Witek misses his train again but meets a fellow medical student with whom he falls in love. They marry, and he lives a fulfilled, apolitical life as husband, father and doctor, until the plane in which he is travelling to a conference explodes, killing all onboard (Ng, 2005: 68–77). Although there are points of contact between Witek's three lives, the radical differences between them are a consequence of blind chance. Ng argues that in Kieslowski's films it is not chance itself but how individuals react to the accidents of fate that defines them (2005: 78–81). Falkowska finds that the protagonists in the Trilogy also have their lives shaped by blind chance. But she reaches a different conclusion, believing that they are at fate's mercy, their willpower and intended actions suspended or rendered irrelevant. For this critic, the last films make a powerful political statement by describing 'man's helplessness in view of history and fate' (1999: 157). But she is mistaken in her judgement that the protagonists are shown to be helpless. For while human fate cannot be escaped in that everyone must die (c.f. the Zeebrugge ferry disaster that ends *Red*), how the characters behave before death – the personal choices that they make – distinguishes them. This is why the contest in *Blue* between Julie and her frozen apathy matters; it gives significance to the contrast between the depressive sadism of Dominique and the vitality of Karol in *White*; and in *Red* it is the burden of the central conflict between Judge Kern's sick, destructive pessimism and the hopefulness of Valentine. Whatever remains in the unconscious, as Jung often remarked, becomes a person's fate.

The plot outline of *Three Colours: Blue* is simple. It opens with a terrible car crash that only Julie (Juliette Binoche) survives while her husband and child perish. The accident is not the driver's fault but the result of blind chance. We can easily imagine alternative versions of Julie's life had the car not developed a mechanical failure. She might have lived the remainder of her days happily married, helping her husband in his work as a composer and bringing up their daughter. Alternatively she might have had to discover that her husband has taken a mistress and deal with that betrayal. But chance shapes Julie's fate and leaves her no choice but to cope (or fail to do so) with her loss of family. She tries to find refuge from her desperate pain through suicide, sex, abandoning her home and possessions, destroying the manuscript of her husband's last composition and withdrawing anonymously into a world where she knows nobody. Ultimately, all these attempts at self-abnegation fail. Chance events such as exchanges (however unwelcome) with her new neighbours break into her isolation. The determination of an old friend to rescue her eventually proves more than she can resist. And (most important of all) the needs and appetites of her psyche cannot indefinitely be suppressed. All these things intervene, reawaken her frozen psyche and in the end bring her back into the world reconciled to the prospect of new life. But although the plot trajectory is simple, complexity abides in its detail. Indeed it abounds with the kinds of rich mystery that interest Kieslowski so deeply.

As mentioned, *Blue* opens with a car crash; but merely stating that fact says nothing about the horror of the accident. From the opening moment, the thunder of tyres on tarmac fills the ears. The long opening take (which commences only after that ceaseless roar has transfixed the audience) is from a camera mounted beneath the body of the vehicle as it speeds down an *autoroute*. Another long take in the same blue-grey dusk, a medium close shot, shows a child's hand sticking out of a passenger window sporting a candy wrapping – a pretty indigo foil that the wind snatches away. We cut to a sequence in red as the car hurtles through a long tunnel.

The traffic's speed smears the passing lights across the screen while the child in the back seat watches. Beyond the tunnel, the car stops by the roadside and the girl runs behind bushes for a comfort break. While her father gets out from behind the wheel to stretch his legs, we cut back to the underside of the vehicle where brake fluid drips unnoticed from a pipe. Something is happening underneath that the family is unaware of. It is analogous to psychic leakage from the unconscious into a reality which is unmapped *terra incognita*. The adults are anxious to move on and the girl is called back into the car.

Another child's hand, this an adolescent boy's, plays *bilboquet* (cup and ball). The sound of a horn draws his eyes to where the automobile, headlights on now, rushes out of fog and past the field in which he stands. A moment of ironic synchronicity: the boy has no sooner placed the ball in his game of chance when a fearful screeching turns him round. In the distance, the car has run off the road and smashed into a tree; a dog streaks out from the wreckage and the woman cries out. A beach ball drops from a door flung open by the impact and blows away across farmland. We cut to a tight shot of the adolescent's feet running, and then to an extreme wide shot of the landscape. The boy stumbles across the field, tossing his skateboard aside as he labours over ploughed ridges toward the accident. After a long moment, the scene fades to black.

The build up toward the crash pulls the audience into an uncomfortable mental frame. Factors in play include the unexpected camera angles, the oppressive intensity of travel noise and the exaggerated reds and blues in the two opening sequences. Adding to these is the selection of moments made strange by their seeming disconnection from any storyline, together with the omission of the familiar conventions of story-telling in the first act such as the introduction of character motivation. All these devices dislocate spectators from the action, a dislocation that anticipates how the sole survivor of the wreck will respond when she regains consciousness in hospital.

The dislocation heightens the impact of everything because we have to strive to find significance in what we are shown. The rhetoric of these opening sequences (the intense colours, the flickering of foil, the escape from the wrecked car of an intact beach ball – relic of the dead child's happiness) thrusts spectators toward the margins of representation. It offers them a place where expressionistically the boundaries of the familiar physical world dissolve and precipitate sensitive viewers into the realm of the imagination – both their own and that of the injured survivor. What follows confirms that Kieslowski intends his viewers to stay in that liminal realm where Julie lies in crisis. After the crash, imagery returns with a cut to bloodless pink. A feather ruffles: a woman is breathing. In extreme close shot, her bloodshot pupil fills with the reflection of a doctor who informs her that her husband and daughter have died in the accident. As Emma Wilson observes, the total isolation of her eye in extreme close up while it looks at what we see suggests that Kieslowski wants us to realise that we are looking through the membrane of this woman's consciousness which he has placed between the viewer and the events of the narration. We fade back to black – another expressionistic rhetorical device. Whenever Julie's overwhelmed mind blanks out, our vision too is suddenly curtailed (Wilson, 2000: 50).

Julie smashes a plate glass window in a hospital corridor and startles the ward nurse. The shattered glass presents a metaphor for Julie's crazed mind and fragmented interior self. When something has not yet moved into a psychological process, people render their feelings concrete through enactment. While the nurse phones for help, Julie slips unseen into the dispensary and stuffs a handful of tablets into her mouth. But she cannot bring herself to swallow and spits them out, apologising explicitly to the sympathetic nurse for breaking the glass, and implicitly for her having to witness the attempted suicide. The nurse says gently that the glass can be replaced – thus communicating her deep understanding of grief by silently acknowledging what cannot be replaced. The desperate, blind need to follow her family into extinction, to materialise, so to speak, the vacuum in her being, has driven Julie's attempt to kill herself. Her utter despair is the first explosion of grief but also, since she finds herself incapable of causing her own death, her first accommodation to life. The very act of hurling through the window a jug of milk (analogous to the container of her own maternal emotions) is an attempt not only to externalise her depression but to get rid of what she has no capacity to hold on to. Wilson says that, although we do not see any images of Julie's memories or imaginings, her emotions are explored externally in both editing and *mise-en-scène*. The breaking pane of glass is a case in point. It opens a series of spatial metaphors where glass, blank walls, whiteness and the emptiness of the clinic allow us to enter the newly emptied out spaces of Julie's mind (2000: 52). The negotiation of space between humans is a familiar function of intimacy: excessive proximity suffocates, too great a distance abandons. Here, however, the omnipresence of absence is suffocating Julie.

A man approaches Julie's bed and places a miniature television set within view. She cannot respond to his inquiries other than to check that the funeral is about to be broadcast. Later she watches the public mourning for her husband, led by an orator and an orchestra. Patrice de Courcy (Hugues Quester) had been an admired composer whose sudden death has left unfinished a Concert to celebrate European unification. His death is the public, collective loss. Speaking of their daughter, Anna, the orator refers only to her age – which he gets wrong. Anna is Julie's private loss, which no one feels as keenly as she. On the television set, white sound and snow rasp out the signal.

Eventually (we are never vouchsafed any indication how much time has passed between scenes – an expressive device that correlates with the timelessness of grief), Julie's search for escape from the crucifying torment of consciousness begins to alter. This happens when the underlying vigour of her body forces convalescence on her, however reluctantly; but her physical recovery is not matched by that of her mind. When a journalist doorstops her, seeking information about Patrice's work, Julie turns her away angrily because the other woman has an agenda – to produce a documentary proving that Julie wrote Patrice's music. The convalescent woman is in the depths of mourning dipping into the well of her internal resources. Whereas the compassionate nurse mirrors her anguish, facilitating her grieving process, the journalist by imposing her own agenda leaves Julie cold. The grieving process requires quiet space for solitary introversion in which the individual may digest the gravity of the loss.

Loss and creating a large enough 'container' to bear the suffering are continuing, explicit themes in *Blue*. A container is the psychological term used to describe the internal vessel that holds our emotional life. But this is not the entire ambit of the film's themes. It had not been the journalist's intrusion that awakened Julie from the easy chair but the opening bars of the Concert for the Unification of Europe – the triumphant music (composed for the film by Zbigniew Preisner) resounding not in the hospital but in her head and ours. As its opening notes pour out, the natural colours of the scene become deeply suffused in blue. How can this irruption into consciousness be comprehended? Julie is not an agent in its production. On the contrary, the music is a bolt from the blue, spontaneously disrupting her catatonic state; but arguably for her as for the audience, it is also something else.

Julie's return to the family's home, strong again in body, once more focuses only on key disjointed fragments as if recorded by a violated consciousness. She goes upstairs to a blue room, which she has ordered her staff to clear completely; but a small chandelier has been left. She snatches angrily at the crystals with which it is strung and a handful comes away. They are the deep translucent blue already a familiar motif. Downstairs Julie finds the housekeeper weeping. She asks her, 'Why are you crying?' and the old woman responds, 'Because you are not.' In order to function and make decisions, Julie has in effect split off her sorrow. Splitting is a primitive defence against unwanted feelings, an unconscious process in which what the individual finds acceptable is divided from the unacceptable, as in Melanie Klein's theoretical cleavage of the good and bad breasts. As Julie perseveres to maintain some semblance of ego strength in order to survive and absorb the psychic trauma, the housekeeper embodies her split-off, grieving self. By this time, the audience cannot have missed that Julie is a poised and intelligent woman; but the stoic exterior protects a rage that in its raw state is too dangerous to touch. Nevertheless, changes in her psychological condition continue whether she likes it or not, and her failed attempt at evacuation of memory has been willed rather than involuntary.

After glancing cursorily at folios of the incomplete composition of the Concert, she squats at the top of the stairs and does not move when voices below announce the arrival of two men. As she sits there, blue–white glints refracted by the crystals in her hand play across her forehead. Their colder tone hints at her chilly state of heart. Later, when the man who visited her in hospital (now known to be a professor of music) comes up the stairs, her blank glare sends him away. When she does go down, it is to give instructions to her attorney to sell the house with all its contents, and to arrange lifelong care for her mother and the domestic staff. She declines to take anything herself, whether mementoes or proceeds of the sale. It is an act that illustrates the analyst's dictum that old psychological structures must be shifted in order to make space for the new.

Alone in the house, she picks out the opening melody of the Concert, reworking what looks like a first draft sheet as she goes. But while she follows the music in her mind, her hand plays with the prop that supports the lid of the grand piano. It crashes down, narrowly missing her fingers. Julie is locked in an ambivalent state of mind – part wanting to die, part to live. A high degree of ambivalence, according to Freud, is a special peculiarity of neurotic people. Her *left* hand (that of the unconscious) has invited, then dodged self-harm. Meanwhile the *right*, is holding onto the music, the part of her that wants to live. She has to slam the lid down because she is not yet capable of assimilating the feelings that the music causes to well up. It is a reminder that recovery from grief (like recovery from ill health) is a process in which reversals are inescapable.

Julie retrieves from a *rédactrice* the handwritten music sheets of the Concert scored for chorus and orchestra and trashes them. Still determined to finalise her separation from the past, she telephones the music professor Olivier (Benoit Régent). She has guessed that he loves her and invites him to join her in the house from which everything has been taken but a mattress. Is the pale blue light shining on her face his projection on her of his muse – his anima or soul? Or does it imply the coldness of her obsessive compulsion masked by sweetness? Probably both. In the morning she wakens him and thanks him for the kindness he has shown her in making love; but she tells him quietly that he now knows she has the physical properties of every other woman and therefore will not miss her. Her self-description figures herself as a soft machine with interesting cavities, but nothing more. In effect, she is telling both him and herself that love is a matter of physical doing and that it is a delusion to think of being in love as anything more.

Gentle and affectionate though she has been, it is not hard to see that curing Olivier of his passion was not Julie's motivation for seducing him in the remnants of the marital bed. It can be better understood as not only a deliberate act of infidelity to her husband's memory but also as moved by her unconscious desire to cure herself. According to Freud, the testing of reality by the bereaved having shown that the loved object no longer exists, requires that all the libido shall forthwith be withdrawn from its attachment to this object (in Mogenson, 1992: 19). Although they know it to be irrational, bereaved partners often feel that they have been betrayed by the death of their lover. To this extent her night with Olivier is Julie's revenge against her husband. Given what we have already seen, it will also be a deliberate attempt to renounce the memory of Patrice's physical presence – and hence another step intended to sever her from him. Having tried to exorcise both her late husband and Olivier (by organising what the latter must think and feel), Julie walks away from the house for the last time. Yet the agony written on her face shows that she has failed to dull the pain. Nor does scraping her knuckles along the wall of the lane help. It is another effort to bring the pain from the internal out to the external. The pattern of rejection and self-harm repeats itself here; but this time does so only after she has engaged in what in her own mind appears to be a pseudo-adulterous seduction. Still crazy, she enacts a repetitious compulsion, an ungovernable process originating in the unconscious. She has placed herself in a distressing situation that repeats an old experience without recognising that she is doing so (Laplanche and Pontalis, 1973: 78).

Julie emerges from the underground into the streets of Paris. Suddenly the vivid greens, oranges and reds of an open-air fruit market and the cheerful racket of street life invigorate these sequences. She locates an estate agent and rents an empty flat, her one pre-condition being that children not be permitted in the building. A pleasant pale green light filters through into the entry windows, and the living room has a wall of glass through which the afternoon tints the room in a soft pink tone. But the only thing Julie has brought from her old home is the chandelier with its chains of blue, and she immediately hangs it in the middle of this room. Beyond the memory of Anna, she appears to be obsessed also by what the translucent blue suggests – meanings that she cannot grasp in the way she can touch the crystals. This serves as a transitional object that comforts and holds her together while grieving for the old life to which she cannot now return. As such it resembles the child's teddy bear, a familiar and reassuring concrete symbol that gives him or her something solid to hold and help tolerate separation from his or her love object/ caregiver. (More about transitional objects follows in *Trois Couleurs: Blanc*.)

With Julie's move to the flat there begins a time when she cannot always shield herself from life. She prefers solitude and becomes an habitué of a café the furnishings and décor of which bathe her in warm russets. The shadows turning across the crockery mark the hours' tranquil passing. Nevertheless, the world begins to intrude on Julie and cracks open the carapace within which she has barricaded herself. The adolescent who witnessed the crash makes contact through her doctor, wanting to return a cross and chain that he took from the wreck. He offers, perhaps to ease a bad conscience, to tell what he saw, but Julie stops him abruptly. The screen crashes to black briefly before she dismisses him with the necklace. Antoine (Yann Tregouet) has sought to give her back what she has lost, but her losses cannot be redeemed. Her insistence that he keep the necklace tells him wordlessly that what he has seen and done is his trauma and must be his cross to bear.

One night, fighting in the street beneath her apartment wakes her. The victim of the attack runs into her tenement stairwell and hammers on her door, desperately begging for help. Immobilised by terror, Julie is unable to respond. When the rumpus has died down she does venture out to peep over the banisters. A gust of wind slams her door and she is locked out. Just as she cannot offer help, she is incapable of asking for it – a hallmark of emotional health. She sits out on the stairs overnight, frozen in icy blue, locked out of any meaningful relationships by her inability to allow herself the painful experience of connection. Ultimately this misadventure forces her to make contact with some of her fellow tenants – some friendly, others less so. One neighbour solicits her help in evicting from the tenement a woman whom she says is a prostitute. Julie declines, saying that it's not her problem. In her detachment, she accidentally ensures that the young woman accused cannot be abandoned on the street. Lucille (Charlotte Véry) promptly befriends her.

Counterpointed against these sequences, in others she swims across a pool saturated in deepest ultramarine light. The trails of water that spill lusciously from her strong arms resemble the chandelier's crystals. In fact, refractions of blue light and fragments of the Concert encroach into several of the episodes in her new existence. But one time, just as she is pulling herself vigorously up out of the swimming pool the music not only engulfs her, but progresses beyond the sections that we have heard before. The great size of the pool, containing the healing qualities of the womb's amniotic fluid, provides the metaphorical liminal space holding the enormity of her loss. New bars of music spontaneously rush in on her – an indication that she has digested a little more of the trauma. Instantly, she regresses back into the water, floating like a corpse. In this transitional moment, for the first time, she feels the visible and the audible with equal impact; but while the rich colour draws her backwards, the fragment of glorious music leads her forward, although she does not yet know it. Music will prove to be the only container large enough to hold her grief. The moment represents the forward and backward motion of the grieving process, anything but a linear progress. (Both Freud and Jung insisted that psychic realities do not follow laws of time.) Julie has long since been physically restored, so when the dead claim her through the music, it is her soul not her body that is possessed.

Julie is sitting in sunlight on a bench when a stooped old woman hobbles by on high-heel shoes to recycle a bottle into a green bin. Only with the greatest difficulty can she reach the aperture and even then she cannot get the bottle to drop before we cut away. The incident allows the spectator to draw the analogy with Julie's emotional circumstances and the near impossibility of recycling grief so deep.

As the titles of the trilogy anticipate, Kieslowski constructs image clusters as a means of expressively, sometimes symbolically pointing toward meanings that are in play even though they may escape both the diegetic societal register and easy verbal labelling. The colour blue has indelible associations in Western culture with grief, with cold and, by extension, with the nearness of death – all associations that are inescapable here. Pure colour is potent and conveys an energy resembling that of archetypal images; and also like archetypal images, colours have a spectrum of potential associations some standing in opposition to others. Blue, as the refracted glimmers playing on Julie's temple remind us, also has strong links with clear, azure skies and water; by extension therefore with healing, inspiration, and hence the spirit. That particular chain of symbolic associations links graphically but also mysteriously in various narrative directions to the foil in Anna's hand/wind/breath/pneuma/the feather on Julie's hospital pillow/life – and, through the specific conjunction that Kieslowski creates, to music.

A street musician (Jacek Ostaszewski) plays opposite Julie's café and soothes her reveries over coffee. He looks like a tramp who makes the street his home; and on one occasion, seeing him asleep on the pavement, she fears he may be unwell. In fact he is contentedly drunk. When Julie helpfully pushes the flute case toward him for a pillow, he mumbles, 'You always have to hold onto something.' The instrument is equivalent to her chandelier – a transitional object that endows him with some sense of connection. The instrument case (as a kind of mothering pillow) also carries her own projection since she too is *psychically* homeless and in need of comfort.

One day (out of the blue?) Olivier finds her in the café after searching across Paris. They are exchanging a few stilted phrases (all that Julie's instinctive *froideur* seems to allow), when the flautist arrives at his stand. He has been brought there in a chauffeur-driven limousine by an elegant woman who embraces him before going on her way. Julie (who is doing her best to ignore Olivier as if hoping he might disappear) has her eyes fixed in bewilderment on this scene, when the musician starts to play a melody like the Concert. Julie and Olivier share a furtive moment of recognition before the latter slips away.[1]

Indeed, she hardly notices Olivier's departure because her attention is wholly focused on the melody. But when she asks the musician where he learnt it, he replies that he likes to invent tunes. One possibility is that he heard the motif when the public funeral was telecast and is aggrandising himself with a small lie. The shimmering uncertainty surrounding his nature gives him the qualities of a trickster – a crucial archetypal figure who triggers transformation by shaking and unsettling the old order of the psyche. It ties in with his trickster nature that the music found by both the flautist and Patrice (which complements the repeated invasions of blue light) was so to speak 'in the air' – where it most certainly now hovers for both his widow and Olivier. In other words something in the collective unconscious has been contacted, which for the first time is leading Julie beyond the personal.

More fragments follow. The discovery of mice in the flat transfixes Julie with fear. She is unable to kill them herself because the nest holds a mother with its newborn litter. Instead, drawn by a sudden need, she visits her mother (Emmanuelle Riva) in the luxurious care home where she lives. The reunion between parent and child is bizarre. As a victim of dementia, the old woman cannot hold in mind that her visitor is her daughter and not her long-dead sister. Yet many of the things that she recalls about the latter – for example that Marie-France is dead – apply metaphorically to Julie. Reflections and refraction of images within the room and beyond the windows add to the sense that the encounter between mother and daughter is not firmly registered in the objective world of daily events but hovers somewhere near a world of the dead. And the old woman's attention keeps drifting back to her preferred window, the television set which she says opens onto the whole world. At the moment it shows men, one of them an ancient fellow, throwing themselves into the void on the end of bungee ropes – a reckless challenge to feel the exhilaration of life. Yet the endless flow of television images seems to soothe her mother. Perhaps they fill her mind and keep at bay the terror of the unknown. Meanwhile, because Julie has nothing left after the death of the two people whom she loved so dearly, she says that she intends to have nothing in the future. Anything else – memories, possessions, friendship or love – is a trap. In other words, she intends to continue as one of the living dead who populate this scene. Thus, mother and daughter are held in the same liminal space between life and death.

Although her mother continues to mistake her for Marie-France, an irony of the scene is that Julie appears to have come to check a memory of her own childhood, namely whether she was afraid of mice. After the old woman has confirmed it, Julie makes her mind up, borrows a neighbour's cat and puts it in with the pests. This small domestic crisis is significant because, although unforeseeably, it cracks open the stout shield she has put up against emotion. The horrible clash between her terror of mice and the knowledge that she is murdering them torments her. Worse, the guilt she suffers as a survivor for continuing to live resurfaces and intensifies her feelings. She dashes headlong from the apartment to cleanse her conflicted feelings in the pool.

For the first time since the crash, her feelings are out of control and therefore she has to accept help when it is offered. Lucille notices her despair, comes to her and embraces her – the first physical contact the widowed Julie has experienced since quitting her old home. The young woman's warmth gives Julie the courage to reveal the shattering impact of her phobia; and Lucille comforts her with the reassurance that it is normal both to fear and exterminate unwanted mice. She takes it upon herself to clean up Julie's flat.

Kieslowski cuts direct from this scene of Julie's despair in the pool to a panicky phone call from Lucille waking her in the middle of the night. The obligations of friendship have re-entered Julie's life and will bring unforeseen psychological consequences. Julie responds reluctantly to Lucille's urgent appeal for help and finds her new friend preparing to perform for the customers in a sex show. Contrary to the stereotypical expectations of a decorous member of the professional middle classes such as Julie, Lucille unabashedly enjoys her work. Indeed, while accounting for her crisis to Julie she gently masturbates her stage partner to ready him for their performance, a casual physical service with no emotional content.[2] Symptomatically, she never wears knickers (whereas Julie would surely always do so). However, she has called Julie in panic on seeing her father among the voyeurs in the audience. Although he has left in the meantime, it is evident that she has a powerful father complex that holds the imago of 'the authority'. Whatever the past history between Lucille and her father, she lives out her unhealthy sexuality in unconscious reaction to this authority figure – and his unexpected presence in the sex club has confronted her with taboo material inherent in the complex.

These signs indicate that Lucille mirrors Julie's shadow. Both share attachment and abandonment issues but function, so to speak, from opposite sides of the pole. They live out their sexuality in very different manners – a metaphor for their dissimilar psychological make-up and contrasting relationships with their animus. Lucille lives unconsciously and unprotected as a shadow figure, constantly exposed to dangerous situations. Julie lives in such a protected way she is unable to take any risks – yet it is risks that ultimately promote growth (as we saw in Frankie Dunn's case, Chapter 4). Julie's recourse to celibacy contrasts with Lucille's sexual availability and fear of sleeping alone. In contrast, Julie, prior to meeting Lucille, has been locked in a manic defence, unwilling to allow herself to depend on anyone. Although there is no implication that Julie is drawn toward imitating her friend, this midnight encounter at the sex club immediately presages the reawakening of Eros as one of the irresistible forces that will return her to life. The erotic ambience is designed to stir longings in the club's customers. Since sex is the most primitive way in which we connect, it cannot but begin to awaken something in Julie: libido. Freud described libido as psychic energy. It is not pleasure-seeking (the limits of Lucille's interest in sex) but object-seeking and Julie will seek connection with others.

As with so much in the grieving process, the return of sexual knowledge to Julie's life happens in a painful way. While they are talking, Lucille glances at a television screen and, of all things, notices footage of Julie. The programme – about Patrice's life and work – transfixes the astonished widow. She discovers two things from it and suspects a third. First, a copy of the manuscript of the Concert has survived her attempt to destroy it. Second, Olivier is trying to complete it, though he does not know whether he will succeed. Finally, photographs she has not seen before show Patrice with a young woman unknown to Julie. The emotional impact of these linked revelations amounts to a *bouleversement*, a turning upside down of Julie's carefully ordered universe. She pursues Olivier along a street (matching her fury, a scarlet fire engine flashes past in the background) and rages at him as having no right to take over the music. She has not, however, anticipated his riposte – that he has done it to stir her out of accidie. The tornado of angry passions gripping her collapses when she perceives that Olivier has read her rightly. She accepts his invitation to hear what he has written and swiftly becomes engaged in the work, drawing to Olivier's attention things that Patrice had in mind that the other man did not know. It is a fundamental turning point for Julie.

The epiphany into which (moved by his love) Olivier has inveigled her amounts to more than a discovery of her own split-off emotions. It encompasses also the moment in which she simultaneously buries and resurrects her dead husband. The revelation of his infidelity through a relationship that has lasted for years unavoidably shows her that she has been grieving for an incomplete mental image of the man and the marriage. Although the physical man is dead, she cannot ignore, given that her image of him has altered so radically, that something in herself is waking.

> The fact that a portion of libido remains committed to an object long after that object has ceased to exist in the world of 'really real reality' may mean that something else is going on. Perhaps, the energy is changing its form and being utilized in another way. Perhaps, the bereaved widow brooding over the image of her dead husband is making him into a part of her inner life, a part of her soul… From the point of view of 'reality,' of course, her husband has become extinct. From the point of view of the imagination, however, he is now eternal… The very man with whom she once explored life, or rather, his imago, is now initiating her into the imaginal.
>
> *(Mogenson, 1992: 20)*

Closely associated with this breakthrough, Julie's attitude to the Concert transforms. Hitherto she has tried simultaneously to destroy it and at the same time hold onto it tenaciously (since it visits her head in every emotional crisis) as her own secret possession. Now she recognises Olivier is right to say that the people who loved Patrice's work have a claim on his music (not to mention its intended inspirational political role). In terms of her own inner life, the Concert has been the one imaginal residue of her marriage, constantly forcing through her grief's agonies. What is more, unlike her imago of Patrice, it has not become stuck or reified in unchanging form. Rather the great chords have extended their range through the weeks of mourning. She starts to take a leading part in developing the music that, through its vital participation in her inner life, has proven itself unquestionably to be her legacy from Patrice. All of this signifies, indeed is predicated on, an opening out of Julie's soul as her imaginal life begins to flourish once again. Music as soul is the only true, limitless container for the enormity of her grief.

Julie still has to deal with the pain that her husband's infidelity has inflicted on her. She tracks down his lover (Florence Pernel) and discovers that she had been much more than a plaything for Patrice and was loved by him. Since his death, the young lawyer has discovered that she is carrying his child. Deeply distressed, Julie flees to her mother but, seeing through the French windows that the old woman is preoccupied as usual with her television (it is showing, appositely to Julie's case, someone performing a high-wire balancing act), she turns away without entering. Her personal mother can no longer help her find her way (any more than Maggie's was, Chapter 4). Instead she must look for the archetypal, collective mother who can nurture her back to life. Like the tightrope walker on screen, Julie focuses forward, struggling to keep her psychological balance. But as she leaves through the nursing home gardens, we see nurses and patients framed in the dusk by the pergola as if in boxes or a painter's still pictures. Tactfully, Kieslowski hints at the impossibility of breaking out – but breaking out of what? It is a theme with which the film deals in its finale.

Julie calls on Olivier, and they work with gathering enthusiasm on the Concert. She suggests alterations in the instrumentation that Olivier has proposed and the music comes to life majestically on the sound track. Meanwhile Slawomir Idziak, the director of photography, racks off focus so that Olivier's room becomes a warm, oceanic blur. As the two characters move around in long shot it is not unlike the ultrasound image of the child in the womb that we shall see in the coda. It is also the first time that the film has blanked out to suggest the diminution of Julie's consciousness other than in anguish. This is the redemptive moment in which conscious control gives way to the creative indirection of the id – and after this moment everything changes.

Julie offers Patrice's mistress the family house and her husband's name for the coming child. Julie's face reveals that the conversation with the other woman is not easy for her, with the painful recognition that they each had their own separate relationship with Patrice. Yet her gesture reflects an expansion of herself rather than the contracting instinct that comes from loss. At the end of the conversation, the young woman reaches out to Julie and tells her, 'I'm sorry.' It is a redemptive moment of clarification, an acknowledgement of what belongs and what no longer belongs to each of them.

Ownership also momentarily becomes an issue on the night when Julie finishes the Concert and telephones to invite Olivier to collect the manuscript. Unexpectedly he refuses, saying that the music can either be his – a little heavy and awkward – or hers. But the public would have to know. Accepting this, Julie rings off. But a few moments later she calls back. We may guess that in the interim she has felt his loving sacrifice in renouncing any claim to his contribution. Perhaps too she remembers the many other indications of his feelings. She calls back to check that she is right. Olivier assures her of his love (with touching respect, they still use the formal 'vous' form of address rather than the intimate 'tu'), and with tears in her eyes she rolls up the manuscript and goes to him. As she leaves, the Concert resumes at its culmination, on which she has been working. The camera cranes up past Anna's lamp: Julie's exit (quitting her solitary existence) is suffused with both the familiar blue (now a glimmer of hope) and the chorale that brings the music to its climax.

The Concert was originally credited to Patrice alone, but following the combination of Olivier's work with Julie's inspiration, it 'belongs' to all three. However, ownership at this stage of Julie's grieving process is no longer relevant. By releasing any narcissistic claim on her dead 'love possessions', Julie has discovered a destiny beyond her tears. In fact, far from insisting on her ownership of the Concert, she gives it to the people – in the plot, the unseen multitudes of Europe; in the cinema, the audience whom it now envelopes in glory.

The coda to the film moves beyond this one woman's adaptation to her pain and encompasses something majestic in scale. First, it confronts spectators with puzzling uncertainties at the very moment they anticipate relishing the straightforward resolution of Julie's anguish in the ritual of the lovers' union. Julie and Olivier do indeed make love, but in her supple delight she rubs her face awkwardly against a pane (pain?) of glass through which we see her. Even if it concerned nothing but this image, the scene would be abstracted from the world the lovers inhabit. The tight framing of Julie's face delays, until the camera slowly moves, our seeing that it is pushed against the bedroom window. Therefore the image is perceived as if it were almost detached from the storyline, an emblem of her long travail. The pressure of her head against the glass at the moment of her ecstasy brings to mind the constraints that inevitably impinge on everyone. People must either confront these constraints and grow or, to protect against them, develop a defence that makes them contract, inhibiting growth.

The finale of the Concert, however, widens the perspective from the moment that Julie leaves her apartment so that the frame of reference far exceeds the predicament of this one individual. It sets as lyrics the well-known words from Paul's First Letter to the Corinthians, 'Though I speak with the tongues of angels, if I have not love, I am become as hollow brass.' Even in today's secular society these words instantly move beyond the mundane and take in the sacramental. The camera cranes quietly outside the window and superimposes reflections that make it seem *as if* the lovers are both in bed and underwater. Then what look like grass roots descend from the top of the frame and press down on the image of the couple. With Olivier scarcely visible, Julie, her sexual passion undiminished, is simultaneously seen *as if* in her grave. What Jung termed the *coniunctio oppositorum* – the meeting of opposites – here allows the audience a view of the psyche in its fully rounded potential, adapted to both life and death, attaining a depth of insight with clarity that surpasses consciousness. Still young enough to conceive new life, Julie's ecstatic vitality in the arms of her lover is locked in conjunction with her mortality.

This is the first of a series of vignettes of the characters that, accompanied by Paul's words, impress on us a vision of the characters' spiritual nature, deeper than consciousness. 'And though I have enough faith to move the highest mountains, if

I have not love, I am nothing.' The vast scale of both the music and the text make it impossible to ignore that more than the love of one man and one woman is involved. Here the specific characters whom we have got to know through the duration of the film now take on a generalising function as illustrations of recurring human predicaments. Although the words 'for now we see through a glass darkly' (Corinthians 1, 13: 12) are not heard, the way the vignettes are framed surely brings them into play. We are in the realm of mysteries.

The glass panes seen in many of the vignettes suggest firstly, the constraints that film and television screens place on insight. Secondly, they form a transparent barrier between the outer world of observers and the inner world of the observed. The glass reminds spectators that we all live in these two worlds and that those we observe can only be perceived or comprehended in a refracted manner.

Out of blackness comes a dream image of Antoine being awakened by an alarm clock in the blue middle of the night. He touches the cross around his neck that had been Julie's before the crash. ('Love is patient, love is kind. It bears all things.') This is his moment of moral awakening when the full realisation of what he has seen and done (as both witness to violent death and remorseful thief) falls on his shoulders. It is the burden he has henceforth to carry – his cross – and yet another indication that suffering is a transcendent function.

We pan off into blackness. ('Love never fails; for prophecies shall fail.') Then pan on to triple reflections of Julie's mother sitting absently in front of her television screen. ('Tongues shall cease, knowledge shall wither away.') The old woman closes her eyes – pre-echoing her death – and a nurse runs to her from the garden. ('Love never fails.') There follows a glimpse of Lucille in the strip club where she gazes into the dark. We pan once again out of blackness onto Patrice's lover and an ultrasound picture of her baby, near term and full of energy in the womb. ('And now shall abide faith, hope, love; but the greatest of these three is love.')

After the next black space we find an extreme close up of Julie's eye that mirrors her awakening in hospital after the crash. Now light is visible in the pupil. Through the black experience of anguish, light is shed upon the unconscious – again the transcendent function of suffering. To love truly requires letting go of the past and ultimately acceptance. The grieving experience has forever changed the way Julie sees and lives. The final shot is a close up of her behind the windowpane, which now reflects the dawn sky. In this quiet moment, she is at last able to weep. As part of the love she feels, grief as well as erotic passion has established its right of way.

Not firmly anchored in either narrative time or space, this cluster of vignettes has a visionary quality that is hard to deny. But whose vision is it? Self-evidently Kieslowski has the first claim. He had announced he would retire after completing the Trilogy, and it stands, therefore, as his artistic testament. Then, since the characters appear to be abstracted from their daily lives to some degree and contemplating their fates, it involves them too. Finally, the vision is also the audience's, an assessment corroborated by the rich and various emotional impact of the coda. Spectators may feel joy, relief, compassion, dread of loss and isolation, the fear of death.

Although isolation is constantly emphasised in these vignettes by long moments when the screen is dark, the totality of what is represented amounts to another *coniunctio oppositorum*. The antithesis of isolation is inclusion; and if the Concert for Unification is to have meaning, then Paul's words with their emphasis on love must be taken into the reckoning. The chorus sing the Greek word for love 'agape'. It refers to the sacramental communion feast of the Lord's supper, and thence indirectly to transcending (or transpersonal) love. Zbigniew Preisner's music soars, lifting the emotions to appropriately high intensity. As Toh Hai Leong says, at the end the Concert 'rises and drowns the audience in a wave of climaxes and anti-climaxes,...' a demonstration of what Buddhists call fate or destiny at work (1996).

Throughout the trilogy, art takes the place of religion, revealing the sacred in humanity. In *Blue*, Kieslowski's consummately realised narrative, character development and aesthetics have the capability to trigger waves of affect and feeling. They inseminate a quasi-religious sense and function as a mirroring guide with therapeutic value for spectators' own sufferings. So the on-screen characters and the audience in front of the screen are connected both in the imaginal and deeper still, beneath the arena of consciousness, at the archetypal source of those images.

Notes

1 From a Jungian perspective, Olivier occupies the position of her animus figure, the male imago in her psyche. When the contrasexual archetypes (as animus and anima are known) are active (or constellated), they present a person with aspects of his or her psyche culturally associated with people of the other sex. The archetype has great power and can lead an individual to discover the Self (Ulanov and Ulanov, 1994: 123–31). Olivier's love for Julie makes it clear that he is projecting onto her his intensely constellated anima. However, Julie's animus is not at present sufficiently constellated in her mind for her to project it onto anyone.

2 Women who are attracted to these environments may feel their sense of power through their physical sexuality. The lack of integration inhibits them from feeling empowered psychologically. Shadow material usually seeks stimulation in unhealthy ways, witness Lucille's attraction to danger.

6

TROIS COULEURS

Blanc (1994)

Like the others in the trilogy, *White* starts with a noise associated with movement – the rumbling of an airport baggage conveyor. Presently the camera picks up a massive, old-fashioned trunk moving down the channel. Not until a third of the film has run, however, can we see that the shot is out of sequence – this despite the fact that (unknown to us at the start) the film's tepid hero is locked within it. Encased of his own volition in this metaphorical box, Karol Karol (Zbigniew Zamachowski) is committed to a journey, but has surrendered control of its destination.

The plot has started *in medias res*, a device that alerts us to the fact that we need the back story – the true, invisible source of present action in family and cultural history – to let us understand the present. Just as Karol in his trunk occupies a transitional space, so in its own way does the audience because we cannot yet establish the significance of what we see (Abram, 1996: 320, 322). Since Karol is himself at a transitional time in his life (so lacking in energy that he can be described as a *puer*), D. W. Winnicott's theories focussing on what it means to feel real are deployed to help show how his personal and cultural history has hindered his psychological growth and threatens to lock him in perpetual grieving for a love object that he has never truly possessed.

On the baggage conveyor, the dominant tones are green and russet. Throughout the trilogy, green is so seldom on screen that when it does occur, even in so unlikely a setting as this, the gratified eye picks it out with relief. As the colour associated with fertility and natural growth, it adds to the sense that moving through psychological transitions is a natural aspect of personal growth. It is all the more noticeable because, when the plot commences to unfold, we see careful references to the colours in the trilogy's titles. White is frequently caught between blue and red: for example, among the vehicles in a car park, or in the clothes worn to court by Karol's wife Dominique Vidal (Julie Delpy). Perhaps this device (since white is the palette on which other colours may be laid) hints that not only is the hero in transition but that the film itself represents a way marker in the progress through the trilogy.

We enter Karol's story as he arrives at court to defend divorce proceedings instigated by Dominique. A pigeon flies up as he crosses the quad and his eyes follow, looking perhaps for an omen of peace and love; but from on high the bird drops white shit on his shoulder. Colour coding, here as throughout the trilogy, spans associations ranging across archetypal opposites. Denotatively the film variously registers white in bird shit, Dominique's car, the couple's wedding, a porcelain figurine, grubby snow and ice, and stylistically in fades to white screen. White's associations and connotations will develop to include traditionally positive qualities such as femininity, delicacy, innocence, purity, beauty, truth, transcendence, virtue, the Madonna, milk and spirituality. Often the characters' behaviour (as when Dominique forces Karol to listen on the phone while behind her white curtained window she brazenly fucks a new lover) negates these values by running quite contrary to them. But even this cruelty fails to shake Karol's need to believe in his wife's essential purity. Yet, as this painful episode insists, the obverse facets of whiteness are in play too carrying associations with surrender, loss of blood or passion, the couple's unconsummated *mariage blanc*, coldness, emptiness, fear and death. The film plays with both these sets of values, finally extending them (by fading to white when finally Karol and Dominique do achieve orgasm) to suggest the coming of light and rebirth.

Richard Dyer (to whose work on whiteness the foregoing lists are indebted) remarks that, unlike every other colour, white as a designated hue is generally accepted to have an opposite, black (1997: 48). Indeed, in opposition to its title, this film is commonly referred to as a black comedy. The colour black figures in its own right. It does this visually with silhouetted images; with scenes of deep *chiaroscuro*; and through fades to black when Karol's mind blanks an intolerable memory. Thematically, black embellishes Karol's work in the black market, the recurrent contact with death, the unconscious and his false funeral.

Confronted in the divorce proceedings by Dominique's charge that he has failed to consummate the marriage, Karol proves painfully passive. Impotence pervades every aspect of his life; but he tells the court that things were different when he and his wife met. Their back-story emerges only after Dominique has won her divorce, but it confirms what Karol has said. Formerly a prize-winning hairdresser, he met her at a competition where she was modelling for one of his rivals. In his Polish homeland in those days he abounded in creativity, an authoritative figure, while she was his beautiful idol. At that time, their love-making was mutually pleasing.

Karol's confidence sank after they moved to Paris. Although he had to cope in a language in which he is far from fluent, Dominique's actions the moment she secures her divorce prove that this was far from the only cause of his downfall. After the hearing, Karol (so dependent on her that he has not even memorised his PIN) tries to withdraw cash from an ATM. It rejects his card: Dominique has frozen him out of their joint account. She retains possession of the hairdressing salon (despite the fact that it must have been established on the back of his expertise) and boasts cruelly that she now controls everything. However, although she has seized financial power, we need to note that Karol had already surrendered it. Thus, his impotence is not simply sexual: with his tacit permission, if not active encouragement, his pale wife has taken his money. Despite his implicit collaboration in his downfall, this is one of the factors that will pressurise him to change his idea of her from impossibly pure wife to whore.

Karol's family history has encouraged his assumption that expressions of devotion should infallibly bind her to him. He has learnt from childhood to ingratiate himself in this way, as we can tell when his brother Jurek (Jerzy Stuhr) acts in the same manner to get Karol to oblige him. But, adopted as the habitual mode of response, fawning ingratiation leads by definition to the development of a false self. D. W. Winnicott described this phenomenon as one of the most successful defence mechanisms in protecting the true self. It performs that function at high cost to the sense of feeling real, however, because when the individual's operational centre is in the false rather than true self, a sense of futility arises (Winnicott, 1971: 292). 'An individual may be successful in the world, but success based in the false self leads to an intensification of the sense of emptiness and despair' (Winnicott in Abram, 1996: 84). And again, 'the false self, however well set up, lacks something and that something is the essential central element of creative originality' (Winnicott, 1960: 152 cited in Mitchell, 1993: 23).

Whilst every healthy individual owes his or her development to a mother figure's devotion without which that development could not have occurred (Winnicott in Abram, 1996: 125), this differs from Karol's obsessive behaviour. Fawning devotion such as his presents as having been founded during childhood in desperate attempts to assuage the mother. That behaviour ultimately formed a complex that freezes Dominique out of their relationship because it prevents her being understood for whom she is. She tries to tell Karol this the morning after the divorce when she finds him asleep in the salon. Newly homeless and broke, he had sheltered there the previous night. Although Dominique's first thought is to call the police, Karol seduces her with sly humour and they commence lovemaking. But then the intense anxiety aroused in him by her need for the sense of connection that he cannot supply lets him down once again. Dominique, both angry and sad, tells him (in what amounts to a catechism of their failed relationship) that he has never understood anything between them: 'If I say I love you, you don't understand. And if I say I hate you, you still don't understand. You don't understand that I want you – that I need you.' And when she asks whether she scares him, Karol can only stammer that he doesn't know. Dominique tests his mettle by setting fire to the salon's curtains (fire perhaps acting symbolically as an agent of cleansing) and telling him that she will inform the police that he has done it. Rather than trying to put the flames out, the coward runs away. The horrid debacle confirms that divorce has merely enacted the dynamic of their relationship.

What has brought about the reversal from their early time together in Poland? Although Karol is wholly focused on Dominique, the only thing he can say when asked to describe her is that she is beautiful. No less striking, he has made no friends or acquaintances in Paris and now has no one to turn to. It seems that Karol's mother complex became activated from the moment he fell in love with his goddess and regressed into a position of being wholly dependent on her.

Karol can think of nowhere to go except the subway station across the road. Like many other heroes[1] he has to go underground to discover what darkness lives in his unconscious. Inevitably, some days after she has kicked him out, he turns back to Dominique. He phones her, hoping that the silhouette of a man shadowing her white curtains is not a lover. Far from reassuring him, she congratulates him sardonically on his timing and forces him to listen while her moans and cries pitch toward an enthusiastic orgasm.

Almost immediately after this gross humiliation, Karol steals the plaster bust of a young woman wearing a mob cap. Carrying it with him in his retreat to Poland, this grotesquely romantic figurine becomes a transitional object for Karol – a concretisation of the cold white goddess ideal (part mother, part lover of impossible purity) which Dominique represents to him. In psychoanalytic theory the term 'object' refers to whatever is an object of attraction, love or hatred for the subject – as in 'the object of my passion'. The contingency of the object does not mean that any object can satisfy the instinct. Rather, according to Freud, the instinctual object, often distinguished by highly specific traits, is determined by the history of each individual subject and particularly by his or her childhood history (Laplanche and Pontalis, 1973: 273–5).

The bust's significance as a transitional object can be amplified through D. W. Winnicott's theoretical work critiquing the commonplace thought that there are two realities, inner and outer. Winnicott explored an intermediate area of experiencing to which both inner reality and external life contribute. Here the distinction between perception and apperception takes on significance. Apperception requires conscious perception with full awareness and is the ultimate goal of individuation. It has been described as 'an inner faculty which represents external things as perceived by the registering, responding psyche; therefore, the result is always a mixture of reality and fantasy, a blend of personal experience and archetypal imago' (Samuels et al., 1986: 25).

For Winnicott, 'creative apperception more than anything else... makes the individual feel that life is worth living' (1971: 65). By using apperception to relate an object to past experience, an individual can discover newly observed qualities in that object and gain fresh understanding. Consciousness achieved via self-reflection is a creative process that integrates understanding with affect and ultimately releases psychic energy from difficult complexes. Winnicott's model marries with Joseph Campbell's argument that the aim of individuation is not to search for the meaning of life but to feel our own aliveness (Campbell and Moyers, 1988: xvi). In theory, the more we work through our personal histories and psychological angst, the more we should feel that life is worth living. Such a thrust toward personal growth is the obverse of Karol's psychological recidivism.

According to Winnicott, developing infants tend sooner or later to weave other-than-me objects into their personal pattern. They identify these so-called transitional phenomena at an intermediate state between their initial inability and their developing capacity to recognise and accept reality. To some extent these objects stand in for the breast and thus belong to the realm of illusion. They become vitally important as defences against anxiety, especially anxiety of the depressive type. The relevance for *White* of this phenomenon lies in a variant manifestation in which the need for a specific object sometimes reappears regressively at a later developmental age when deprivation threatens. The depressive Karol undergoes just such a regression after the breakup of his marriage (1971: 5).

Winnicott summarises the special qualities in the relationship with a transitional object, several of which touch on Karol's use of the bust. The infant assumes rights over the object just as Karol possessively keeps the figurine to himself. Nevertheless, some abrogation of omnipotence is a feature from the start: Karol only seizes on this marble piece because he has lost Dominique. The object is affectionately cuddled as well as excitedly loved or even mutilated; and it must have qualities that seem to show it has a vitality or reality of its own. Just so, late one night back in Poland, while trying to improve his French to impress Dominique, Karol is almost magnetically attracted to the bust and kisses it tenderly. A transitional object must never change, unless changed by the infant – witness Karol's distress when the thugs who steal his trunk toss the bust onto a rubbish heap and break it. Finally, transitional objects are gradually decathected: in the course of years they lose their energy charge and become not so much forgotten as relegated to limbo. They lose meaning because the transitional phenomena have become diffused and spread over the whole intermediate territory between inner psychic reality and the external world, that is, over the whole cultural field (Ibid.). This too eventually occurs in *White* when Karol moves toward a healthier relationship with Dominique and the bust (hitherto the frequent focus of his lonely, nocturnal attention) becomes peripheral to his life.

The bust represents an early stage on Karol's journey from the purely subjective narcissistic wound he experienced from Dominique's rejection of him, to one of objectivity (or the movement from perception to apperception already mentioned). The bust as transitional object is what we see of Karol's progress towards experiencing realness – and it gains additional significance from the fact that he has felt the need to steal it. For Winnicott, thieving by a child originates in emotional deprivation and expresses profound need. The deprived child who behaves in an antisocial way is in fact more hopeful than the child who cannot behave badly. For the latter, hope has gone and the child has become defeated. So the antisocial tendency implies hope (Winnicott in Abram, 1996: 47), an early sign that something positive is stirring in the psyche of the hitherto infantile Karol.

Dominique's sadism, meanwhile, is driven by rage and despair over their failed relationship. Responding to Karol's projection onto her of his colourless, empty anima – the cool white goddess – she expresses her hungry needs by taking to bed a lusty human lover. The stark contrast between her beauteous perfection and her calculated cruelty driven by the irresistible need for completeness makes her resemble a character in a fairy tale, a phenomenon to which we shall return.

Later we must examine how the trauma of the humiliating phone call to his sexually active ex-wife triggers Karol's own reaction. However, his anguish carries with it more than personal suffering. As Slavoj Zizek remarks, *White* is the most political film in the trilogy, being embedded, as Janina Falkowska notes, in the context of the unequal relationship between France and Poland (Žižek, 2001: 177; Falkowska, 1999: 147).[2] The film's story world repeatedly touches on the political and economic impotence from which Poland was emerging in the late 1980s when France (and Western European capitalism) seemed to many Poles to provide a clean, white ideal (see Falkowska, ibid.). This vision of purity is instantly obliterated when Karol returns to Poland and coincides with the breaking of the bust.

Yola Schabenbeck-Ebers describes 'history' as the key word for every Polish intellectual. They subscribe to a well-established set of ideas about Poland in the nineteenth century – ideas driven by the nation's experience of partition between three great neighbouring powers and the subsequent tragedies of failed uprisings in which every new generation lost its most noble characters. The belief held in common was that this suffering was not in vain and that God had chosen Poland to suffer for other nations in the war against despotic, oppressive empires. Through fighting those powers the nation was supposed to attain democracy for the whole continent. Although World War II smashed Poland's newly won sovereignty and its outcome did not bring full independence, the same pattern of thinking continued to prevail through the twentieth century: sustaining the totalitarian rule of the Cold War period would reinstate the nation's dignity (Schabenbeck-Ebers, 2006). As Norman Davies, says in the concluding words to his monumental account of the nation's re-emergence,

> To everyone who knows its history, ... Poland is a repository of ideas and values which can outlast any number of military and political catastrophes. Poland offers no guarantee that its individual citizens will observe its ideals, but stands none the less as an enduring symbol of moral purpose in European life.
>
> *(Davies, 1982: Vol 2, 642)*

The parallel between Poland's relations with France and the unbalanced marriage of Karol and Dominique is plain. Complete relationships, whether personal or international, must be equal in nature (which does not mean that they occur often). This brings with it the uncomfortable thought that suffering and sacrifice are necessary to the quest for completion. This is what Dominique and Karol both long to have, but a complete relationship must bring the feminine and the masculine together in a natural fit like the symbol of yin and yang.

The unselfconscious, yet ingratiating defeatism evident in Karol's behaviour as an expatriate Pole maps neatly onto the backdrop of the nation's ideological history. If confirmation were needed, it comes from the intervention of a sombre fellow-expatriate visiting Paris to make money as a bridge player. Mikolaj (Janusz Gajos) stumbles over Karol in the underground station. The latter's inanition has reduced him to a lamentable parody of a busker, with only a trunk for his few possessions.

To gain coppers for survival he renders on his comb a highly appropriate, mournful tango, famous among Poles of a certain age. According to Marek Haltof, the suicidal lyrics of 'This is our last Sunday', though voicing desperate hope for a last chance, contemplate separation forever (2004: 133–4). Mikolaj (who, naturally, recognises this sorrowful tune) soon mentions that he has a faculty essential for a bridge player – an excellent memory. But in the context of the Polish nation's history prior to the fall of Communism, memory is also an essential trait of the archaic sorrowing Pole because the national culture has imbued him or her with the knowledge that suffering cannot be escaped. And so it proves with Mikolaj when, much later, he reveals a desire for assisted suicide, explaining that he wants less suffering. Locked into its ever-increasing fund of memories that he cannot let go, his psyche ceaselessly augments his pain. Not until he grows in maturity through individuation will he develop an internal container large enough to bear his pain. Then he will cease to feel the impulse to act out the process of ridding himself of his suffering. Prior to that, like other would-be suicides, he just needs it to end.

Now, however, early in the acquaintance, Mikolaj (perhaps seeing his own suffering mirrored in Karol) generously offers to repatriate him. Easier said than done because Karol has mislaid his passport (a nice metaphor for his lost identity) and believes the police are after him (his paranoid projection of internalised Polish fear of oppressive, despotic powers). However, this time he does not succumb to misery, thanks ironically to Dominique herself. He makes the fateful phone call only after trying to show off her beauty to his new acquaintance. Unlike the devotion-blinded Karol, Mikolaj notices that she has another man with her. Although Karol cannot release his anger while she forces him to listen to her orgasm, when he ends the call he lets go for the first time ever. The phone box withholds his change and his awful humiliation explodes in rage, albeit displaced onto a surly official. Nor does his fury wither quickly. Forced to a psychological turning point, Karol can no longer passively accept suffering this extreme. Anger awakens a trickster in him and he shows his new friend how he will get into Poland as passenger baggage, enclosed in the trunk – metaphorically a coffin for his past self and womb from which his future will gestate.

No sooner does Karol touch down in his parental homeland than thieves steal the trunk, discover him, smash the figurine and (pausing only to knock him around when he tries to stop them stealing his last two French francs) tip him onto a snow-covered rubbish dump. 'Home at last,' the battered pauper murmurs, not one whit surprised at a less than propitious re-entry to the world that drops him right back into the Pole's familiar painful lot.

He staggers back to the ladies hairdressing salon that his brother still operates. Once recovered from his physical injuries and the first shocking wave of trauma induced by Dominique, Karol (more popular with the clientele than Jurek) resumes work to pay his way. He is already beginning to get in touch with the feminine by re-connecting to all those women whose needs he has always been able to satisfy by attending to their hair, that symbol of woman's sexuality. However, his mind soon turns to schemes more ambitious than his adipose brother (content with having innovated the salon's name in neon) will ever aspire to.

Karol soon finds that the rapidly changing political and economic environment offers him ample opportunity to greatly augment the limited income that hairdressing brings in – and, by no means incidentally, to boost the trickster aspect of his personality. He soon takes on a role to which he is wonderfully ill suited as bodyguard to such a man, a wily money changer (Cezary Pazura) who operates on the criminal margin. As Falkowska notes, values and money that previously had no natural home in Poland are filling the disorder following the fall of the Communist regime. Con artists and crooks step in to exploit the vacuum. Harsh juxtapositions result with brash new capitalism already by 1993 sitting alongside rubbish heaps. Corruption, poverty and crime go together with luxurious new houses and cars. 'The country which openly turned to capitalism after 1989 is the country of cynicism, betrayal, failure and disillusionment' (1999: 152). As a nation in transition, the Poles have (in *White*) made a transitional object of the zloty, which they intend to convert to Euros and US dollars at the earliest opportunity. Just like Karol's new boss snatching at piles of banknotes when a gust of wind threatens to blow them out of his steel container office, they lunge after hard currency whenever the opportunity arises.

Karol's intense desire for cash sprang from a revelatory moment when he tried to throw away the two-franc piece he got in the Paris underground. It stuck to his palm which he took as an omen, swiftly embracing this new transitional love-object so that wealth takes on high significance for him as an object to be used in service of the greater goal of securing love. Meanwhile the passions locked in the bust will require more devious pursuit; and their magical powers, although by no means wholly decathected, are beginning to diminish – witness Karol's clumsy attempts to restore the broken figurine. Grubby cash from the black market is beginning to alternate with 'pure' white desire as the means to deal with Dominique.

Karol's pursuit of riches does not lack deviousness. He eavesdrops on his boss and an associate who plan to exploit advance information and buy agricultural land cheaply where some of Europe's biggest supermarket chains intend to build outlets. Armed with this knowledge, Karol outpaces them and buys a small plot of land from an old peasant farmer (Jerzy Nowak) who, after a lifetime grubbing a livelihood in the backbreaking manual labour of his forebears, is dazzled by Karol's offer of American dollars. But to him the cash, far from being usable, is a mysterious hoard to hold onto by burying it. For his part, Karol (who arrived in Warsaw broke) has financed the purchase with his brother's savings which, much like the peasant, Jurek had merely stuffed in a box. The difference in attitude between the old money culture and the unregulated commercial behaviour that Karol is adopting exactly illustrates the emergence of a transitional object for the societal collective of the new would-be rich.

Karol's exploitation of money confirms that he is developing beyond infantile behaviour. Winnicott reminds us that the earlier, infantile phase of development, called object relating, is based on pure projection. It is as if the baby creates the breast, which becomes a cathected object. To make the developmental shift toward creating transitional objects, the infant must have developed the reality principle to the point where he or she has a capacity to use objects. That necessitates relinquishing omnipotent control over what he has now to recognise as something separate from the self (1971: 89).

Driven by the appetite for useable wealth, Karol wants to increase his investment by purchasing additional smallholdings strategically placed to frustrate his boss's grand ambitions. Needing more cash urgently, he recalls that in the Paris underground Mikolaj offered him the well-paid 'job' of killing a man who wants to die without sacrificing his life insurance. Karol had previously declined even to consider such an act; but now he smells the money, slyly asserting, 'When someone asks for help – you have to help him.' He has not yet matured to the extent that moral conscience has emerged. His trickster is deluding even him, concealing behind his hackneyed moral phrase an inadmissible urge. Characteristically the archetypal trickster makes mischief to bring dark impulses to the light. The effect is beneficial to the extent that the person moved by those ugly impulses learns to understand them for what they are. This will be the case with Karol.

Mikolaj sets up a rendezvous with the would-be assisted suicide in the Warsaw underground. The deserted subway is still under construction, darker than the French Metro, suggesting that the protagonists are venturing onto new territory in the underworld. And so it proves, for the client is none other than Mikolaj himself. Visibly disturbed, Karol prepares for murder. Urged on by his friend, he shoots him in the chest, catching him when he collapses, while the sound of the shot echoes like life itself departing down the tunnel. However, since accepting the commission the prospect of extinguishing a human life has evidently driven Karol to consider his moral position and he had secretly loaded a blank. A significant silent pun is in play here. White is *blanc* and blank of colour, which by extension becomes the colour of the void. A blank holds a space to think and can be compared to the Buddhist position of emptiness. After this pause, Karol requires his friend to understand that the next bullet is real and asks whether he wishes to receive it. Mikolaj, having touched death's cloak, changes his mind.

The authentic suffering that the two men experience in this confrontation with death alters them, unblocking their depressive state. Suddenly they find it in themselves to face sorrow, exultant, sharing life – boozed up and skidding across white winter ice to Preisner's cheerful tango. The relationship between them matures: Mikolaj insists on paying Karol for the contract 'murder' which, while not a physical event, did kill their dead, depressive parts. Karol accepts the money, but only as a loan. When his investment in land pays off, he insists in exchange that Mikolaj become his business partner.

In all this, the toughening of Karol cannot be missed. When his boss discovers Karol's land purchases, he and his thuggish associate assault the little man. The latter, however, has prepared for their vengeful brutality and faces it with courage. To cite Jung, he proves to be a true trickster by exposing himself to torture and managing to achieve through seeming stupidity what the others have failed to accomplish with their best efforts (1954c: §456). When Karol declares that he has willed his property to the church the heavies realise they have been outmanoeuvred.

No less the con man than they, he sells them the land for ten times what he paid; and in retribution for their aggression reveals with a pleasant smile that he owns more plots than they know.

Suddenly a wealthy man, Karol's image transforms, trickster like. By day, adopting the oiled mane of the high-powered crook, he replaces tatty pullovers and slacks with suits and a double-breasted greatcoat. A new, darker persona – the efficient, ruthless and successful international businessman – soon emerges. Yet the transformation is not complete and at night he regresses as before to the whingeing *puer*. In a further development, at other times his personality takes on a clown's characteristics. For example, as a company director negotiating for an office, he has no concept of the basic technology that every secretary and personal assistant depends on. When this facet of the character presents, it reinforces the comic register of *White*.

As always, the register of a film guides its interpretation and Karol's naivety reminds us that comedy distinguishes *White* from the other parts of the trilogy. It highlights the quirky qualities of certain characters so that, shown up by irony, their complexes stand out in front of the grander backdrop of human potential that they seldom fulfil. In dramas that seek a documentary plausibility, characters' language, speech patterns and gestures are usually constrained by the requirements of realist conventions. Here, Zbigniew Zamachowski occasionally 'over acts' in playing Karol to distance his character from a realist portrayal. For example, when handed a gun and told to guard his money-changing boss discreetly, Zamachowski appears to quote Charlie Chaplin as Karol swells with the delusion of new-found authority and struts his pride so ostentatiously that bystanders shrink from him. In other Chaplinesque scenes Zamachowski makes Karol clumsy, wrecking his pomposity and dropping him into the defensive-aggressive pathos of the narcissism we so often witness.

Jerzy Stuhr inscribes complementary traits even more broadly on Karol's brother Jurek. He proffers the world a morose moon face, but his sympathetic gestures toward his brother do not quite erase his opportunism. Meanwhile Karol's black-and-white mental picture of Dominique (until the film's climax the only available point of view of her) switches so radically between whore and innocent that in Julie Delpy's presentation the character appears to be untouched by routine daily life. Our picture of Karol's wife is his projection from a psychological position entrapped in the age-old male split between virgin and whore from which he attempts to preserve the good mother.

The sharp reversals that transform the protagonists' personalities complement the reversals of their fates and afford further clues to the film's register. The characters live in a comic world that has the qualities of fable. The plot is structured around archetypal oppositions, and these resonate as variants of the enantiodromia familiar in fairy tales. Each of the two unformed heroes Mikolaj and Karol offers to assist the other by 'killing' him; and this exchange of 'deaths' leads to new life for both. The incompetent little citizen wins power (the king or prince of the old stories, becomes the boss here) and then gives it all away. The ice-cold beauty loses her throne (the salon she has appropriated) and ends up (not exactly a maiden, but certainly in distress) locked in a tower (an upper floor of a gloomy prison) looking as though (a necessary precursor to true intimacy) she has surrendered emotionally to their union. The nearness of those older archetypal figures cannot be missed, but Kieslowski undercuts the simple oppositional patterns of the fairy tale allowing his characters to show the complex drives that move them. Karol, the not so handsome prince, far from being the damsel's liberator, has brought about her incarceration through Machiavellian trickery. And the damsel (a virgin in that her psyche has never been broken into by a lover) has been made into a cruel witch by unrequited love. These variations from the old stories speak meaningfully of the psychological development of the protagonists because, as Jacoby, Kast and Riedel put it, 'From the vantage point of depth psychology, fairy tales can be understood as depictions of psychological processes' (1992: 3).

Zbigniew Preisner's melodies colour the fabric of all three movies in the trilogy, helping the viewer experience a flavour of the inner-world landscape of the characters. The drawn-out notes of a clarinet played without vibrato deepen the audience's sense of Karol's feelings of isolation. This lament's function in the dynamic of plot and character development can be compared with the street musician's melody in *Blue* except that the latter bears the promise of grief surmounted. Karol's lament also resembles to some degree the musical accompaniment to Valentine's loneliness in *Red* except that in the latter instance strings lead the melody with ensemble playing that makes an appropriate accompaniment to the young woman's fundamentally gregarious nature.

White features a second musical theme that contrasts the isolation of the clarinet – a tango. To foreign audiences recalling the dance's Argentinean origins it may seem culturally misplaced. In fact, the tango became immensely popular in Poland and by the 1930s had evolved its own, distinctively Polish traits, evoking (no surprise here) both yearning and nostalgia (Placzkiewicz, 2007). However, Preisner's tango, scored for a vigorous string quartet, has abandoned sorrow in favour of a confident, cheeky rhythm.[3] Sustaining the comedic momentum, it underlines Karol's intermittent rediscovery of a cheerful humour. It also alerts us to his growing readiness for the psycho-sexual struggle in which lovers must engage if they are to be equal partners. But as mentioned previously, Karol's advances are not constant. By day ebullient in his role as boss and riding the wave that sweeps him to stupendous business success, his movement toward psychological integration is periodically interrupted when Urszula Lesiak edits in deep low-key shots (silhouettes of Karol and Dominique fading from obscurity to black) and these evoke their despairing fantasies of each other. At night, Karol the *puer*, trapped under the bust's remorseless gaze, is often flooded in narcissistic misery – cue reprise of the lonely clarinet.

Having studied hard to improve his French so that he can communicate with her better, Karol phones Dominique and begs her to speak to him, whereupon she cuts the line without saying a word. He has failed to understand that she does not particularly want him to address her in confident French. She wants to be recognised as the woman she is rather than as an idol of freezing marble that has to be shattered if she is to claim her own true self. But paradoxically her summary rejection of his whingeing call saves him from further pained self-regard. Once again, her callousness pushes him too far, but this time he has the confidence in his new role as a businessman to be able to react effectively. Anger revives trickster wit and he crafts a revenge calculated to reverse the power imbalance between them. He first makes a will naming Dominique as sole beneficiary and then sets about staging his own death. After warning the phlegmatic Mikolaj to expect to see his obituaries in the papers, he instructs his chauffeur to register his death and buy a corpse for burial in lieu of himself. Mikolaj (a man accustomed to unexplained 'deaths') completes the arrangements.

We referred earlier to Winnicott's concept of the false self as a structure first erected in infancy to defend the true self. At that stage in its development the child shapes its defences in response to its early environment. However, when the false self dominates the individual's responses, as with Karol in Paris, a sense of unreality and futility results. The false self, however well set up, lacks something – the essential central element, creative originality. In contrast, the true self feels real. Only it can be creative: spontaneous gestures and personal ideas always reveal the true self in action (Winnicott, 1971: 102, 148; Mitchell, 1993: 23).

Karol and Mikolaj had touched their own true aliveness when the former prepared to kill the latter. Now, delivering Karol his new passport, Mikolaj asks (clearly perceiving the thrust of Karol's plot), whether he is sure he wants to follow through. The echo of Karol's question to him *in extremis* seals the deep trust between them. Meanwhile Karol's rebellious decision to stage his own death indicates the revival of his true self. The difference on this occasion is that the laddish derring-do that characterises his black-market business deals will not suffice in facing the challenge of remaking his damaged relationship with Dominique. A complete renewal is necessary.

Winnicott indicates that invariable compliance with the pressures exerted by other people is incompatible with the true self. Always associated with living through the false self, compliance (Karol's predominant manner in Paris) is connected with despair rather than hope. Yet it attracts individuals because it brings immediate rewards and is thereby all too easily mistaken by parents or authority figures for growth (1971: 102). Nevertheless, although Karol is now acting in accordance with the demands of his true self, it is equally obvious that the person who functions exclusively in self-centred terms cannot be a member of society. Winnicott concludes that to live healthily the infant must develop the ability to compromise; but he or she must also be able to refuse compromise when the issues it faces become crucial. Then the true self should override the compliant self (Ibid.: 149–150). Trickster energy, it hardly needs noting, is invaluable in breaking away from compliance.

Posed in Winnicott's terms, the question that arises at the conclusion of *White* is whether Karol, having veered away from the false toward the true self, has advanced to the point where he can compromise. As a trickster he has arranged to die in order to be reborn – putting an end to the old Karol. When closing the coffin on the corpse that will substitute him, he slips his lucky coin under the lid, his symbolic farewell to money making and the false self that has hitherto formed him. Indeed, he cannot return to a life focused on international business because he has willed his share of the company to Dominique. In the event, though Mikolaj has set him up with a false identity(!) and a house in Hong Kong, he will even abandon his plan to leave Warsaw and bury himself instead in the family home. He has arranged things so that he must be reborn – but will he emerge from his transformation as prince or monster?

Before discovering the new Karol, we need to pay attention to a change in point of view involving Dominique. The shift is striking in that it first occurs only after she learns of Karol's 'death'. At the funeral the viewpoint remains where it always has been, with Karol who, moved by her sorrow, spies on his ex-wife through binoculars from afar. Point of view remains his when she returns to her Warsaw hotel room that night to find him alive and in her bed. Now she is scared by him (just as he has been of her) and they both know it. But once he has supported her through the shock of a reunion from beyond the grave, his confident kindness reaches her and they make love successfully with unfettered passion.

Afterwards she agrees when Karol murmurs that her cries of ecstasy were more intense than with her Parisian lover. So he has not let that humiliation fall from memory and her words now validate their mutually satisfying reunion. Nevertheless, come the morning, he hesitates before leaving. He gazes at her lovingly where she sleeps between sheets of flaming orange that (in the colour's naked violation of the film's repressed tonal scale) cry out the shocking impact of their passion. But although he does not go through with his carefully laid plan in its entirety, neither does he give up his revenge. Fondly he smoothes away a curl of hair blown by her breathing[4] and exits the suite just before the police, summoned by Mikolaj, arrive right on cue to spring Karol's trap.

This moment of getting even and moral reversal, coincides with the change in point of view. Just as Karol had once been alone, a stranger in Paris, so now Dominique will suffer an emotionally similar fate in Warsaw. The switch to her point of view makes her appear all the more vulnerable when she wakes alone and, wrapped only in the orange sheet, answers the suite's doorbell to be faced not by her returning lover but the cops. The police, having received reports that Karol died an unnatural death, have obtained a search warrant. They seize her passport which, despite her denials, proves to their satisfaction that she came to Warsaw before Karol's death. Unleashing the clipped fury that her ex-husband knows all too well, Dominique begins to rebut the charge. However, when awareness suddenly dawns that Karol has falsified her date of arrival to spring a trap, she falls silent, surrendering to his vengeance.

Jung observed that, 'One does not become enlightened by imagining figures of light, but by making the darkness conscious. The latter procedure, however, is disagreeable and not popular' (1954d: §335). John Beebe (2007) parses Jung's observation as meaning that spirit enters the psyche through the shadow – the compensation for suffering that may yet prove as attainable for Dominique and Karol as for the devout contemplative. Their love can't blossom until they know more about themselves and each other. However painful, their suffering will bring the clarification needed to secure their love.

The introduction of a quasi-religious dimension to our analysis responds to a tactful crescendo of signs that are incipient in the film from its start. Here too, a shift in the film's point of view provides a key. Occasionally during Karol's long exile from Dominique's affection and in the depths of his loneliness, his point of view had been intensified by a montage of the mind – the silhouetted image of her entering a dark room and moving into blackness. At the moment they occur these inserted fragments read like sombre waking reveries underpinning Karol's dark side. However, they anticipate an almost identical repetition of the shot when Dominique returns to her hotel suite after the funeral; so these fleeting moments have eventually to be recognised as based in synchronicity. If they comprised an isolated episode, it might be injudicious to claim this, but there are several corroborating moments that imply the shared psychological turmoil of the couple.

When Dominique enters the hotel room after the funeral, the blackness that surrounds her implies the darkness of her own mind, rather than as in his previous visions of this scene, Karol's grieving. But in the next few minutes of screen time, point of view is further disturbed. When their love making climaxes, the dark room fades to black, then mixes through to white before reverting to black and a dissolve back into the room. The device is so unusual that it draws attention to itself. It is congruent with the idea that darkness must be rendered conscious before one awakens, an immolation that Dominique (like Karol before her) now begins to undergo.

Next morning, at the moment of her arrest, a pigeon can be heard flying away from her window ledge – the clatter of wings being accompanied by the lonely tune on the clarinet that had previously haunted Karol. At the same time the recollection of their white wedding thrusts into her mind. The scene links her to Karol not only in the past but also in what appears to be the present (actually the future) as he stands in his brother's window abstractedly gazing at the comb that brought him and his wife together in the first place. While he muses (not for the first time) on this memory identical to her own, we notice that the implement has become grubby through use. Perfection in the mind juxtaposed against imperfection in life.

At the remembered wedding a mob of pigeons scattered as the couple were leaving the church to greet their supporters. The symbolism of the birds has obverse facets. Pigeons also rose up noisily when Mikolaj and Karol first get to understand each other – the latter's first meaningful contact with anyone since Dominique threw him out. All these occurrences, and another in the warehouse when Karol closes the coffin on his substitute corpse, appear to suggest, as Joseph Campbell and Bill Moyers mentioned, that the flight of birds implies the freeing of the spirit (1988: 18). However, we need to observe that while *White* does not refuse that connotation, it does not make the association comfortable. These tough city birds not only shit on people, they survive by scratching through garbage – light and darkness linked again.

The shared evocation of the wedding provides a moment of synchronicity more emphatic for the audience than the characters. The link it forges between the couple masks the chronological elision between Dominique's arrest and Karol in his brother's salon getting ready to visit her in jail – plainly some time later. We perceive that Karol has become snared in his own trap and that his love for Dominique has denied him the escape from Poland he had planned.[5] In *White* (as opposed to *Red* where they are plainly marked), synchronistic moments pass fleetingly. It is as if they hint at meaning the deep value of which, while tied to their mutual struggle, Karol and Dominique's psyches are ill prepared to receive. Kieslowski, in allowing us to observe their fates unspool, gives us a slight advantage over his characters; but while these synchronistic moments hint at the spiritual riches that could open for them following integration, their brevity – their almost unremarked nature – perhaps also suggests that while a positive resolution is possible, it nonetheless still remains uncertain.

A refugee in his home town, Karol skulks along the sidewalks clad once again in drab clothing and keeping away from public transport. Sidling up to the steel portal of a jail, he buys entry with a small bribe of Jurek's freshly made bread and cherry jam. It looks as though among common folk the mores of the old Poland have not expired. We already know that, amplified a hundred thousand fold, greed animates the *nouveau riche*, so when the expensive lawyer hired by Mikolaj and Jurek says to them that 'he sees a little light at the end of the tunnel', perhaps he means that altogether bigger bribes paid to the right people might free Dominique.

The clang of metal doors behind Karol resonates hollowly through the prison's gloomy inner yard. The architecture presents a macrocosm of the emptiness to which want of love has delivered husband and wife. They are now physically so distant from each other (she at her high, barred window, he in the yard below) that to be sure of obtaining a close view of her Karol must once again with unconscious irony use bird-watching binoculars. As the familiar sorrowing music resumes (but transferred to a flute for its more delicate timbre), Dominique mimes their break up, but only in order to negate it. Then, making a circular movement with her hand before dressing her bare finger with an imaginary ring, she proposes that they complete the circle to remarry.[6] Her circular gesture can be read as implying not only the togetherness for which she hopes, but also the circular journey that Karol and she have taken from Poland through France and back to Poland and the sharp reversal of both their fortunes. It corresponds too to the psychological activity that impels change in both of them – namely, the movement to a more differentiated self. Dominique ends by seeking his recognition with a tentative smile, while the melody passes to an oboe (possibly for the hint of confidence that its harder edge communicates).

Winnicott remarks that the change from object-relating to object-use requires the subject to destroy the object in fantasy, yet the object must survive. 'This destruction becomes the unconscious backcloth for love of a real object, that is, an object outside the area of the subject's omnipotent control' (Winnicott, 1971: 94). This is exactly what Karol has had to live out with Dominique in order to make her something real and separate from him. In this journey, as an imago in Karol's psyche, Dominique has developed her own sense of autonomy, in connecting to him more fully. The question that remains is whether Karol has learnt how to live with Dominique as woman rather than archetypal imago. *White* leaves the issue undecided with contrary indications as the contest in his heart pulls him first one way and then another.

True, he knows now that he loves her dearly. True, he weeps copiously when Dominique makes her appeal. True too, he smiles back at her; but just before the image fades for the last time, he averts his gaze and resolve braces his lips. Instead of giving in to his desire to free her, he seems likely to balance it against the recognition that to do so would be premature. He seems to know that she must feel the strength of his new sense of self, just as he was injured by hers, if they are more fully to understand themselves and each other. Thus, *White* ends with hope, but no denouement. That fits not only the state of the couple's relationship but also that of the collective. In resisting any temptation to round off *White* with a fairy-tale ending, Kieslowski has kept faith with the then political circumstances of Poland. In the film it remains a nation still in transition from the Communism it had abandoned only five years earlier in favour of a corrupt and corrupting free market – a period when Poles had hopes but not yet the certainty of entering the European Union. A denouement postponed until the conclusion of *Red*.

Notes

1 Cinematic heroes who go underground include Holly Martins in *The Third Man*, Clarice Starling in *The Silence of the Lambs* and the timorous Dr Bill Harford in *Eyes Wide Shut*.
2 Karol specifically alludes to the want of equality when alleging that the divorce court refuses to hear his case because he does not speak French.
3 Haltof mentions that Preisner consciously incorporated motifs from the tune that Karol plays on his comb – Jerzy Petersburski's 'This is our last Sunday' (2004: 133).
4 The moment recalls Julie in hospital in *Blue*. Metaphorically, Dominique's life is undergoing a slow-motion car crash.
5 Jurek recounts how he and Mikolaj had to identify his brother's supposed corpse after exhumation, and that they and several others would have been jailed if Karol had turned himself in. Evidently Karol has been tempted to release Dominique by sacrificing himself: a severe tug-of-love is rending his heart.
6 Kieslowski and his crew achieve an elegant special effect as she mimes. The camera seems to track toward the window so that its bars open and lose focus to allow a clearer view. However, the camera does not move in relation to the young woman who remains in sharply focussed close up. The unobtrusive device communicates (at a deep level that scarcely engages the spectator's consciousness) the intensity of Karol's gaze, his emotional attachment to Dominique and their mutual desire to free her.

7

TROIS COULEURS

Rouge (1994)

Cultural associations with the colour red are potent in the Western world. They include blood and intense passion, linking to injury and death on one wing of a diptych and to love and life on the other. These connections and others resonate through Kieslowski's *Red* as authentic indications of its themes. Yet in this setting the connotations of the colour are not exclusively traditional because the heroine, a model, will have her image displayed on a gigantic scarlet billboard to promote bubble gum. Unlike *White*, *Red* does not draw international political relations into its orbit, but the politics of capitalism are very much part of its realm.

Like *Blue* and *White*, *Red* commences with raw noise running behind the opening title card – in this case, the racket of drenching rain. That gives way, when a man calls an international number, to a collage of digital sounds woven into a myriad voices. The camera follows the imagined path of the phone signal (through a CGI montage of cables and exchange equipment) down across the seabed of the English Channel, out the other side and along wiring tunnels until – as the beep for an engaged number is heard – it encounters a flashing amber light on which the title *Rouge* is superimposed: communication foiled, at least for the moment.

The caller replaces the receiver and dials again. We cut to Auguste (Jean-Pierre Lorit) thinking he is the same guy, as he takes his dog for a morning walk. But this is neither the caller nor the intended recipient. When Auguste leaves his front door, the camera elevates past a corner shop across the road from his apartment and penetrates someone else's upstairs window. In this flat the phone rings until the answering machine cuts in, but at the last moment a young woman picks up. Michel, her lover, is calling Geneva from England and immediately asks why her phone was engaged earlier and whether she is alone. His confrontational jealousy exposes the insecurities that separation has provoked in him: yet when Valentine (Irène Jacob) tells him how she longs to be with him, he abruptly veers away from an exchange of emotion so that she retreats and chats about the weather.

Throughout the trilogy, when Kieslowski's characters make use of communications technologies the warmth of their personal connection is tested. In *Blue*, Julie uses the telephone as a means of initiating loving intimacy with Olivier. Dominique, on the contrary, deploys her phone in *White* callously to humiliate her ex-husband Karol. In this opening sequence of *Red* the telephone's function in the characters' emotional lives remains uncertain. Will it bring them together, as an instrument of communication should, or does it emphasise their apartness? Michel is never less than tetchy; but Auguste is wholly devoted to Karin his lover (Frédérique Feder), whom we only know for a long time by her telephone identity 'Personal Weather Reports'.

Valentine goes to her window as Michel's call ends, and the framing invites us to see her neighbour and his dog returning home unnoticed by her. A moment later Auguste comes back down to the street alone and drives off in a scarlet jeep so bright that we cannot but have spotted it in the street earlier. Right from the start scarlet obtrudes in shot after shot – in the furnishing of apartments, passing cars, a shop awning, a jacket and a tablecloth. The most vibrant primary colour on screen (frequently in deep contrast with either white or near black tones), it functions differently for spectators and characters. For spectators, prompted by the film's title and the careful placing of red within both the frame and the shots' chromatic scale, it impacts as a summons to puzzle at its significance. Indeed, given that there are no denotative connections between the red objects mentioned, the implicit invitation is to look for what hides behind their colour. As in analysing *Blue*, it seems right for the spectator to respect intuition and respond to the archetypal energies conveyed by this colour. Red, then, frequently implicates the instinctual realm. The characters, however, do not experience these triggers in the same way. Red seems to have no greater (and no less) significance to them than to us when we are outside the cinema. For example, they respond automatically to traffic signals without needing to cogitate on their meaning. The one exception: the vast scarlet background to Valentine's image in the advertisement does catch their attention – and ours too. It leaves us wanting to understand why.

From the start, as Janina Falkowska notices, vertical and horizontal lines isolate the spaces within apartments and houses and divide the landscape of Geneva into fragments of a city. She observes that this framing of shots complements the fragmentary nature of the characters' lives and emotions (1999: 153). Editing adds to the effect. The culmination of *Red*, in bringing together the protagonists from all three films demonstrates that it is not so much their lives that are fragmented as the opportunities we have for looking in on them – just as in the cinema, so too in contemporary city life.

Fitting this aesthetic, Valentine (a professional model) is seen in disjointed moments of a long, tough day. First, a photographer, Jacques (Samuel Lebihan) stands her in front of a scarlet backdrop and, to get the shot he wants, urges her to express sadness by thinking of the most terrible thing she can.[1] As we are to see much later, the resultant image synchronistically anticipates the transforming terror she will experience at the film's conclusion. In a ballet studio during the afternoon, she works her body up to the threshold of pain, benefiting from the discipline that the regime imposes on her. Then evening brings the rapid-change routines of a glittering fashion show. Yet although the audience sees only fragments of these activities, the takes are long, fluid and lit to emphasise the beauty of the young woman's face. Kieslowski establishes much more than the way Valentine earns a living. Unlike the two films that precede it, *Red* does not open on a grieving character. Even when the exercises cause her pain, or she stumbles on the catwalk, Valentine radiates joyous expectancy in her young life. When first encountering the character we might think this an untested delight, but we later discover that although she is the bearer of painful family problems, she does not allow herself to succumb to sorrow. However, she has not yet integrated her own shadow (a prerequisite for a really intimate encounter with another) and this helps account for her still being alone.

When late that night she drives home through quiet city streets, scarlet lights glaze the screen oppressively. Traffic lights flare across her windscreen while the stoplights on a motorcycle and the frame of the vast but empty advertising hoarding catch at her eye. It hardly seems an accident (although it is obviously an irony) that this crossroads (so complex in both its topography and the protagonists' lives, and which will soon be dominated by a vast advert for bubble gum – an image for vacant inflation if ever there was one) is the Place des Philosophes. Pulling away from the lights, Valentine does not notice Auguste crossing on foot behind her. He drops his books in the road and discovers that by chance one has opened at a passage which grabs his eye. Meanwhile Valentine's attention is distracted by what she takes to be a malfunction in the car radio. As she tries to retune it, the car hits something she has not noticed – a large Alsatian bitch. When something strikes us unexpectedly out of left field, as in these accidents, the unconscious has created a moment of synchronistic crisis, a moment in time where there is a meaningful connection between the internal and external life. And so it proves for Auguste and Valentine.

There is in this sequence a rich conjunction of instances of noticing, not noticing and blind chance which will radically change the life of both Valentine and Auguste. Her depth of being shows at once. She stops, soothes the injured dog and lifts it with difficulty into the car. The brown tones and deep shadows of the city streets now predominate, except for the animal's blood on Valentine's fingers, as she searches her street map for the address on its tag. Far from the glamorous scarlet to which we have become accustomed, the blood has a rusted, smeary look. Her searching for direction is analogous to the stirring of the individuation process, as she seeks a first indication of where she must go. In the crisis, as she leaves the neon-bright city centre behind, the drabness of the night prepares the spectator for the ill-lit house that she approaches.

No one answers the knock of the nervous young woman in the shadowed open door. We cut to a shot that tracks uncertainly through gloomy corridors as she tries to find her way in. Once again the takes are long, but the *mise-en scène* remains tightly restricted so that we cannot make out much more than that she is in a

Victorian house. At last she comes to a living room. An elderly man (Jean-Louis Trintignant) sits in front of a console, unaware of her intrusion. Despite the seeming blankness of the encounter, something links them. A whine like a radio receiver searching for a signal hangs in the air, as if trying to find a connection – the very sound that distracted Valentine before her car struck the old man's dog.

All that she makes out during this first meeting is the old man's bitter indifference to the dog's fate. Appalled but not intimidated, she asks whether his reaction would be the same if she had run over his daughter. The misanthrope merely ripostes that he has no daughter and insists that Valentine leave. The scene is not as simple as this brief exchange suggests, however. Although the old man's words are rebarbative and direct, his gestures seem hesitant. For her part, Valentine's unexpected reference to a daughter unconsciously positions her in relation to him. Meanwhile his parting cry, '*Don't* shut the door!' (contrary to what most crusty ancients demand) is like an unconscious admission on his part that he does not altogether want to close her or Rita the bitch out. Both possess a libidinal energy that he badly needs. Valentine slams the door defiantly, which brings the old man to his window. They gaze at each other, drawn (despite their hostility) by archetypal traits in the other to which they need to connect. They are *senex* and *anima* and, as we shall see, each supplies a necessary compensation to the other's dominant mind-set – standing as they do at the polar opposites of spirit and instinct.

Valentine drives Rita to a vet and then takes her home when the wound has been sutured. Undeterred by discovering that the dog is pregnant, she accepts with love the creature that blind chance has delivered to her. Then time shifts back into the earlier highly fragmented mode. She receives another jealous phone call from Michel. Her car alarm interrupts. She returns to the studio to see transparencies from the shoot, and learns that the legend to accompany her image in the bubble gum advert is 'Fraîcheur de vivre'. Jacques, the photographer wants to make love to her, but she deflects him gently, thinking of Michel. She buys a newspaper at her local café and wins money on a slot machine. She and the owner agree that in gambling bad luck is good (a notion that will resonate with the outturn of the ferry disaster that concludes the film). Conversely, good luck connotes misfortune. This seemingly bizarre reversal of the norm actually provides a good example of holding the tension between opposites and recognising intuitively that there is always another side to every circumstance. The rounded individual learns to circumambulate (or look at all sides of) a situation and to stay away from the ills of one-sidedness. The necessity of such a circumambulation of the facts immediately confronts Valentine when she opens the local paper. It carries a front-page shot of her brother fronting a headline story about drug users. Soon after, a neighbour brings money to her apartment that has been left for her anonymously. Troubled, she tries to reach her brother by phone. Time expands again.

Walking the restored Rita through a park, she lets the dog off the leash and it dashes into a church, skitters across its echoing marble floor, runs out and disappears completely. The empty church, home of a *deus absconditus* – a missing god – contains only a priest who has nothing to say in response to Valentine's plea for help. But Rita has followed her instinct and run home (perhaps a hint that ultimately help lies within the self – the psyche's home). Valentine instinctively pursues the animal, which brings her back to the old man's house where late autumn's dead leaves crepitate across the gravelled yard as she approaches the gate. Sure enough, when she rings the bell Rita comes out followed by the old man. Although the bitch has found her own way home and obviously loves her sour master, the animal holds the tension between the two of them in this awkward relationship, with Valentine embodying instinct and the old man personifying damaged spirit. Rita turns her head toward one and then the other.

The old man again offers Rita to Valentine, no longer wanting the animal or indeed anything. When Valentine suggests that he might as well stop breathing, he applauds the sentiment. Nevertheless, she establishes that it was he who sent money to her flat. Having secretly discovered where she lives, he appears to want to gain psychological control over her while remaining legally in the clear – hence he sent much more cash than she needed to pay the vet's bill. It is an over-compensation that brings to mind Jung's dictum that the opposite of power is not powerlessness but relationship. For Valentine, her yearning for relationship always matters more than power and she gives him back the wad.

The old man goes indoors to fetch change, leaving Valentine in the yard. She wanders around and then, unable to raise a response from the disconcerting hermit, enters his house. Once more she makes her way nervously through its gloomy spaces, an area of unconsciousness scarcely better lit than on her first visit. Indeed, all the scenes in this house take on a Vermeer-like chiaroscuro in which the protagonists' faces momentarily surface in murky pools of light before sinking back into the dark. Once again Valentine finds the radio console functioning. But this time, mixed through the tuning signal come the voices of two men, clandestine lovers, sharing a snatched conversation, one begging for an early meeting, the other struggling to ensure that his family know nothing of his second life.

The old man is watching her unobserved. He draws attention to himself and, challenged by a shocked Valentine, admits that he spies on his neighbours. His illegal use of communications technology to eavesdrop emphasises not his closeness but apartness from other people, not only socially but also emotionally and spiritually. He is repellent, but also pathetic. Although he complains when she cuts the signal that the lovers' suffering was just getting interesting, we can deduce (since he has taken no precautions to ensure that his unpleasant obsession remains concealed) that somewhere on the fringes where consciousness verges into the mind's darkness he wants to be found out. Indeed, he challenges Valentine to inform on him to the neighbour. His nervy decisiveness and startling gestures disconcert the young woman, as does his penetrating anticipation of her moral revulsion; but the fact that he has foreseen her reaction fails to shake her certainty that she must stop his sinister intrusion on his neighbours' privacy.

She crosses the road to the suburban villa that he points out. A pleasant woman opens the door and asks her to wait until she calls her husband; but as she stands in the hallway, Valentine notices the daughter eavesdropping on her father via a telephone extension. Horrified by what she knows the girl must be hearing, Valentine mumbles an excuse and leaves.

As she returns across the street, the camera frames the scarlet jeep. Auguste has brought his weather-reporting girlfriend home. The blind, chance intersection of times and lives, though still unobserved by the characters, is becoming more insistent. Valentine's focus, of course, is elsewhere. She charges back under the old man's dispassionate gaze into his house. Leaves reflected in the window make his unshaven face appear yet more haggard and severe. The two protagonists prowl uncertainly around each other in the gloomy house, their reflections caught in various mirrors that make it difficult for the viewer to co-ordinate their movements. Valentine admits that she has been unable to intervene with the neighbour, but asks the old man to desist from spying. Her request deepens the conflict between them and, in the long scene that follows, their faces are for the most part deeply shadowed, with seldom more than one half of each countenance lit dimly.

Coldly, the old man tells Valentine that all his working life as a judge he spied on people (surely a unique description of the judicial role). He has no idea whether he acted for good or bad.[2] This is a profound statement by the old man, realising post-career that he had passed verdicts based in his own subjective state of mind at the time. Those judgements had life-changing consequences for those whom he judged. Yet judgement is connected to the superego in that people usually judge events in their own lives as good or bad. They do so as if definitively, rather than realise that their 'judgement' merely reflects a certain consciousness (personal or collective) which might be assigned meaning at a later time through a process of introspection that would further their own development.

This judge personifies the *senex*, an archetypal figure whose negative aspects stand in opposition to the wise old man. His conservative and authoritarian mental set; his detached assessment of his fellow beings; his melancholic humour and denial of imagination all confirm the attribution of type (see Samuels *et al.*, 1986: 137). No less than his contempt for others, he loathes and deliberately humiliates himself. When Valentine refuses his offer of tea and asks him to stop spying, he pours boiling water on the floor as if he were pissing rather than tipping a kettle. As a voyeur who subconsciously yearns for intimacy, rage boils behind his detached persona. Compounding offence, he invites her to flick his braces against his chest, an ugly mock offer of assisted self-flagellation. Such distasteful behaviour conforms to the *senex* type that Jung found sometimes associated with the sewer (1948a: §269).

Among the gods, the *senex* is Saturn. Associated with the deepest of depressions, he represents the terrifying aspect of the old man in front of whom youth is helpless despite being relentlessly driven by him. As Kronos, he castrated his father and severed the point of contact between male and female (Chetwynd, 1993: 349). This we shall discover holds true (at least at first sight) of Judge Kern, whose responsibility now must be to repair the loss. That will not be an easy task since his career-long exposure in court to endless malfeasance, brutality and evil has left him, like the god, cynical and despondent about human nature. The Judge's professional experiences have equipped him to predict the worst of people and, as he demonstrates to Valentine, he is all too often right. This comes home to her when he divines the roots of the sorrow he has caused her through his relentlessly pessimistic view of the human condition, and locates them in her own family. Yet she has the courage to admit that the source of her pain is her brother's discovery aged fifteen that he was not his father's son, a betrayal that led to the teenager's addiction to heroin. In thus laying herself open, Valentine mirrors the Judge's self-exposure: filaments of trust begin to form between them.

Just as Saturn's day heralds Sun-day (Jung, 1948a: §301), new light will eventually spring from the torpid figure of the Judge. The depressive nadir of life, as Chetwynd notes, ultimately liberates that which is essential from the dross, affording the chance of transformation (1993: 349). Then, positive *senex* features (which include balance, generosity towards others, wisdom and far-sightedness) may be integrated.

Suddenly the old man asks the girl to pause for a moment. Late autumn light brightens the gloomy interior of his house and Piotr Sobocinski's cinematography accentuates the change. Silvery notes overlay what could be the sound of a distant lighthouse while, as the rays of the setting sun flow under the eaves, the roof appears to journey across space. The combined effect is magical. Seeming to anticipate a shift in the planets' order, it prefigures just such an alteration in the interpersonal sphere. The *enantiodromia* (or reversal of opposed values) of darkness into light anticipates the reversal of personality. But the moment does not last long, and soon the faces of the two characters (as they regress, resuming their familiar, opposed personae) are again bisected by dim light striving against deep shadow. The brief episode can be compared with the moment in *Blue* when Julie sinks underwater in the swimming pool – regression in the service of further integration.

Actually the illusory foghorn announces another phone call coming through Kern's eavesdropping system. A woman contacts Personal Weather Reports and inquires about the forecast to cover a long journey south. This conversation, very different from that of the anguished gay lovers, radiates mutual respect and kindness between caller and service provider. Two women who do not know each other are nonetheless connected by the telephone. Valentine is enchanted and, equally to the point, drawn into auditing the parade of unseen characters as surely as if she had been watching them pass by on the street. When a second call comes through, Kern announces before the caller speaks that it will be the weather reporter's lover. Valentine is hooked: although she eventually does cover her ears, she delays until she has overheard the young man expressing his wonderment at the previous night's lovemaking. The extent of the change that has come over her becomes plain when the Judge points to another neighbour strolling in his garden using a mobile. Kern alleges he is Geneva's biggest dealer in heroin, untouchable because the police can get no evidence against him. Valentine promptly asks for his number and, driven by the suffering the drug is causing her family, calls the dealer and tells him that he deserves to die. The man runs into his house, afraid.

What has got into Valentine? Her sudden rage has hitherto been a disavowed part of her self that resides in her shadow. Her action disgusts her; yet when the next call comes in just as she is leaving the Judge, she stops and listens without hesitation, desolated by an elderly woman's bitter complaints that her daughter neither visits nor shops for her. Kern turns the moral screws on Valentine by suggesting she do the old woman's shopping to ease her own feelings; then traps her into admitting that she rescued Rita because she would have felt guilty had she left the dog injured on the road. The Judge has tapped into Valentine's unconscious, pressing her to face the complexities of reality. But although guilt was an element that motivated her, the Judge misses noticing that it was not the main driver moving her to rescue the dog. That arose from her developed sense of owning and taking responsibility for her own conscience: the accident occurred when she was distracted from driving by correcting the tuning of her radio. Thus, rescuing and taking responsibility for the dog anticipates her rescuing herself and eventually the Judge.

When she drives back to the city, Valentine weeps – perhaps for loss of her innocence; perhaps because she sees how easily she has been drawn into the Judge's voyeuristic web; perhaps out of pity for the Judge himself, so skilled at seeing the worst in humanity, so blind to the complex motivations behind the actions of most people that lead them to mix good and bad purposes. Whatever else may have caused her tears, the feelings of powerlessness that triggered her shadow rage are key: she must give up the fantasy (which Judge Kern has sardonically proposed) that she is responsible for other people's misfortune. Omnipotent fantasies like those of saving her brother have trapped her. Now she must learn to live with her own survivor's guilt – *that* will be her responsibility, to save her soul and thus her self.

The pain Valentine is holding over her brother and the dynamics of her original family are also reflected in her present relationship with Michel. To this extent the judge was not lacking in psychological insight. Michael Friedman (1985) recognised a pivotal role played by guilt in arguing that individuals are hard wired to be concerned about other people altruistically, to a much greater degree than is commonly understood. Survivor guilt, according to research conducted by O'Connor *et al.* (2000), encompasses guilt about feeling better off than others, or about any sort of advantage a person may think they have when compared to others. They propose that survivor guilt has been selected by evolution as a psychological mechanism supporting group living. In addition, according to the Control-Mastery perspective, survivor guilt, although indeed altruistically evolved, has links with submissive behaviour and may extend to causing depression and the individual's failure to progress toward his or her own goals. The motive thought to be responsible is concern about harming others by outdoing them (Clinical Update, 2005: 8). All of this speaks volumes about Valentine's suffering.

Valentine is not alone in being disturbed by the clash with the Judge. Just as Saturn is identical with the negative aspects of Mercurius, Kern also has a Mercurial temperament that undergoes swift change. It seems that these bruising encounters have sprung *enantiodromia* in him too: he sets about writing letters confessing his illicit spying to his neighbours and the police. A kind of painful enchantment is occurring with each character taking on some of the qualities of the other in compensation for their own lacks.

Hitherto our analysis has accepted, without unduly pressurising the evidence, that the story's coincidences have simply been a matter of the kind of chance on which many scriptwriters and novelists depend for their well-rounded plots. Indeed, other coincidences of that type occur when Valentine gets home, still distressed by her clash with Kern. She phones her brother, but he cuts conversation to the bone. Needing comfort, she no sooner murmurs her yearning for a call from her boy-friend, than the phone rings. However, it is not Michel but Jacques and she accepts his invitation to go bowling. Unknown to her (her ears having been covered at that moment), Karin the weather reporter has persuaded Auguste to go bowling too. But when the camera tracks across the lanes from Jacques's party and we expect to find this couple, it halts not on them but a table with a shattered beer glass – a mute augury of Auguste's soon-to-be broken heart.

In addition to the unnoticed coincidences that happen in everyone's life, consid-erable evidence is mounting up that phenomena of another, energy-charged kind are occurring. When Karin tossed a coin at her end of the phone line to decide how she and her lover should pass the evening, Kern flipped his own money – and it too came up tails. At one level this incident is undoubtedly an example of Kieslowski's interest in blind chance (see Chapter 5), since neither party could have influenced the fall of the other's coin. However, although we do not yet know what its mean-ing might be, it impresses us as having significance because we see how Kern's coin has landed before Karin reveals how hers has fallen. Remember too that the Judge knew who was calling before Auguste spoke. Both incidents furnish early signs of a phenomenon that will recur.

Jung called this phenomenon synchronicity. He used the term to refer to 'an acausal connection, through meaning, of inner psychological states (such as dreams, fantasies, or feelings) with events in the outer or material world' (Mansfield, 2002: 122). Roderick Main points out that although Jung's formal definition did not extend to cover sets of events either solely between two inner psychic states or solely between two outer physical events, he nonetheless applied the term to them also (2004: 40). The extension of Jung's definition in this way permits the term synchronicity to be used in connection with events in *Red* where, for example, one character has prescient knowledge of the likely behaviour of another. Jung described as characteristic of synchronistic events that they 'cannot be considered from the point of view of causality, for causality presupposes the existence of space and time in so far as all observations are ultimately based upon bodies in motion' (Jung, 1952: §836). Synchronistic events are neither linked in time (witness Kern's fore-knowledge noted above) nor in space (such events occur where no physical or material connection exists between them) (Ibid.). As Victor Mansfield says, the inner state neither causes the outer event nor vice versa (2002: 123).

It is important to understand with Mansfield that no transcendent principle, whether god, angel or archetype, acts as the cause for synchronicity. We cannot attribute what happens in the empirical realm to what goes on in the transcendent realm (Ibid.). This specifically applies to the collective unconscious which, to cite Marie-Louise von Franz, 'is not at all an expression of personal wishes and goals,

but is a neutral entity, psychic in nature, that exists in an absolutely transpersonal way'
(1992: 231).

If the connection that links psychological states with events in the outer world
is meaning, what is its nature? We may begin by noting that the meaning latent
in a synchronistic event requires time, effort and contemplation in order to be consciously assimilated because, in this context, meaning is of a deep order connected
with the unconscious. And the chief form of interaction between the conscious
and unconscious is compensation, in which the unconscious psyche purposefully
corrects the restricted perspective or even blindness of the ego (Mansfield, 2002:
125). For Jung, 'All psychological phenomena have some such sense of purpose
inherent in them…' (1948b: §456). At the personal level that purpose is the fur-
therance of individuation – the coming to selfhood.

Jung argued that dreams and fantasies offer the individual unconscious compensation for imbalanced positions in which the ego is stuck. The more one-sided the
conscious attitude, the more likely that vivid dreams with a strongly contrasting
and purposive content will appear as an expression of the psyche's self-regulating
function (Ibid.: §488). People who pay attention to their own internal lives may
recognise and respond to the correctives that they offer. Given that dreams have
this potential, why do synchronistic experiences occur? Mansfield observes that
such events are usually preceded by some activation and disturbance in the unconscious: they are more likely to occur in periods of deep difficulty and stress.
Synchronicity may forcibly deliver an emotional and psychological awakening to
the individual who has not responded at a deep level to less dramatic signals from
the unconscious. It does so with the purpose of transforming that person through the
process of individuation (2002: 126–9). The synchronistic event is the transforming
agent. Mansfield adds that although positive experiences can also contribute to
transformation, the suffering that human experience inevitably delivers is the surest
point of access to change: 'only when we are broken open, only when the ego is at least
a little crushed, can the most powerful transforming experiences occur' (Ibid.: 135).

While personal transformation is what principally occupies Valentine, the narrative invites audiences to follow the Judge's engagement with revelations of shared
or transpersonal import. His experiences affirm that synchronicities may extend the
register beyond that of the personal psyche by conveying numinous, prophetic
messages, a discussion we shall develop later.

Since in the cinema the audience cannot stop the film and contemplate in full
the as yet incompletely revealed personalities of *Red's* protagonists, we cannot at this
point make out what unconscious compensation may mean for them. It is already
apparent from their behaviour patterns that compensation is occurring and matches
Mansfield's observation that the unconscious is not always encouraging (Ibid.: 126).
Judge Kern's persona is too darkly devoted to voyeurism for the synchronistic
knowledge he presents to Valentine to be anything other than painful. He has been
living in his own shadow. Like the priest in the vacant church, he is a counterfeit
spirit,[3] disguising an absence of connection behind the appearance of being in touch
with all those around him – but espionage is not contact. And unlike Valentine,

who has taken risks (for example, entering his house uninvited) he does not allow himself to be vulnerable – not, that is, until he waits by his radio receiver for her to enter his house again. By then allowing the intrusion of another person into his private domain, he opens himself up to the possibility of discovering his deeper self. We cannot individuate alone: the opus of the soul needs relationship to advance.

> 'Know thyself' is the philosophical axiom from which psychology was birthed, but it is only through revealing ourselves that we may heal. 'Know thyself' will be insufficient for a creative psychology. Not 'Know thyself' through reflection, but 'Reveal thyself,' which is the same as the commandment to love, since nowhere are we more revealed than in our loving.
>
> *(Ortega y Gasset, 1957: 82–3)*

Valentine and Joseph Kern do not lose contact. She reads a newspaper report of his trial and hastens one evening to his house fearing he might think that she had betrayed his grubby secret. The Judge assures her that he wrote his own confession in response to her wishes.[4] However, Valentine had asked him to do nothing more than stop spying. So he has over-compensated again, albeit this time making a conscious correction integral to his personality by surrendering to the Law. Although his confession moves his personal transformation onward, the Judge's attempt at entering into relationship with Valentine is clumsy. Rather than consciously open himself by contacting her directly, he has calculated (correctly) that reports of his trial would bring her to him – behaviour that smacks of manipulation. Nevertheless, he reveals his backsliding and confesses his own want of probity. Then he challenges Valentine to do likewise and concede that, when previously she had spoken of pity for him, she truly meant that she felt disgust. She acknowledges the hit.

As they converse, Sobocinski's camera tracks onto a billiard table laden with antiquated junk. While Kern's house at large offers an emblem of his autumnal psyche pushing into old age, the long-abandoned table displays a particular feature of his inner turbidity. This is the decay of freshness (in contrast to the implications of Valentine's billboard). According to Winnicott play is the hallmark of developing the ability to be relational; so the Judge's inability to play games, is an emblem for his aloneness and lack of relationship. Yet there is too something new in the house that signals rebirth. Rita has produced seven pups; and at Kern's invitation Valentine stays for a while, enchanted by the little creatures. Clearly his heart too has been stirred by the arrival of the litter. Sensing this, she accepts warily his offer of a celebratory glass of pear brandy. Then shockingly, in another rude volte-face, the egregious old man promptly toasts neither the dogs nor her but himself.

Valentine has decided to travel to England. She makes it sound as though her plans are to leave forever, telling the Judge she feels she is abandoning her family. The exaggeration reveals that she has adopted the false posture of omnipotence to compensate for her inner powerlessness and guilt. Kern counters by shifting into a quasi-fatherly role (thereby substituting her absent parent). He advises (his words rising to her out of near total darkness in both the room and her own mind) that she must simply *be* and live out her own destiny rather than those of her brother and mother. To parse this psychologically, she must discover a new level of integration and maturity to shift from continued personal responsibility for the burden she took on during adolescence to a self-directed life. That process involves differentiating between duty and obligation. The former is more externally focused and ruled by superego impositions of right and wrong. Obligation depends on an internally driven, self-reflective position considering both the other and the Self. It has a truly relational potential which holds the whole Self and all ego states.

In parallel processes during this third encounter, the Judge and Valentine draw each other out from where they were previously stuck. As he turns on a lamp, it fails. The image blacks out, then blinds with excessive light before Kern shades the replacement bulb and restores chiaroscuro. The harsh visual oscillation encapsulates the emotional switchback through which their dialogue is pulling the unlikely pair. The topic of conversation switches to the role of judges when Kern reflects that one of his best decisions lay in acquitting a guilty man who subsequently made an honourable life for himself. Musing aloud about the nature of justice, Valentine discovers the thought that there is a vanity (a worldly futility) in attempting to determine what is and is not true. A person remains psychically calcified when using only reasoning determined exclusively by cause and effect. A higher mental functioning includes intuition, trusting the self, the source of Judge Kern's verdict in this instance. So Valentine's idea leads the old man toward a mode of understanding human kind that moves beyond the frames of reason and righteous morality. While he is impacting on her sense of self worth, she is rousing a more acute sense of personal ethics and value in him: each leads the other toward a spiritual awakening.

By chance Valentine has turned up on his birthday. Following their fruitful discussion, warmth has grown between them and she drinks to his health. In response, Kern celebrates her innocence. But no sooner have the words passed his lips than a stone shatters a window. Kern asks Valentine to add it to his collection of projectiles hurled at the house since the trial. Dropped into a pile, it cannot quite be the solitary philosopher's stone from which alchemists might make spiritual gold; in *Red*, both the characters and their society cannot scale the commanding heights of philosophy, so these are the stones of an imperfect moral philosopher. Kern keeps them as reminders that in his neighbours' place he would do the same, that were his circumstances those of the people he had adjudged guilty, he too would have stolen and killed. His ascetic amoralism compares with Valentine's innocence in that both positions are too one-sided, the former overwhelmed by shadow, the latter trying to exclude it. The synchronicity of the shattered window can be read as indicating (to refer back to Mansfield's observation) that something in each needs to be broken before transformation can take place.

Synchronicities have by this time begun with increasing emphasis to involve more characters. Auguste passes the final examination that admits him to practise as a Judge. He has been helped by revising the topic presented to him when his book fell open at the Place des Philosophes crossroads a few moments before Valentine's car hit Rita. She, of course, knows nothing of this, but later Judge Kern will recount a similar fortunate incident of *sortes Virgilianae* that occurred when he dropped a book decades earlier during his own preparation for his final legal exams.

Other incidents make for chance connections within the plot. For example, Karin celebrates Auguste's success by giving him a fountain pen exactly like the one that the Judge broke some nights earlier when writing his confession. This the latter had owned since taking up office: but now finally the phallus of Logos and the Law has failed him. Will the new pen have similar consequences for the young man? Indeed speculation about Auguste's future grows when the Judge's confession brings him and his neighbours to court. There, almost at the edge of the screen, Karin meets another young man (Paul Vermeulen). We cut hard to them shopping together for CDs at the very moment Valentine is sampling the Concert for the Unification of Europe on the next set of headphones. Although these coincidences do not have the characteristics of synchronistic events for the protagonists themselves, we experience the strangeness of these decreasingly random, but increasingly frequent and purposeful connections as synchronistic. As yet, their meaning remains to be discerned; but periodically, by recalling generic musical devices from science fiction movies, Zbigniew Preisner's non-diegetic strings add to a sense that the material world conceals actualities deeper than can be seen on the surface – and that the surface is dissolving to reveal the potential of what lies hidden.

The most dramatic synchronicities link Judge Kern and Auguste, but these can only be appreciated after the younger man's love relationship collapses. Auguste and Karin had used the phone freely to utter intimacies that they could not say face-to-face. This typifies the way that communications technologies are deployed in the trilogy. They change the nature of human connection – they extend the possibilities of reaching across time and space but also constrain the messages that can be sent. By abstracting one channel of communication from the others, they amplify its emotional tenor (whether positively or negatively) and thereby intensify whatever happens to be the current tenor of the characters' relationship, rather like the communication pattern between the conscious and unconscious. Now, however, Karin's phone is always engaged, denying all communication. In a frenzy of anxious suspicion amplified by her silence, Auguste hurls his jeep along the roads to her apartment. When he gets to her door he decides instinctively against knocking and scales risky exterior ledges to gain her window where he sees her in bed with her new lover. To take the risk called for in the search for one's own truth is to be deeply committed to growth whereas fear suppresses it. Every painful encounter (especially if synchronistic) holds the possibility of further growth.

Dominique in *White* betrayed Karol. But Karin's lie, like Patrice's silent betrayal of Julie, cuts deeper than the deed itself. Karin violates fidelity by not letting Auguste know *why* she has taken another lover. Her unwillingness to share what is in her mind hints at her distorted rationalisation that she is protecting him from the truth. Actually she is only protecting her own self-image – an indication of her psychological immaturity, her narcissism. The lie stops Auguste from moving forward and keeps him, as the victim of deception, living in a space of not knowing – a betrayal of the self. Although her leaving him in a more truthful manner would still feel like betrayal to Auguste, it would have provided him with an opportunity to learn more about the Self, with his suffering holding transformative potential.

Like many newly betrayed lovers, Auguste suffers an erotic injury, misery so boundless and irremediable that (if it cannot be turned outward in anger against the traitor) it must be answered with some self-humiliation. He follows Karin and her new lover to a restaurant, taps on the window to get her attention but hides when she comes out to speak to him. Then, as if replicating the damage done to his libido and willing his own animal warmth to die, he chains his beloved dog to a roadside post and abandons it.

While eavesdropping on Auguste's loving phone call to Karin, Judge Kern had said to Valentine that the weather reporter was not the right woman for him. Now we can see why. Although she is in her thirties, in developmental terms Karin behaves like an adolescent in hoping that she can get away with cheating. She lacks a sufficient sense of responsibility, unlike Valentine who has it to excess. Engulfed in her fantasies, her immature carelessness shows to the extreme in her final forecast. The Judge has inquired about the weather over the Channel in a week's time. He has divined that is when Valentine will board the ferry for England. Karin paints an idyllic picture, ignoring the storm clouds (both meteorological and metaphorical) gathering overhead. In her self-absorbed state of prolonged adolescence, the prospect she projects of sunny breezes completely ignores external reality and has everything to do with her idealisation of an escape across the same waters on her new lover's yacht. Unlike the Judge (when confessing to spying) she has not learnt to take responsibility for her actions.

Why does Judge Kern inquire about the weather when he expects Valentine to be on the ferry? It confirms his awareness that he has prophetic powers, but is wise enough to realise that such powers can be erratic when it comes to foretelling a specific incident. Von Franz argues that divination cannot foretell specifically what will happen. Rather, 'prediction only refers to the quality of the moment in which a synchronistic event might occur'; it might give a broad indication such as 'unexpected bad luck' (1980: 101). Only after events have been played out and his story is told in its entirety can we deduce that the Judge, contemplating the rejuvenating impact of Valentine on his life, must have fallen into a reverie reflecting on his own pursuit of a lost love. In summoning the past, he has divined the future – that a storm will endanger this young woman. It explains why he asks to see Valentine's ticket the night before she leaves – a request that would otherwise seem intrusive. He wants to be sure she *is* to sail on the day he anticipated because, relying on Karin's accuracy, he is confident that his foreboding was mistaken and that Valentine will be safe if she travels then, but not if she goes at another time. Karin's carelessness has betrayed him (and perhaps herself too). As a diviner, Judge Kern is better attuned to the world than the personal weather reporter. He is transforming from *senex* into wise old man.

Before she leaves for England, Valentine invites the Judge to a fashion show in which she is modelling. On the runway she is at her most sure-footed, as beautiful as a goddess; but close-ups reveal her sadness when she cannot spot him in the crowd. However, Kern has watched the event from on high in the balcony – his lifelong custom in this theatre, and a reminder of his habitual elevated perspective on the human parade that came before him as a judge. Yet after the event, when she exits the dressing rooms on the catwalk and he has descended to the front stalls, she towers over him. As they shake hands warmly, he draws her down to squat cheerfully on the platform, so that she is not so far above him. Later, relinquishing her role as public performer and her image of perfection (as he in retiring had given up his public role), she steps down from the stage and stands beside him. As Jung wrote of individuation, 'Wholeness is not so much perfection as completeness' (1958a: §452). Their movements enact growing mutual respect in which neither dominates the other. Their relationship contrasts with their previous lives. Kern (like Auguste) had placed a woman on a dais from which (like Karin) she inevitably fell, a calamity for the pedestal builder. Valentine has found awareness gradually dawning that, as Michel's jealously guarded love object, she has been held geographically and emotionally at a distance, a posture not too different from being on a plinth. As long as people idealise they do not have a real relationship with the other.[5]

The strangeness of the meeting in the theatre cannot be missed since Valentine herself speaks of it. The characters' solemn parting gives it the tone of a final farewell despite the fact that they also anticipate her return to Geneva after two weeks' absence. Their deep-felt sadness in saying good-bye reminds us that every new loss brings to mind all previous losses. Taking leave of someone in a manner that promotes personal growth entails completing the encounter by expressing to the other person who they have been and what they have meant.

Valentine has not mentioned that she will visit her boyfriend, possibly because, having tasted authenticity with Kern, she doubts the relationship with Michel. Instead she asks the Judge to enlarge on his dream of her as a middle-aged woman waking happily alongside a man. He assures her that this prophecy will come true. His words are both a gift to her and the root of healing for his own wounded anima. Yet his prescience disconcerts her because she senses something important happening over which she has no control – fears that signal the kind of psychological disturbance which might precede synchronicity.

Comforted by Kern, she sets her fear to one side and (whereas he has intuited the future) makes his past her text. She breaks into it decisively, guided by empathy with his suffering. Threaded secretly behind her words, Preisner's delicately suspended strings (as during their previous meeting) subtly abstract the audience from any decreasingly relevant concern with the mundane and inculcate a readiness for further shifts in the orders of reality. Valentine's penetrating reading of Kern's sorrow shows that she has seen behind his persona no less surely than he through her disguises. Under her prompting, he fills out his story. Although the events he recounts precede Auguste by thirty-five years, the younger man's recent history has closely replicated them: the *sortes Virgilianae* with the dropped book; the love of a lissom blonde; her betrayal; and his spying on her. Although the parallels are not complete, the older man's subsequent lifetime of grief-locked rage, humiliation and espionage signals plainly the danger to which the younger man will be exposed if he does not resolve his anima obsession.

A storm interrupts the Judge's story and once again the smashing of a window breaks into their intimacy. Valentine battles to secure the wind- and rain-lashed French doors and the curtains wrap her ominously as if in a shroud. Kern looks on, the anxiety this sign triggers augmented when he perceives that she was expecting this storm. Has she heard a forecast that contradicts Karin's blithe prediction of calm? The harsh weather both intensifies and acts out the protagonists' states of mind fittingly since the words for wind and spirit (as with the Greek *pneuma*) are closely aligned in many languages (Jung, 1934: §663–4). Here the Judge, revisiting acute past agony and conscious that Valentine's empathy makes it safe for him to do so, experiences the rushing wind of the spirit breaking open the ego (Mansfield, 2002: 135). He wonders whether Valentine may not be the woman whom, after the disaster with his first love, he never met. Beyond question, their emotional and spiritual affinity empowers her to steer him toward further transformation.

Indeed, like a healer, Valentine perceives that Kern has more to confess. It concerns Hugo Holbling, the rival whom the Judge saw as having stolen his only love. Many years later, this person was arraigned before him, charged with the death of several people in a building's collapse. Kern ought ethically to have declined hearing the case but could not resist exercising power over the man he still considered his enemy. Although Holbling's guilt was not in question and Kern delivered the correct verdict, he had exploited his office for the secret satisfaction of extracting revenge. Behind the obvious moral issue (which his immediate retirement did not extinguish), the Judge's confession reveals the extent to which inability to process his archaic grief had exposed him to the shadow archetype.

The trauma suffered in the betrayal of love provoked a splitting in Kern from his shadow. As Jung said of this phenomenon, 'The tendency to split means that parts of the psyche detach themselves from consciousness to such an extent that they not only appear foreign but lead an autonomous life of their own' (1937: §253). All those years fused in frozen rage he has been unaware of projecting self-loathing onto his enemy. As complexes do, in Kern's imaginal world his former rival has taken on the autonomous behaviour patterns of a seemingly independent being (Ibid.). In its obsessive quality, his spying on the neighbours arose from the Judge's need to fill a painful lack – to reunite with the split-off shadow that he had displaced onto Holbling.

As Kern confesses to the cold, self-seeking calculation that lay behind his final case, his account is interrupted by the theatre's gruff janitor. Somewhat irritably the tired functionary is searching for the cleaner so that he can lock the building. But when he finds her, he ceases grumbling and insists that she hand him her buckets because they are heavy. His generous stance is, from a psychoanalytic perspective, relational. Had it been otherwise, rather than wishing to help share the burden (a relational stance), the janitor would have insisted on his own agenda, namely to get away home. As played out here, however, his role in cleaning up garbage is analogous to the necessity, if an individual is to be complete (as opposed to perfect), to gather and connect with the contents of his or her own shadow.

Valentine, despite the glamorous persona she adopts as a model, also has a humble capacity for relation. One further incident, this one relating to a scenario that recurs in each part of the trilogy, confirms it. Julie and Karol in Paris and Valentine in Geneva each see a bent ancient struggling to push a bottle into a recycling bank (a repeated scene so unusual that it seems in deceitful memory as though it must be the same individual in the same city).[6] Only the last person receives help – from Valentine – just as, undeterred by old age or his bitter humour, she risks her peace of mind to help Judge Kern. Indeed, it is because of the comfort Valentine gives Kern that his shadow releases its deepest obscurities. Their last moments together present evidence of his inner growth. Valentine offers to have her brother take him her unwanted television set and the Judge replies that he looks forward to knowing him. He could never have welcomed meeting a heroin user without advancing in self-knowledge.

In due time, Valentine boards the ferry for England. So does Auguste, who has recovered from his trauma to the extent that he has reclaimed his dog. But scarcely has the ship left port than it capsizes in the storm, and almost 1500 people perish. We take up the Judge's point of view as, aghast, he devours televised news footage.[7] Immediately we find it impossible to deny a thought triggered by the first report of two people who have drowned after their yacht capsized that they might be Karin and her new lover. Our making this statistically improbable connection confirms that the film has drawn us into its synchronistic structure. Soon the transmission freezes close ups of the few survivors as they are brought ashore. The reporter identifies Auguste as one of only two Swiss citizens to have been found alive; and then, cold and exhausted, Valentine steps onto dry land. When her eyes lock with Auguste's we see (aided by the Judge's precognition) that surviving the horror will throw them together – and that they are right for each other.

Having watched the coverage, the old man looks out from his window and, for the first time in decades, grief pushes through his defences as he weeps healing tears. Given what we now know about him, his tears signify not only his joy at Valentine's survival, but also relief at the playing out of his prevision. No less important is the confirmation for his spirit that his anima has not perished after its lovely re-illumination.

The final shot, a freeze frame, pointedly mirrors Valentine's image in the advertisement and therefore reverberates with complexity. Auguste had found her image striking when seen on that enormous billboard where it undulated in the breeze, giving the illusion of life. By the time of the disaster, it has been imprinted on his mind for some while. As they disembark from the rescue launch, its replication before his eyes implies that he has found the woman whom he has, without knowing it, been waiting for – the woman on whom to project positive attributes of his anima in what will become a love relationship.

Valentine is not interviewed in the television coverage, but she has survived disaster, seen many die and faced real terror brought on by the impersonal forces of a destiny that she has no power to challenge. These experiences can only have diminished her fantasies of omnipotence. When her rage exploded at the drug dealer, her over-weighted omnipotence was produced by the powerlessness she could not acknowledge. In this calamity she has found strength enough only to save her own life and cannot deny her helplessness in the face of the storm. Thus, the integration of her shadow is tactfully signalled.

The conclusion of *Red* goes beyond the personal transformation of the protagonists to draw attention to the cultural and archetypal spheres. When Judge Kern was driving to Valentine's fashion show he passed her advertisement on the Place des Philosophes. At last its legend is revealed: 'En toute circonstance: Fraîcheur de vivre'. 'Fraîcheur' has several connotations and refers equally to a blooming complexion, the blossoming of a flower and freshness of spirit. An ad for bubble gum offers the consumer nothing less than transformation! In part, indeed, the advert attracts through this bogus implication that gum will transform the purchaser into a cynosure of youthful beauty like the young model. In part it achieves potency through the glamour of the image as opposed to the product (the agency rejected the shot where Valentine blew a pink bubble). Several factors endow the poster with this glamour: the size of the billboard; the suffusion of scarlet to an intensity not found in nature; the beauty and youth of the woman; and the artful disarray of her hair that speaks (as does her expression) of life lived to the full but still within control. Paradox lies latent here in that, to gain the effect of living life to the full, the photographer asked Valentine to think of something terrible as he took this still. Thus, two countercultural readings of the advert would be, first, that a little terror creates stimulation; and, second, that there is nothing to fear except not feeling one's aliveness through the fraîcheur that bubble gum excites. These readings converge in that (like so many advertisements) both invite the consumer to a constant and ultimately unhealthy need for stimuli experienced as an end in their own right rather than as the trigger for passionate action. Meanwhile the hoarding's location presents us with a culture in which philosophers have been sidelined by the commercial imperative.

This image so engaged actual audiences that, cropped to frame only Valentine's profile, it became the icon fronting the marketing campaign for *Red*, featuring on posters, DVDs and videotapes – where meanings available to those who had yet to see the film bore no reference to gum but focussed on imperilled, youthful beauty. Within the film's narrative, however, the giant poster focuses the tension between celebration of Valentine's beauty and the cultural abjection of emotive appeals to puerile commercial values. The effect on viewers, nevertheless, is so striking that it calls to mind Gilberto Perez's thought that beauty has the power to do no less than sway, move and persuade (2005: 38 and see Chapter 9).

After the denouement, the audience cannot but look back in time and recognise that the poster (in an *enantiodromia* or reversal of opposed values) has by negative implication predicted the terror. It is the film's most disturbing evocation of precognition. However, although the final televised freeze frame strikingly resembles the advert, it is not an exact replica. The billboard no longer exists because, when the storm worsened, workmen took it down. While, intercut against the ferry putting to sea the men lower the image, Valentine's face buckles and sags as if waves were washing over her – another forewarning synchronicity. It warns not of her death but the collapse of her old self. The final televised frame (a minute, low resolution image compared with the hoarding) starts as a two shot with Auguste until we zoom in on Valentine; salt water has soaked the dishevelled woman; shock has dropped her jaw; a coarse first-aid blanket replaces a stylish wrap in the original photograph; and the background is the matt and scuffed red of a rescuer's jacket, not the ad's vibrant scarlet.

Not for the first time (an earlier instance being the accident where Rita bleeds), Kieslowski has extended traditional readings of redness to distinguish between the brilliant scarlet that technology can produce and less glamorous reds. The former, highly saturated and pure colour (which imbues not only advertisements but also lights, furniture, vehicles and clothing) *can* convey traditional values. However, it may also reflect a hyped register that not only goes beyond actual human experience (of itself an entirely appropriate means of engaging with the archetypal) but tends to a one-sidedness in which endlessly, greedily to desire becomes the goal rather than the means to knowledge of the world and self. Less glamorous reds, by contrast, never exceed the archetypal values associated with the colour in older traditions of Western culture.

Blind chance recurs dramatically in the final sequence in that Julie and Olivier, the lead protagonists in *Blue*, are numbered among the handful of survivors together with Karol and Dominique from *White*. Through their presence, the three films converge so unexpectedly as to require audiences to account for the connections between them. The shock of this last-minute entwining of the main characters' fates directs our attention back to the other carefully rendered links between the parts of the trilogy. Those links (as in the bottle bank scenes) may at first sight be deceptive in implying connections in time and space. However, careful scrutiny dissolves any such notion and the impossibility in most cases of a causal connection invites spectators to cogitate on the true underlying meaning of these moments. In terms of the emotional impact relating to the three couples, one thematic implication is that to find real love individuals must be survivors of their own personal storms.

The conclusion of *Red* invites us to recognise but then look beyond the personal dimension. The wreck featured in the final sequences had actually occurred some years earlier, a fact that intensifies our need to explore chance connections. Although the crew's failure to close the bow doors (which caused the *Herald of Free Enterprise* to capsize in 1987) is only hinted at in *Red*, and the numbers actually drowned were fewer, most Europeans would not have failed in 1994 to feel the closeness of recent history. In the film, the impersonal forces of nature govern the fates of *Red's* main characters; by extension to the other principal protagonists, those forces become transpersonal in the trilogy's conclusion.

Spectators who have empathised with the suffering and joys of the main characters in *Red* will be aware that the process of being drawn through the ingeniously dovetailed narrative also creates a vicarious form of stress in us. We are being played through the flux and rupture of emotionally charged cinematic time which, for any spectator engaged in a film, is by definition imaginal time. Conditions in these three psychological narratives are, then, ripe for the audience to experience virtual synchronicity.

Among the characteristics that Vic Mansfield identified in describing trans-formative self-knowledge experienced through synchronicity, some, duly adapted to take account of the moviegoer's vicarious engagement, help us understand the level of experience that *Red* opens to those spectators who do indeed register its synchronicity. First, such experiences always involve an inner intuition that the events are meaningful, albeit the articulation of meaning may take much time and effort (Mansfield, 2002: 133). Not all audience members will have such an intuition – only those who, at a puzzling, deep level, experience blind chance as meaningful in *Red*. Second, the experience of synchronicity is always arresting and numinous – and therefore has the potential to bring sacred knowledge. This may be of a cosmic nature; it may be teleological in expressing the compensatory function of the unconscious; and it may bring holistic knowledge by giving us a personal expression of the unity underlying soul and matter (Ibid.: 133–5). As mentioned earlier, the impersonal forces of nature govern the fates of *Red's* main characters. When the principal figures from the trilogy's other films are involved in the wreck, the transpersonal dimension cannot be missed. If deeply moved, we have the opportunity to perceive an underlying unity: the ordering of life seems on the surface random, but those who attend well cannot miss revelations of the numinous.

As *Red* reminds us, with its relentless juxtaposition of the wonderful against the tawdry, numinous revelations may be positive in the affirmation of life and the glories of human culture that celebrate it, but they may also be hideously negative. This is true when human artistry elevates something so vacuous as bubble gum into a cultural object of spuriously high significance. It constitutes a psychological betrayal (through a carelessness of the psyche, a lack of consciousness) the endless repetition of which through the insistent pressure of universal advertising clogs the inner growth not only of individuals but also whole societies. The psychological carelessness inculcated by the advertising industry in *Red* bears a share of responsi-bility for the culture's developmental and spiritual immaturity.

A comparable human carelessness contributes to the shipwreck. Where indiffer-ent human labour is overturned and punished by storm, the forces in play are so dramatic that they can be recognised as having a cosmic, transpersonal quality. In that wider context, a symbolic reading touching on the condition of the European psyche can be offered. The ferry should have carried its human cargo between one land mass and another. Its movement can be interpreted as a journey from one state of consciousness to another (as it should prove, whether they know it or not, for the couples from all three films). However, in this symbolic paradigm, the sea, as one of the most common symbols of the unconscious and emotional life, cannot be ignored when almost 1,500 people drown. The transpersonal significance of the disaster arises therefore from all these souls having been sucked into the ocean.

Powerless to break free of the sinking vessel and swim to the nearby shore, the great mass of passengers seems, reckoning their fate symbolically, to have been wholly unprepared for an encounter with the unconscious.

Extending our reading in the collective register, how can we understand the synchronicity of our six protagonists all surviving this horrendous and yet numinous catastrophe? Inevitably their continued existence reverberates with echoes of their own stories. Julie and Olivier have not only been liberated from grief through their love and music. They have also completed composing music commenced by the dead – its purpose to celebrate the uniting of Europe and touch the political psyche of the continent. Success in his personal affairs has enabled Karol to move on from what had in its moment been an empowering transformation into an entrepreneur. Now he has put aside his passion for money. Given that Dominique's double incarceration in both her own cruelty and jail was due in part to their shared lack of psychological development, his freeing her and renewing their union demonstrates their growth. Implicit in their rapprochement is the anticipated remarriage of Poland to its continental neighbours as accession to the European Union approached. Yet the wreck of the ferry implies, as indicated earlier, the perilous uncertainty of human affairs (political as well as personal), as the warfaring history of Europe over the centuries has demonstrated time and again. When people go to war, the conscious and the unconscious are far from being in relationship – be the battle personal and concern a couple such as Dominique and Karol, or collective and have to do with the overwhelming of nations (so often Poland's terrible fate).

Perhaps it is no accident that the trilogy concludes with the anticipated happiness of a Swiss couple – their nation one of the very few in Europe to have a fine record of neutrality in times of war. Like the other survivors, Valentine and Auguste have also suffered through difficult relationships; now as the vectors of their stories converge, we cannot doubt they will become lovers. Thus, what their story might mean for collective humanity registers in terms of what can be taken from disaster. The psychological shipwreck that all six characters have in their various ways endured has brought about a measure of transformation in their lives. All have been steeped in the unconscious by the pain they have had to undergo. That in turn has endowed them with the potential not only to love, but also to gain deeper understanding of their spiritual natures. Therein lies the symbolic justification for their survival. Whereas greed stimulated by commerce leads to a ceaseless appetite for empty possession, these lovers have acquired something infinitely more valuable, a sense of belonging to each other. The numinous significance of their survival is transpersonal in that they are simply fulfilling their destinies.

Red ends with the distinctive engine note of a light aircraft passing over the Judge's house as we watch his tears of joy and the final freeze frame of his rescued protegée. The noise that occasionally intervened when he and Valentine were conversing, it hints tactfully at the self-transformation that follows suffering.

Notes

1 The scene pays homage to David Hemmings's calculating photographer in Antonioni's *Blow Up*.
2 Judge Kern is professional kin to the Parisian justice who presided over Karol and Dominique's divorce in *White*, focussing on legal niceties rather than the parties' wellbeing.
3 The term is a concept developed by George Rosch.
4 The Judge's betrayal of his neighbours' privacy can be compared with the behaviour of three other characters (Valentine's mother, Karin, and his own former lover), all of whom cheat on other people.
5 As an example, when do parents become real to their children? The latter must break free from idealising, which should happen during adolescence in a good enough environment where they can separate from the parents in a healthy way. Trauma inhibits this process from occurring (as with Valentine and her brother finding out the secret about their mother and father). Only when the young shift from a dependent psychological position do they really start to see their parents as real people with strengths and weaknesses and their own histories.
6 The recurrence of this motif across the trilogy draws the spectator's attention, endowing the action with significance. In the recycling process, old bottles become the source of something fresh and new – perhaps a metaphor for the fragility of human life or the psyche's transformation at its end.
7 Valentine's brother must already have visited him.

PART 3

Transcending the personal

8

THE SON'S ROOM (2001)

Philip French makes the point that *La Stanza del Figlio* (the Italian title of *The Son's Room*) carries a pun. In addition to 'the room' explicit in the English version, in both languages stanza also means a verse, thus suggesting the idea of 'a poem or part of a life left standing' (2002). In this pun lies the key to what makes the film special. On the one hand it deals with the lives of an ordinary, educated middle-class family, the Sermontis; on the other, it does so with a quiet approach that achieves its impact through a restrained script and performances by the five leads so sensitive that irresistibly they command viewers' empathy. Peter Bradshaw astutely observes, 'the essential happiness of their bourgeois existence is the happiness that, in the Russian phrase, writes white on the page. Its unassuming contentment is all but invisible' (2002). Bradshaw rightly implies that the film leaves such memories; but that is all the more interesting in that we are almost from the beginning led into a devastating crisis that could have resulted in the fragmentation of a family.

Giovanni Sermonti (Nanni Moretti) is established as a healthy man who runs to take care of himself (both physically and emotionally) and to balance the long hours he spends with clients in practice as a psychoanalyst. He jogs along the harbour past cargo ships owned by Costa Container Lines – it's a real company but its name provides a metaphor for Giovanni's role as a therapist and also anticipates problems he will face. Professionally and psychologically organised to provide a container for other people's emotional worlds, in his personal life he will prove so self-contained as to make it extremely difficult to be vulnerable when he most needs others. Since Costa is Italian for coast, the full name may hint at the position he will find himself in, on the edge.

Giovanni is called urgently to a meeting at his son's school where his boy, 17 year-old Andrea (Giuseppe Sanfelice), has been accused of colluding with another lad to steal a fossil from a science laboratory. Although Andrea denies the allegation, the head teacher believes that he has sufficient evidence to prove his guilt and suspends him for a week. Despite this, the love and strong family rituals that bond the Sermontis are not disturbed. The parents have the capacity to respond to their children's emotional needs and provide a safe holding environment that encourages their growth, maturity and testing of limits even in the face of the uncomfortable allegation. Giovanni, his beautiful wife Paola (Laura Morante), their daughter Irene (Jasmine Trinca) and Andrea continue to gather at meal times and enjoy each other's company. We cannot but notice, however, that Paola's unconditional maternal love (she faithfully believes her son's innocence) differs from the necessarily more objective, conditional stance of the father which serves to teach his teenagers into adulthood.

The parents pay attention to issues as they impinge rather than allowing problems to go underground – another sign of a thriving family. The evening after his son's exclusion from school, Giovanni takes Andrea to a meeting between the families concerned. One boy had told the head teacher that he saw the missing ammonite in the bag of Andrea's friend who has also been suspended. The father of this last boy puts pressure on the accuser until he retracts. The issue seems resolved except that something causes Giovanni unease. He says he feels the other father has been too aggressive, but as the days pass it becomes clear that he has private doubts about Andrea's innocence – doubts that he does not voice to his son.

Notwithstanding the school incident, the family remain by and large well attuned to each other. One evening, for example, Giovanni and Paola help Irene with some tricky Latin homework. And it is not only the parents who are aware of their young. Irene observes her father's body language after Andrea's suspension from school. Realising that her father is not wholly convinced of his son's innocence, she teases Giovanni into sharing her own good humour. Her sensitive reading of his discomfort suggests that she recognises her father's anxiety.

Giovanni is a kind, if slightly weary psychoanalyst with a clientele who keep him fully occupied. His counselling room is reached from the family apartment. Opening the double doors that lead into the office is a weekday morning ritual since they mark the liminal psychological and emotional boundary between his very connected home environment and the pain-filled emotional lives of his patients. Such are the idealisations of those coming for therapy that they make it hard for us to think of the family as anything but blissfully content – and normal. Giovanni bears the heavy weight of his profession the more willingly because in the evening the quiet ceremony of switching off the lights mirrors that first moment of the day as, with growing pleasure, he returns to the warmth of family. His devoted service to his clients is amplified by the stability of his loving and connected family. In this respect, he and Paola are alike, both having a passion for their work. They differ in that her career as a publisher not only gives her a fulfilling independent professional life but something she can share enthusiastically with her husband; by contrast the details of Giovanni's work must be kept to himself.

The separation of Giovanni's family life from the long hours he spends with his clients is significant because he has to keep the lives of those on either side of the double doors apart. In the consulting room, skilled therapists allow themselves an *essential* vulnerability in order to take in the patient's experience, while simultaneously holding their own mind as they help the client to mentalise.[1] It is this most rigorous component of the therapeutic process that we will come to see Giovanni must confront. Giovanni does take in his clients' worlds; but not until after his son's death, when he announces he is closing his practice, can he allow himself to let go and make physical contact with a client who desperately needs connection. When this angry man rages against the abandonment he feels, Giovanni hugs him, an authentic moment of real contact that signals the psychotherapist's own defences breaking down at last and releasing unresolved grief for both of them.

Although he has patients who have deep-rooted traumas, the majority of Giovanni's clients suffer neuroses to which the prosperous middle-aged, middle classes are prone – paying the price, as George Boeree (2002) says, for 'poor ability to adapt to one's environment, an inability to change one's life patterns, and the inability to develop a richer, more complex, more satisfying personality'. One woman comes week after week to share the anguish of having to make decisions – any decisions. Another gnaws bitterly at the uselessness of the therapy she receives, heaves a sigh of pleasure when she has puked up this nasty mental hairball and leaves, promising cheerfully to return in a week's time, when (as her analyst notes) she will neurotically repeat. A no less derisive client expunges the ravaging memories of her sessions (blighted, she wrongly believes, by Giovanni's failure to understand her) by profligate shopping (a routine excess for which, naturally, she blames him). All these hypochondriacs verge on the ludicrous, blind (when viewed superficially) to their self-absorption. Apart from these, emotionally struggling individuals come for help and Giovanni offers such reflections as they are able to take in. For example, he advises a patient who feels excessive guilt that he should try not to control everything but learn to relish idleness and thus reduce anxiety.

And then there are the more serious characterological problems. A man addicted to child pornography and promiscuous sex with prostitutes both male and female appears to have made some progress; but when Giovanni congratulates him the client is instantly caught in a complex and overwhelmed by guilt and shame. He unleashes pent-up anger and furiously describes a scenario of dangerous sexual exhibitionism to which he is drawn. Analytic mistakes are inevitable and Giovanni's response has ignited a transference neurosis, releasing the patient's bad objects from his unconscious – one of the most difficult processes of therapy. As part of the healing process, whatever happens outside the therapy room needs to be re-enacted in the room between the therapist and patient, a process known as acting in rather than acting out. Giovanni, however, appears neither to have intended nor anticipated the event: at times driven too much by his own superego construct, his limitations blind him. Yet the more a therapist is aware of what is going on inside himself, the better he can make conscious therapeutic interventions. These connect clients to their own inner lives, helping them get unstuck from old psychic patterns.

Among Giovanni's patients there are those who naturally reflect parts of *his* personality, some of which are patent, but others still hidden. The woman who complains of boredom cannot see from her place on the couch that transference is occurring. She inflicts boredom on him to the extent that he fantasises showing her all the many shoes he keeps for the sports he enjoys. If only, rather than keeping his fantasies mute, he were able to use them as part of the therapeutic process (as his supervisor suggests regarding a different client), movement might occur. The excessively guilty patient who tries to control everything foreshadows Giovanni's ungovernable attempts to turn the clock back after Andrea dies: as the therapist he seems unable to demonstrate what he has told this client. Finally, the traumatised patient's abandonment tantrum resembles Giovanni breaking damaged crockery when feeling abandoned through his son's death.

Another patient, sad Oscar (Silvio Orlando), brings dreams to the analyst's couch. In one, people quitting a party leave him alone in a large building; but before Giovanni can investigate the dream with him the client defensively dismisses it – and analysis – as boring. When another nightmare confronts Oscar with a ship of the dead, he insists all is well despite thoughts of a renewed attempt at suicide. Although hindsight reveals that Oscar's dreams forewarn him of his future, Giovanni finds it hard to pierce this patient's defences to work with him. Yet the mysterious parallel process that sometimes takes place between client and therapist appears once again to be occurring here in that Oscar's dream bears not only on his own life but also Giovanni's since the ship of the dead foretells the fate that is closing in on him.

All these cases, which we join *in medias res*, appear wretchedly intractable. No matter that Giovanni practises in the small Italian coastal city of Ancona, his clientele seem little different from those who might be expected to visit psychoanalysts anywhere in Western Europe or North America.

Giovanni cannot quite set aside his worries about his son, doubtful that he is acting as a normal boy of his age should. When Andrea enters a tennis tournament, Giovanni is deeply bothered by the adolescent's relaxed attitude in playing so casually that he loses. An intuitive and psychological man, Giovanni is aware that a competitive spirit contributes to developing a sense of mastery and control. Andrea finds his father's sporting competitiveness amusing because he himself plays casually for pleasure. Despite the close affection between them, their personality differences are apparent here. Father and son do not relate in their attitudes toward competition and need for control.

Giovanni is almost always so emotionally contained that he may be difficult to reach in a deeply felt way. It fits with Andrea's psychology that, as an adolescent boy who identifies with his father and seeks his approval, rather than disturb a shared moment when his father is feeling happy, the boy confesses instead to his mother that he and a friend did take the ammonite. They had meant only to play a trick on a teacher, but before they could return the stone, they dropped and smashed it. Although a typical adolescent prank, the joke may have undertones of father transference, in being Andrea's attempt to elicit from the science teacher an emotional response difficult to get from his father. As we have seen, Andrea, perhaps by way of compensation, is interested in playing: his attitude toward games has more to do with connection than opposition. Contrary to his father's frequent isolation in private practice, he is surrounded by male companions.

When Andrea confesses to his mother, Paola reacts by asking a few pointed questions and then gives her boy an affectionate hug. She offers the unconditional love which, since the father has to prepare the children for the external world, he archetypally cannot. All the same, Giovanni's stoicism seems to have preceded the nurturing of his offspring. Not uncommon to the personality of the therapist, it may stem from his own personal history to be emotionally so well contained.

Moretti keeps us focussed on the family and we never find out what happens at the school. Come Sunday morning, Giovanni wants to show his affection for Andrea and asks him to go running. He repeatedly ruffles his son's hair as if to reassure the lad that, despite the debacle with the ammonite, he is secure in his father's love. But beneath this obvious motivation there appears to lie his own natural need to feel connected to his family.

Despite this, as a therapist Giovanni struggles with the conflict between his own needs and those of others. And for that reason the run never happens. Oscar telephones while the Sermontis are still at breakfast, so distraught that he claims he cannot wait for his next appointment. Giovanni, rather than transfer the call to his office, answers from the kitchen, breaking the physical boundary that helps him separate work and family. Rather than fully assessing his patient as a suicide risk and responding accordingly, he reacts from his own anxieties. Psychologically organised to respond to the needs of others, he is unable to hold the internal tension projected inside him. He gives way to his patient's intense sense of urgency, which takes precedence over pleasure-seeking and his need for connection with Andrea. Submitting to feelings of responsibility, he agrees reluctantly to make an immediate house call. This is at the cost of disappointing his family – possibly a familiar dynamic faced by the Sermontis.

As he drives out of town, the family occupy themselves in different pursuits, yet each experiences a *memento mori*, a reminder that existence is tenuous (Armstrong, 2001). At an antiques street market a thief escaping pursuit barges into Paola. Irene, on her scooter, fends off some crazy friends who ride alongside and kick out at her machine for fun. Both moments are synecdochic, miniature forewarnings of the ruin that sooner or later impinges on every human life. They hint too at the discernment necessary to respond consciously in times of decision when the shadow may be present. Meanwhile Giovanni listens to Oscar who has been diagnosed with lung cancer and is certain he will die.

In the late afternoon Giovanni returns home and is met at his door by weeping friends who break the news of calamity. Andrea has drowned while scuba diving. In complete shock, Giovanni goes to a basketball hall to find Irene. There she is, playing in a match, running blithely in complete control of the ball. She grins at her dad with pride before registering his traumatised face. Horror freezes her to the spot. An opponent steals the ball and both teams sweep back past her as if she were no longer there – which to all intents and purposes is true.

In their first paroxysms of anguish, during the immediate hours after Andrea drowns, the three survivors weep together. As non-believers in a Catholic nation, they have no rituals for taking leave of Andrea. There is no funeral ceremony.

Instead, in a harrowing scene, they are constrained to watching in the hospital morgue as impassive undertakers seal the beautiful young man in his coffin. They will never see him again.

Soon the grief of the surviving family members pulls them in different directions. The devastating isolation of bereavement: all the rituals that have bonded them as a family break down. For example, although Irene tries to keep the old patterns alive, they no longer gather round the table at mealtimes. For want of an alternative secular ritual, she proposes the family should ask for a Mass to be said so that Andrea's friends have somewhere to commemorate him. Her parents agree, but the memorial is a ghastly affair. A priest who knows nothing about Andrea doles out the dogmatic bromides of a sclerotic faith, adding to the family's wretchedness. Here we have a paradox: a warm family engaged in its own daily rituals that create a deep sense of connection is confronted by a lack of connection to a spiritual life that might provide a larger container for a loss of such magnitude. The disjunction echoes the start of the film when Giovanni watches a group of Hari Krishna dancers going through the streets, puzzled by what they are doing. Yet Giovanni's stupefied anger deafens him to the potent resonances of the priest's words when heard psychologically: they are a reminder that the marriage of the psychological and spiritual completes the self. The priest intones,

> If the master of the house had known in what hour the thief was coming, he would have watched, and not have left his house to be broken through.
>
> *(Luke 12:39)*

In raising the biblical metaphor of theft, the priest draws the authorised moral that we cannot know when God will come for us. This for Giovanni is so inapposite that he rages against it. Yet theft has become a motif (Andrea and the ammonite; the moment at the market; the ball stolen on the field of play from Irene; Andrea's life stolen from him; the lad snatched away from the survivors). Furthermore, switching registers, Giovanni is the master of the house, unconscious of the shadow consequences of the choice he made by reacting to his patient's cry for help and breaking the agreement to go running with his son. That, psychologically speaking, left his home vulnerable to potential loss – a spiritual theft.

When Paola's suffering overwhelms her, pain pours out in terrible howling to which she gives way completely. As the days go by, she neither locks herself away from what has happened nor tries to deny it. In externalising her pain she looks to be more devastated than either her husband or daughter – but this is not the case. Rather, in releasing herself to suffering as it takes over her whole being, her weeping becomes a means of recovering the lost object in order to obtain the strength and help of others. She surrenders to the mourning process, which prepares the way for the eventual change that will come over her when she finds it possible to resume her life and move on. Paola's process is a painful sign of emotional health as she reaches out not only for her lost son, but the other relationships that matter to her.

Giovanni is different and tries to cope alone, cutting himself off emotionally from his wife, daughter and clients. Mourning alone, as Furman stresses, is 'an almost impossible task' (1974: 114). His behaviour displays his ego's fierce attempt to preserve its fragility. He first tries to deaden his mind by overloading the senses in a solitary visit to a fairground, which becomes to his ears and eyes a cacophonous pit of garish chaos mirroring his own inner state. Whereas Paola takes time off work to create the space to fall into despair and let her grieving find its way, he goes back to his patients at once. He immediately fills the space with distractions, the ego's first line of defence. John Bowlby, to whom we turn for assistance in understanding the grieving process in the inner life, suggests that the primitive defences of denial, splitting and repression all contribute to 'An inability to mourn [which expresses] an inability to tolerate being in a position of weakness and supplication' (1961: 319). This is the moment to note that whereas Kübler-Ross focuses on the stages of grieving, Bowlby emphasises the psychological processes one goes through.

The doors to Giovanni's office become an obstacle. Irene goes there wanting to share sorrow and calls her father to breakfast. But faced with the blank barrier, she cannot bring herself to go through when he does not reply. She is left alone to cope with her distress as best she can. Soon Giovanni begins to manifest obsessive behaviour. One evening when all three sit in Andrea's room, he plays over and over again a discordant few seconds from one of the lad's CDs. His actions indicate a repetition compulsion, a searching for an unremembered memory. The annoying cacophony distresses Paola and Irene, but he appears to be attempting to make a connection with an emotional, split-off part of himself that he cannot contact, in contrast with the women's ready access to their emotional lives. Blaming himself for the choice he made, which led Andrea to his death, he tries to reverse time by repeatedly playing the fragment of music. He fantasises a revised memory of the Sunday morning phone conversation with Oscar. In his imagination he refuses his patient's request for a home visit and goes running with Andrea, which prevents his son from scuba diving. Then he convinces himself that Andrea's diving equipment must have failed – until Paola reminds him that it has been checked and found to be in good order. Longing to regain the lost object is integral to sadness and grief and Paola has managed to accept what cannot be controlled in life and take in that the incomprehensible happened: Andrea drowned in an accident after getting lost in an underwater cave and taking his tank off to find his way out.

However, nothing reconciles Giovanni to the loss of his son. He remains locked in a state of that peculiar amalgam of anxiety, anger and despair which grief is. Edith Jacobson writes that the happier the relationship with the lost object has been, the easier it is for the bereaved to experience sadness and the less does aggression intrude to create conflict and difficulty (in Bowlby, 1961: 327). Read superficially, this would imply that father and son were not at ease with each other – clearly overstating the case. For Giovanni the complicating factor is the complete failure of the omnipotent fantasies that he has, like many therapists. The resultant guilt stokes an aggression which, though directed at the world around him, is actually aimed at himself. He will be able to experience his sadness and this aggression only when he breaks through his own defences.

Ultimately, as Bradshaw (2002) notes, the Sermontis have to endure their pain without convenient fantasies to fall back on, which makes *The Son's Room* all the more convincing. As Greg Mogenson reports, nothing weighs so heavily upon a mourner's heart than the passing of a life that has been incompletely lived. The more truncated the life, the more difficult the grieving for it in a depressive search for the meaning of that early death (1992: 103). And as Oscar (of all people) will remark when he returns to therapy with Giovanni, the grief of parents who are predeceased by their child is almost beyond bearing. It hardly needs adding that Giovanni's circumstances as a psychoanalyst seriously compromise the essence of his work, namely his capacity to be fully present to the suffering of his clients. As we witnessed prior to the death of his son, the doors provided a symbolic function separating his happy family life from the psychic demands of his work. Moving back to work so quickly was his unconscious treatment plan to stay away from his own devastated life, evacuating his grief-stricken self into the troubled lives of his clients. How can his mind not be occupied by the command, 'Physician, heal thyself'? The remedy will require Giovanni to be present to his own pain and eventually seek out the strength and help of others.

For her part, Irene focuses intently on her school life and the basketball tournaments to which she has returned soon after Andrea's death. She has lost both her parents' presence during this time so returning to her friends and exterior life is both natural and necessary. Yet the untimely trauma is experienced 'as an incomprehensible and overwhelming assault that strikes at the core of the adolescent's intrapsychic and external world' (Sussillo, 2005: 499). Irene's activity is not enough either to ease or govern her suffering. Her rage bursts out on another Sunday afternoon when her team is playing away before a hostile crowd (her parents isolated in their sector of the stadium are her team's only supporters). When an opponent fouls her, Irene protests unavailingly and then starts a fight with the other girl that escalates into a messy ruckus both on field and off as she performs an Eric Cantona and attacks some of the razzing spectators. In effect, Irene is experiencing the loss of being psychically held by both parents who are understandably destabilised from the shock of losing Andrea. As Sussillo observes, 'When grief intrudes in bursts, the adolescent's experience in the absence of emotionally attuned others may be alarming, profoundly isolating and despairing,' (2005: 500). Many aspects of Irene's milieu are experienced as violently altered and irrevocably different, even though some external realities – her school, friends and activities – may look the same. However, she regains her life more swiftly than her parents, whose identity as parents has changed forever.

Communication between Giovanni and Paola approaches a nadir. He prowls their seemingly immaculate kitchen picking out items of crockery that are chipped or cracked. Lifting his favourite teapot, he remarks how well they had repaired it after it had been dropped. No sooner said than he deliberately shatters it in a furious gesture that enacts a painful reminder of what is broken beyond repair. His aggression intrudes a new, uncharacteristic dynamic into their marriage, a first indication Giovanni cannot contain his grief. Perhaps, as Bowlby suggests, a further increase in aggression that might lead to even stronger outbursts of anger is prevented by the memories of a happy past and of a previously rich self (1961: 327). Bowlby describes the behavioural sequence of mourning which demonstrates that Giovanni's anger, Paola's despair and Irene's protest all present normal reactions to loss. That sequence 'begins with anger and anxiety, proceeds through pain and despair and if fortune smiles, ends with hope. Both feeling and behaviour oscillate violently especially in the early phases of grief. Yearning, protest and rage alternate with blank mute despair' (1961: 330).

Mail arrives addressed to Andrea. Paola opens the envelope and reads a love letter from a girl with whom he had spent a single day at a summer camp. The deep emotion Paola feels in discovering an aspect of her son's life that she knew nothing about reveals two things about her grieving. The first is that Giovanni's own difficult mourning process has alienated Paola, moving her further into a depressive state. The second concerns the risk identified by Mogenson that an image of the dead person taken from the past may atrophy, with the consequent atrophying of the mourner (1992: 29–30). For both Paola and Irene, Arianna's letter regenerates Andrea's image. When the girl writes that his silences do not make other people feel awkward, they recognise something they had forgotten.

Giovanni, however, does not allow the process of renewal to commence. He remains locked to memories of his son on that last Sunday morning (mixing the actual past with wish fulfilment). When he suggests that rather than Paola phoning Arianna he should write a letter telling her about Andrea's death, that in part accords with his sensitive need to protect the girl as well as his need to control (an expression of his inability to tolerate being in a vulnerable position); but it also indicates that he is beginning to get stuck with his existing idea of Andrea as if (to use Mogenson's phrase) it were an image in a museum (Ibid.: 30). Indeed, despite many attempts, Giovanni proves incapable of writing the letter in terms that he can accept. Paola gets it right in saying, 'You think talking about Andrea means losing something.'

As we have said before, Elisabeth Kübler-Ross (1969) describes mourning as having five stages: denial; anger; bargaining and negotiation; depression; and acceptance. Giovanni's fluctuation shows that it is a non-linear process involving a moving back and forth from one stage to another until the mourner finds him or herself in a new psychological place of acceptance. Having oscillated between denial, anger and bargaining, Giovanni now sinks into the depressive state. When Paola talks about wanting to meet Arianna he intervenes to dissuade her, but she can no longer cope with his blocked obsessions and soon they are sleeping separately in the house.

Things have meantime been getting worse in Giovanni's practice and he realises that he can no longer face his patients with any conviction. A turning point comes when Oscar seeks Giovanni's endorsement of his belief that a positive attitude helps cancer sufferers like himself to fight off the disease. Rather than deflecting the issue by saying the belief is common but unproven, Giovanni coolly rebuts the notion, his once positive attitude lost in his private suffering. Whatever his medical knowledge of lung cancer may be, it is plain that Giovanni cannot separate self-blame from anger directed toward his patient for having pulled him away from his family that fateful Sunday. Giovanni seeks supervision from a colleague who addresses his counter transference toward Oscar. The other counsellor advises Giovanni to tell Oscar about his own emotion as grist to the mill in hopes of mobilising what now silently sits between them. But Giovanni cannot conceive of communicating his still too raw, unprocessed emotions.

Surrendering to his grief and understanding that he cannot help his clients, Giovanni tells them that he must discontinue working with them. Faced with the necessity to find a new therapist, their reactions are intriguing. The indecisive woman (whom Giovanni has been offering techniques to help her adjust) accepts the challenge and decides to postpone further analysis until he resumes his practice. Oscar (to whom Giovanni has given no account of his feelings) has already made his decision and thanks his analyst before bringing the therapy to an end because everything has changed for him. Notwithstanding Giovanni's scepticism he intends to focus all his energy on making a physical recovery and expresses deep gratitude to Giovanni for helping him. However, the disturbed sex addict is nowhere near ready to cope with his therapist's absence from his life. Feeling completely abandoned, he screams abuse and in a violent rage starts smashing the office furnishings until Giovanni finally allows himself to hold him; at which point the other man lets go, sobs uncontrollably and hangs onto his therapist like a grown child.

We are left with the question how Giovanni himself will cope. He will lose his income, and perhaps his profession and wife too (as he and Paola silently acknowledge). At the root of all this lurks a grieving process so badly blocked that there is no obvious way for it to resume. Idle at home, he prepares an evening meal. But home is now too cold a place for the others and Paola stays on at her office desk working late while Irene chats to a friend in a bar. As Giovanni cooks a dish, it splits on the hob – an echo of his smashing the teapot, and perhaps the deepest hour of his depression. Yet at the time of this nadir, and before help arrives from an unexpected quarter, he goes to his son's favourite record store to buy a present for Andrea and asks for help in buying a CD that the boy would have liked. It is a moment of sweetness that at last marks a turning point when the mourning process begins to supplant unrelieved grief.

Meanwhile the strong urge to communicate with the unknown girl who had loved her son has not left Paola. Fed up with waiting for her prevaricating husband to write, she telephones Arianna. As Giovanni had foreseen, the unexpected news of Andrea's death delivered by his sobbing mother so shocks the girl that she hastens to bring the phone call to an end, swiftly declining Paola's invitation to visit or have further contact. However, Giovanni had not anticipated that the girl would not only be observant, passionate and subtle (as her letter had revealed) but she would also possess considerable emotional resilience. The Sermontis know nothing of that until without warning Arianna (Sofia Vigliar) arrives at their door. Now it is the turn of the adults to be shaken. At first they find it difficult to open their feelings to her but she has brought with her exuberant photos that Andrea had taken of himself in his bedroom. For Giovanni these pictures kick start the revitalising of his internalised image of his beloved son. For the whole family the fact that Arianna has come to see them brings comfort; but more than that, her presence is illuminating. It is worth noting that Ariadne (from whose name Arianna derives) was the figure in classical mythology who gave Theseus the ball of thread that enabled him to find his way out of the Labyrinth after he slew the monster.

Arianna has called by for an hour or two only, interrupting a hitchhiking trip to France. She is travelling with a friend Stefano (Alessandro Ascoli). Clearly her life has moved forward and she has accepted and absorbed the loss of the boy she cared for. That of course is easier for a teenager whose romantic feelings are based on a single day and a passionate correspondence than for close family. Nevertheless her example points the way forward for the Sermontis – Giovanni in particular. Despite the fact that mourning is always experienced as a letting go, it is not, Mogenson writes, about getting rid of 'lost objects'. The mourning process does not rid us of our attachments but of our projections so that finally we see those we have lost for who they are (1992: 98). As a direct consequence, it also allows mourners to see themselves more clearly too.

It is this process that strengthens when, that evening Paola, Giovanni and Irene drive the young travellers to a service area on the *autostrada*. But no cars stop for the hitchhikers, so they all drive forward into the night, with Giovanni extending the journey far beyond his first target while the three teenagers sleep in the back seats. As they go on, his love for Paola and Irene reawakens and his affection for the young visitors deepens. Come the early morning light, they reach the Riviera with only the adults awake. Irene wakes up, astonished to find herself on the French border (edging, as it were, onto new psychological territory). She asks her parents rather fiercely if they have forgotten she has to attend training for her first game back with the team. Giovanni and Paola look at each other and their daughter, amused by her intensity, and begin to laugh.

When the incongruity of her irritation dawns on her, Irene joins in the laughter. The family are beginning to share their emotions again and the good feelings continue as they take breakfast with Arianna and Stefano. When the young travellers board a coach to continue their journey to Paris, the Sermontis wander onto the beach. As the film ends there is space between the three of them but they are relaxed, separate yet together. We are reminded of Nietzsche's vision of the tragic condition of humanity in which to live to the fullest is to build sandcastles passionately, all the time aware of the incoming tide. The contrast with the last scene of *Birth* is striking.

The desolation of the bereaved is for Mogenson in part a consequence of the bankruptcy of secular cultures. Giovanni had found it impossible to help himself partly because as a non-believer in a culture dominated by Roman Catholicism, he has no structures of ideology or belief to support a focus on the imaginal presence of the dead. Pointedly, the grieving of the Sermonti family does not move out of the personal into the archetypal realm. As Mogenson notes,

> Even when dealing specifically with issues of loss and bereavement, psycho-
> therapy tends to ignore the dead. Mourning tends to be conceptualized first

and foremost as a parting and letting-go. The therapist experiences the bereaved as bankrupt and depleted by their loss, and empathizes with their desolation.

(1992: 130)

He argues that to focus almost exclusively on the trauma of loss is not entirely appropriate. Mourning becomes a less desolate process when supported by a culture embodying religious and spiritual ideas that provide the dead with a place of repose in the Beyond. The pain of loss may remain acute, but the meaning supplied by faith and tradition may help it be borne (1992: 130–1). This we find reflected in the Korean film *Spring, Summer, Autumn, Winter… and Spring.*

Note

1 The term refers to the process by which people realise that having a mind mediates their experience of the world. It is an essential feature of emotional self-regulation and thus a core aspect of human social functioning. It allows individuals to 'make sense of' or understand themselves and others.

9

SPRING, SUMMER, AUTUMN, WINTER... AND SPRING (2003)[1]

The visual register of *Spring, Summer, Autumn, Winter... and Spring* is persuasively naturalistic. The aesthetics of its framing and editing contribute lusciously to building the sense that we are gazing at a dependable representation of a physical world located in a specific space and time. Wide shots across a lake, the setting for the entire film; tripod-mounted or leisurely tracking camera; a steady pace of cutting that respects the measured chronology of the seasons; and inserts of landscape shots that interrupt coverage of the characters' actions all contribute to this effect. For the most part the soundtrack features the soft sounds of the elements and bird song. Dialogue is sparse. All in all, the dominant aesthetic register endows the narrative with plausibility even when incidents occur that do not fit with secular Western notions of the caesura dividing physical existence from spiritual states. As a consequence of the pervasive naturalism, such moments do not alienate a Western audience.

This is the more striking in that each of the film's parts featuring a new season begins on an ornate pair of doors mounted within a portal. A pair of warriors is painted on the woodwork, guarding the entry. When the doors open to announce the start of each chapter they permit a view of the lake in which they stand and provide formal access to the small Buddhist monastery that floats in the middle. Meanwhile, those who leave the monastery see the reverse of the portal doors on which are depicted a pair of goddesses. Emmanuel Levinas refers to the maternal psyche as the inspired self, deeper and higher than egoism, concerned for others in its very being – and we shall experience the truth of this when discussing the absence of tenderness in the film. The goddesses remind visitors to carry with them as they leave the grace they may have found in this tranquil place. Doors in *The Son's Room* serve as boundary markers separating one socio-psychological area (the house) from another (the therapy rooms). In the Korean film, as we are about to confirm, they serve a ritual, spiritually oriented function. Doors in *The Tree of Life* represent the transitional domain that incorporates both the psychological and spiritual.

The portal is only one of a number of structures that function as threshold markers rather than openings in walls. The doors that demarcate the monks' sleeping areas are attached to no walls and do not obstruct sight lines across the monastery interior. However, even though there is nothing to stop the monks looking into each other's space, they use the doorways like conventional openings through walls. Over and beyond the arena of social relations, the strangeness of these functionally redundant doors implies that they also act as boundary markers between the physical and the spiritual. They mark out the liminal, signifying the apartness-in-sharing of each individual and implying that the acceptance of separation is a precondition for transcendence. They can thus be understood in the context of the director's (Kim Ki-duk's) remark that a house floating on water does not have a fixed orientation. When one wakes up east may have become west, south have become north (2004). Where space fluctuates in this (and as we shall soon see) other ways and where life measured in the years' cycle is transient, the doors provide a point of reference whose moral and spiritual analogue is to be found in a person's maturity. As we shall see, people who choose their own direction create the opening to become conscious of their existence.

The aesthetic register impresses the more because of the film's visual and aural beauty. Gilberto Perez has described the impact of beauty in actors in a way that readily transfers to cinematic landscapes and helps account for the persuasive nature of Kim Ki-duk's film.

> Beauty… acts on the beholder. It is not, as some suppose, an object passively sitting there to be looked at. The art critic Dave Hickey talks about beauty as rhetoric, as an agency that sways and moves us. Beauty has a manifold capacity for suasion… Film is an art of images, of appearances, an art that works on us through the look of things. Looks are as various as individuals, however, and small differences can make a big difference. The camera always specifies – every face is a particular face, every gesture a particular gesture – and we must attend to the specifics of beauty on the screen.
>
> *(Perez, 2005: 38)*

Perez's delicate appreciation of the subtle yet robust influence of beauty on screen enriches our understanding of the pleasure that Valentine's image communicates in *Red* just as it deepens our wonder at the image of the monastery moored in an exquisite lake. Set among thickly wooded hills, it appears to have been there for many decades. A knotted tree of great antiquity rises from the water and overhangs the portal. The conjunction of these elements and the gently rippling water immediately excites in the spectator the rich pleasures that representations of landscape can stimulate. It is a genre that (over centuries in both the East and West) many artists have deployed to invoke the spiritual. The aesthetics in the film silently transmit its meaning. Dylan Thomas's phrase in 'Fern Hill' is apposite: 'Time held me green and dying.' Steven Mitchell interprets this as meaning alive but changing, growing and disappearing, caught by the constraints of flux and temporality but singing (2003: 200).

As the beauty of the film invokes us, we transcend ordinary reality, creating a more capacious regard for the self and the world. Elaine Scarry notes that when 'We apprehend a beautiful thing outside its customary context... it opens up into infinite possibilities' (1999: 48). Beauty is the bridge between reality and fantasy that crosses into the infinite – conveying what is more than we can know. That bridge is what makes rapture possible.

The film opens in springtime, sensually heavy with trees' greenery. It seems idyllic as the Master (Oh Young-su), a man in his late middle years, rows his young Buddhist apprentice (Seo Jae-kyeong) to the shore to pick herbs. The latter is a happy and bold child, completely at ease in his natural surroundings and unafraid when a snake surprises him. He collects greens enthusiastically but still has to learn from the old monk which plants can be eaten safely. Having observed how his master rows, he takes the boat for an exploration and rows it to shore – backwards. James Hillman recalled that

> Jung says we must look at the intentionality of the characters and where they are heading, for they are the main influence upon the shape of the stories. Each carries his own plot with him, writing his story both backwards and forwards as he individuates.
>
> *(1983: 10)*

At this stage in the life cycle, the boy needs to learn not only practical skills but also discernment, an important psychological task that develops wisdom. Soon his solo adventures take a mischievous turn. He amuses himself by catching a fish, a frog and a snake, crippling them by binding each to a stone. Meanwhile, unseen by the boy, the Master peers across the boulders at the boy's play and observes these cruelties. The Old Monk's presence, although (as he labours over the rocks) self-evidently physical, simultaneously insists upon his spirituality. The child has taken the only boat yet the old man has followed him from the monastery without the need to swim.

Back in the monastery that night, he binds a heavy stone to the sleeping child's back. When the boy awakens, his Master tells him that his distress is no different from the creatures he has maimed. He must free them before he himself is untied. The boy rows back to shore under his sore burden, and struggles across the rocks. As on the previous day, the Old Monk overlooks the boy's actions, his expression blending sternness of purpose with compassion. The Master's severe warning that if harm has come to the creatures the boy will carry the stone in his heart as long as he lives now echoes through the child's heart. He discovers the frog has lived but the fish and snake have died. The boy buries the fish and, when he finds the broken bloody snake, sobs inconsolably. His wailing and the lively stream are the only sounds heard as the chapter ends. The Master has made his novice face and comprehend for the first time the consequences of his actions. As a child he has participated in the amoral nature of nascent humanity, being equally capable of good deeds and bad. Before spring ends, he learns the rudiments of morality with the suffering entailed when he must abandon the darker side of his being. However, there will be an unfortunate consequence of the teaching he receives.

Although intended as spiritual teaching, the Old Monk's first lesson on morality focuses on compassionate responsibility toward the creatures of nature. His instruction has underlying hints of universal applicability, but his words lack understanding of a child's inner life. Specifically, the apprentice may unconsciously have been attempting to play something out in fantasy. Doubtless his cruelty was in part typical of his age, as Klein noted: '…such phantasies occur very early, and… in very young children they are at times idyllic and other times violent, terrifying and bizarre' (in Britton, 1998: 31). But in this case, with the boy's face clearly revealing his guilt and despair at the damage done, there is likely to be some additional cause. We have to assume the boy has an early history of profound loss in accounting for how he came to live with the Master.

In the developing consciousness of an individual he or she must realise that the shadow exists and must master and assimilate it. Unfortunately, the unconscious acts of caretakers, as in this instance, can contribute to pushing it underground, thus inhibiting this processing. Thus, the Master's response has obstructed the natural wish of a young child to repair the damage he has caused. Klein comments that in instances where a child's wish to make reparation fails, he or she may deny the damage – which then seems to be restored magically by omnipotent manic reparation (Ibid.). Given the boy's emotionally complicated early life, this situation puts him at risk of developing oedipal or pre-oedipal pathology, thereby prematurely terminating the necessary working through of the oedipal period of development.[2] The Monk's response further weakens the structure of the boy's narcissism by fortifying a suppression of hate and an exaggeration of love.

The noisy coursing of the disinterested stream, with its associations to life flowing on uninterrupted, sets the child's damaged self (all encompassing in his own world) against a vaster panorama. Come summer, if confirmation were needed that the chapters feature the seasons of human life, the Child Monk has matured into an adolescent (Kim Young-min). With the season's change, new sensations stir in him. His gormlessness cannot be missed. When a worried mother (Jung-young Kim) brings her teenage daughter (Ha Yeo-jin) to the lake, he shows them one of the resplendent and ancient trees that grow out of the water and promises that the girl will soon be as healthy as it. But his words sound as if he is mimicking his Master and the mother ignores him. Instead she asks the Old Monk to restore her adolescent child to health and he leads the two women in prayer. Deep into the night after the Old Monk has gone to bed, the mother continues her excessively anxious devotions. The old man no doubt perceives that the mother's obsessive state has something to do with the girl's illness; but he confines himself to telling the woman that when her daughter's mind is at ease, her body will get better. The mother leaves and her daughter whiles away the rainy days in listless silence with only her prayer sessions before the stone Buddha marking the hours' passing.

The girl's presence awakens the Young Monk's desire, but he has no idea how to negotiate the gulf between sexual appetite and self-disciplined monastic life.

One wet day, finding her asleep in front of the Buddha, he thoughtfully puts a cover over her, but then, unable to hold back, feels her breast. She wakes and slaps him, but then reaches out a consoling hand. As the days pass, he tries to get close to her and alternates playing like an unruly puppy with jejune sexual advances that she rebuffs without rancour. After she tips him into one of the pools where he had played as a child, he repays her by pulling her off the temple raft into the lake and then rows her to shore. At the pools, with the stream pouring past them, they become lovers. This first lovemaking is brutally physical, a male-dominated sexual encounter. The young man takes his pleasure with relentless vigour, disconnected from the pain he causes the young woman; and the young woman, though excited, hurts from her summertime deflowering on the rocks. They do not express tender feelings through so much as a single kiss – an absence that foretells the fate of their relationship.

> For a healthy relationship desire must be mediated by another aspect of love – tenderness... Tenderness works in opposition to the great threat that comes from the sense of death and loss. One could say that our deepest feelings of violence and tenderness are connected by the never-ending fear of losing the other.
>
> *(Carotenuto, 1989: 71)*

We cut away from their passion to the Old Monk writing on a stone, his brush laden with water rather than ink. By the time he finishes each line, the calligraphy at its start has evaporated in the afternoon warmth. The water's swift absorption into the air evokes the transience of human affairs but also the eternal. It hints that the lovers' relationship is not founded in eternity; and it also suggests that the Master's words become one with the universe, evaporating like smoke carrying prayers to the heavens. While the Old Monk focuses on his devotional task, the Young Monk, his body language contorted by guilt, rows the girl back across the lake and lands on the decking.

Mitchell says that 'a contrived sense of guiltiness can serve as a psychological defence against a more genuine sense of pathos or sadness for oneself' (2003: 155). The Young Monk's body language reveals he has yet to understand that in order to respond with true compassion to others he must also feel sympathy for himself. If the Master's spiritual teaching had been kindlier when as a child his novice had injured living creatures, it could have acted as a balm to start the healing of his narcissistic wound. Instead, the old man's severity seems to have reinforced the child's feelings of responsibility for the loss of his mother – belief that his badness made her leave. Had the Master offered a more inclusive response, with both a spiritual and psychological perspective, he could have helped the novice process his suffering, teaching him that he was playing out in fantasy the deep hurt of abandonment he had suffered as a young child. Now the Young Monk's grief will remain frozen into winter.

The Master does not look up from his occupation as the young people return, but remarks sharply that the boat is drifting away. With the same tangential vision, he already knows of the liaison between the couple and that not only the boat but they too are adrift. At the moment people enter the realm of love they become disoriented and lose their bearings – interestingly since a state of disequilibrium is a prerequisite for potential psychic transformation.

The lovers take every opportunity to be together – whether on the temple raft or by the pools. Nor is the Old Monk unsympathetic: witnessing their horseplay one day, compassionate amusement lights his face. However, the audience cannot fail to notice that when by night the Young Monk leaves his bed and goes to the girl, he violates the temple's symbolic harmony by failing to leave their shared sleeping area through the door because it creaks noisily. The metaphor is clear: his passions are leading him to disregard the principles of self-discipline incumbent on a monk to transform desire into the spiritual life. Seduced by love, he is willing to risk all.

> To be seduced means to go off course, to be derailed... But it is precisely from this perspective, in conflict and crisis situations, that we have the possibility of becoming authentic. Seduction thus involves a psychological state that allows us to understand aspects of ourselves that would otherwise remain unknown.
>
> *(Carotenuto, 1989: 42)*

Read symbolically, the girl has a potentially ambivalent function (as always when the archetypes are summoned by the great events of life). She could become the Young Monk's agent for knowledge and growth. However, as Aldo Carotenuto writes, when a lover is bewitched and obsessed by the image of the other that obsession may take on a compulsive character (1989: 15). Compulsion drives us to the edge of an extreme condition – the desire to incorporate and be incorporated by the other. Citing Goethe's *Faust*, Carotenuto argues that when this happens the archetype of the mother appears in a form that imperils the lover (Ibid.: 69–70). This invokes the dichotomy familiar through Jung's writing between the loving, nurturing aspect of the Great Mother and her fearsome face. The individual who experiences this second, terrible aspect has an ego-consciousness that has begun to emerge from the womb of the unconscious, but which is struggling to secure the necessary separation. The thrust to achieve maturity depends upon the evolution to the fullest capacity of consciousness, the distinguishing mark and *sine qua non* of the human species. However, the urge toward growth has to fight against the psychologically fatal attraction of continued submersion in the unconscious. That attraction holds out the false promise of a safe return to an earlier, known state, together with escape from the fears that come with the enforced adventure into the developing world of consciousness (Neumann, 1954: 39–101). Symbolically the devouring mother who destroys her offspring represents this desire to regress.

Notwithstanding the lovers' violation of monastic order, the girl's relationship with the Young Monk has brought her back to health. Looking back with a touch of irony on her former sickly life, she joyfully describes her transformation as a miracle. Jay Greenberg's hypothesis of a dual instinct theory grounded in conflicting human needs fits her case. On the one hand individuals need a sense of grounding that feels completely known and predictable, a reliable anchoring, a framework for orientation and devotion; on the other hand, they feel a longing to break out of established and familiar patterns, to step over boundaries, to encounter something unpredictable, awe inspiring, or uncanny (in Mitchell, 2003: 39). The boy's monastic life expresses his need for orientation and devotion; but in stepping around the boundary of the door and discovering romantic love, he responds to a longing to transcend the boundaries of the psychic enclosures that have hitherto confined him. He thus enters the course of his life that must play out directed by the Self. As the organising, guiding, and uniting principle that gives the personality direction and meaning in life, the Self is both the quintessential archetype and where Buddhism and Jungian theory intersect.

The girl's 'cure' leaves it open to us to speculate that she may previously have repressed her budding sexuality because of an inner conflict between, on one side, attachment to her mother and the security of home, as against the developmental need to separate, leave the parental home and find herself. In this all-too human story of separation and individuation it is likely that the girl's depression was symptomatic of an unhealthy dependency between mother and daughter. Nevertheless it was the mother's fear that set off the daughter's need to fight against her parent's unconscious resistance to her growth. For Carotenuto, 'Love and fear go together precisely because they have the primitive quality of that which is unknown' (1989: 31). This is equally true of the emotions linking parent and child as those between lovers.

In their lovemaking the young couple enact what from the mother's perspective they 'ought not' (Ibid.). Thereby they clear the psychological obstacle and create an opening to follow a path more personal to them. According to Mitchell, romantic passion emerges from the convergence of these two currents, since human beings crave both security and adventure. Romance imparts to life a sense of robustness, a quality of purpose and excitement, a feeling that one's life is worth living, cultivating and savouring (2003: 25). Yet, as Carotenuto insists, fear remains an inescapable component of love: 'A sign of our true involvement in this rapture… is the accompanying fear that something destructive may happen' (1989: 28).

As usual, the Old Monk does not miss a thing. He discovers the couple sleeping in the drifting boat after a night of lovemaking as the little vessel moves randomly at the behest of light airs. A tame cockerel lives on the temple raft, its usual associations with rampant sexuality restricted by the absence of a mate (ironic comparison here with the young man). The Master flies the bird onto the boat's prow with a cord attached to its leg. By this means he draws the boat back to the raft, intending to restore to the Young Monk direction compatible with the disciplines governing monastic life. He pulls the drainage bung, and the water flooding the sleeping couple cools their ardour and scuppers, so to say, the illusion that seduction alone suffices to keep lovers afloat.

The lovers have no choice but to return to the relative stability of the raft and the Old Monk's ascetic disciplines – relative rather than complete stability because the floating platform turns softly in the breeze as the Master talks to the embarrassed pair – and nothing remains unchanged. He dismisses the young man's cringing apologies, saying that lovemaking is natural and, since the girl is now well, they have discovered the best medicine for her. However, he decrees that now she is cured, the young woman must return to her mainland home. To his apprentice's cries of protest, the Master responds with the sutra 'Desire leads to attachment. Attachment leads to the intention of killing.' These words suggest, firstly, that he foresees the path his headstrong apprentice will follow – something hidden from the audience until after it has occurred. Secondly, his rigorous words reflect the discipline required of the Buddhist monk. They echo the second Noble Truth, which holds that suffering inevitably follows craving because we crave things we cannot have (Cooper and James, 2005: 42).

> The essential point is that suffering is portrayed as depending upon spiritual ignorance, which means that the overcoming of spiritual ignorance will lead to the stopping of craving and hence the cessation of suffering.
>
> *(Cooper and James, 2005: 43)*

In this connection, Mitchell describes romance as filled with longing; intense desire always generates a sense of deprivation because the precondition of romantic passion is lack, desire for what one does not have (2003: 56). Fitting, then, that Eros's mother Penia personified poverty, since the individual who feels deprived of something will search for love (as the Young Monk will do when pursuing his girl). However, Eros also has associations with gaining knowledge because it is the nature of romantic passion to strive to overcome the lack it generates (Mitchell, 2003: 56). Carotenuto says, 'There is no introspection, no other experience, equal to love for putting us into contact with the unconscious. Only through love can we really get to know ourselves' (1989: 48). And Denis De Rougemont writes:

> Passion means suffering, something undergone, the overbearing power of destiny on a free and responsible person. To love more than love's object, to love passion for its own sake, from the *amabam amare* of Augustine up to modern Romanticism, means to love and seek out suffering. Love-passion; the desire for that which wounds and annihilates us is its victory. This is a secret the West has never allowed to be revealed, continuing stubbornly to suffocate it.
>
> *(De Rougemont in Carotenuto, 1989: 28)*

In psychological terms, discovering the difference between attachment and love, seduction and relationship is an emotionally charged spiritual journey. Recognising and accepting this supports the individual in understanding that dependency is not a 'holdover from childhood [but] constitutive of desire for a real person' (Mitchell, 2003: 138). To mature is to come to terms with childhood's archaic dependency needs and confront one's own narcissism including feelings of abandonment and neediness.

Marriage brings the illusion of permanency. Typically, newlyweds reaffirm over and over 'you are mine', as if to reassure themselves that their being in love is forever. However, a securely based relationship must navigate the perilous transition from the ecstatic state of 'being in love' to loving. The partners need to bear the frustration and emotional tension created by the alternation between separation and reunion, love and hate. Dealing with ambivalence necessitates that the couple gives up the expectation of finding an ideal relationship that might be realised in the material world and therefore recognise the difference between aspiration and expectation as well as the distinction between the psychic and the material. Living truthfully develops from combining different emotional views of the same person, thereby making the relationship feel real. When their capacity to do this grows, the healthy couple discovers that a real relationship is not an unchanging thing guaranteed to last forever, but a continual achievement. As they embark on what amounts to a process of individuation (Jung) or enlightenment (Buddhism) they find that it must be attended both by Eros (the principle of relatedness) and Logos (the rational principle), aiming as it does at the total transformation of personality, the consummation of the union of opposites, in order to create a new life. In the contrary case, which occurs here, understanding does not develop.

> If the frustration cannot be tolerated... the absence of something is perceived as the presence of something bad... and with this goes the notion that it can be got rid of; hence the belief that a state of deprivation can be remedied by abolishing things.
>
> *(Britton, 1998: 33)*

The slow turning of the temple raft taken in conjunction with the Master's words reinforces the thought that while nothing is permanent, life can be brought into order by understanding that 'a balance between security and adventure can only be a transitory equilibrium, a temporary pause in our struggle to reconcile our conflictual longings' (Mitchell, 2003: 56). Although the Young Monk has learnt not to inflict suffering on other creatures both for moral reasons and because witnessing them suffer inflicts pain on oneself, he is not conscious that much suffering will continue to follow his early attachment loss. His passion blazes too brightly for him to feel a scintilla of doubt that it will endure forever. And when the Old Monk rows the distraught young woman back to the landing pier, the wind rises in concert with the lovers' distress at parting. Over the next hours, try as he may to ignore his feelings, the Young Monk cannot quell them. So he leaves the temple and follows his girl, taking with him the Buddha statue and the cockerel. Heavy in his backpack, the Buddha recalls the stone he had to bear in childhood. The burden symbolises the weight of teachings that he has only partially understood but – as he will discover far in the future – cannot escape. The cockerel represents what he will be called upon to give up in his future, but not yet. To Mitchell, 'because we are dislocated within nature, our conscious control over our minds is limited. We are also our unconscious processes, we are called upon to give up some hubris' (2003: 24).

At present, the Young Monk is unable to renounce sexual desire and attachment to the girl in favour of the spiritual life. As he was her cure, she is his and therefore he must follow her. Carotenuto again:

> Anyone who wants to experience *psychic infinity*, that aspect of ourselves that transcends the limitations of physical existence, must enter the realm of love. At that moment we are disoriented, lose our bearings. But it is good that this is so. We must lose them. The fact of our being outside everyday reality, enclosed in what might be called a double narcissism, impels others to close ranks against us. We are lost to their lives, we have deserted, gone over to a different world.
>
> *(1989: 18)*

The Old Monk does not abandon the young man in the moment of his dawn departure although the latter does not know it. The wind has remained strong since the girl's departure and the boat is drifting without mooring, yet it presents itself in precisely the right place for boarding just as he is ready to go. This can only be because the Old Monk has so willed it. Indeed, as the young man pulls away across the water, the Old Monk, who had been feigning sleep, rises from his bed to pray. In his wisdom, he knows that the novice must follow his fate and his redemption must result from lived experience.

Come the autumn the Old Monk learns that, having married the girl after leaving the monastery, the young man has now murdered her for taking a lover. Foreseeing his novice's return from the outside world, the old man tailors monk's clothes for him. On arrival, the young man looks like a fashionable city dweller, but in reality is a fearful refugee from the police. Although he has brought back the stone Buddha and restores it to its old place, terror grips him. Also in his bag is the gory knife with which he killed the girl; and when unabated rage overwhelms him he stabs it murderously into the floorboards. Surrendering wholly to his passions, he revisits the pond where he first made love to the girl and rages against nature. Once again the Old Monk watches over him, as when he was a child.

Reckoning the young man's behaviour from a Jungian perspective, we can see that he has suffered a calamitous inflation of the anima. Jung himself wrote,

> Within the soul of a man with a negative mother-anima figure the theme 'I am nothing' repeats. Such dark moods can even lure a man to suicide, in which case the anima becomes a death demon.
>
> *(1964: 178)*

Unable to free his mind from the despoliation of the imago on which he has projected his romantic passions (longings that have depleted the self, all value located in the other) the young man attempts suicide. But when his Master finds him, far from consoling or offering counsel, he chastises him fiercely with a heavy stave, then trusses and suspends him from the temple roof until a candle burns through the rope by which he hangs. Just as the Master identified the young man's manufactured sense of guilt over his first sexual experience, he now recognises a contrived sense of self-pity serving to displace a more genuine sense of guilt. This punishment symbolically pre-enacts the Buddhist's understanding of death in that it can neither be escaped nor deliberately precipitated; nor is it terminal, but rather leads to rebirth into a new life governed by the karma earned in the previous existence. In concert with this, the Old Monk prescribes a restorative programme avoiding any intellectual bromides. Rather than explore and amplify the young man's anima complex, the Master imposes a rigorous discipline. It is intended to have the effect of altering the young man's view of the world. While he still swings on the rope, the old man begins to paint on the raft's boards a Buddhist sutra the theme of which is control of the mind. Rather than revert to the means by which he wrote the prayer, the Master dips the tail of the monastery cat in black paint and outlines the characters with this unique brush despite the little creature's mild protests – an eloquent emblem for the way animal nature can be tamed. The young man emerges from enforced physical suffering, shaves his fashionable hair and dons monk's clothing, ready to surrender to monastic discipline. Thereupon the Old Monk instructs him to carve the painted sutra. The young man gradually releases his rage as he gouges the characters with his bloodstained knife.

Concerning the work a person needs to do to advance individuation Jung wrote,

> If... [a man] does this consciously and intentionally, he avoids all unhappy consequences of repressed individuation. In other words, if he voluntarily takes the burden of completeness on himself he need not find it 'happening' to him against his will in a negative form.
>
> *(Jung, 1950: §125).*

It goes without saying that the young man had committed an appalling crime in his calamitous reaction to his wife taking a lover; but the grievous experience of betrayal turns out to have been a formative step in his journey. Sophocles's version of the Oedipus Myth helps us understand the Young Monk's predicament. The Greek dramatist did not begin with Oedipus the lover and murderer, but with his abandonment by his parents in infancy, the identical root to the Young Monk's personal story. Like this mythological forebear, the young man remained fixated in a pre-Oedipal mindset which (because Oedipal guilt had not been aroused) resulted in sociopathy when he suffered a second betrayal. He re-enacted in his marriage his childhood trauma as unconscious longing carved out his fate.

Carotenuto describes the psychology of jealousy in terms that help us understand what the Young Monk has been through. He calls it a feeling immutably tied to love which produces anxiety. This intense and dramatic reaction is a concrete re-enactment of our experience in the primary relationship with the mother. When jealousy grips, it calls up a whole series of psychological devices that have to do with aggression and these are motivated more strongly by the fear of loss than by sexual infidelity (1989: 71–2). Thus (just as the Old Monk had asserted), aggression is the underbelly of desire, bringing out the shadow in full force.

> At the moment of betrayal a wound is opened in our most vulnerable spot – our original trust – which is that of a totally defenseless infant who cannot survive in the world except in someone's arms. This is the primitive and basic reality of the child; it is embedded in the psyche to the point we can never dominate it.
>
> *(Carotenuto, 1989: 79)*

The capacity to contain aggression is a precondition to loving truly, but the young man's desire for his wife came from a need for possession rather than a deep sense of devotion. Mitchell remarks, 'One of the motives for monogamous commitments is always, surely, the effort to make the relationship more secure, a hedge against the vulnerabilities and risks of love' (2003: 46). It is a painful reminder that fear is love's partner in crime. As Carotenuto observes,

> this fear is justified because it is difficult to accept that the worst pains and sufferings that we inflict and are inflicted upon us mostly occur in the realm of love. Nor can it help but surprise us to discover that we inflict a mortal wound on the very person to whom we have dedicated our life. We can even commit murder.
>
> *(Carotenuto, 1989: 28)*

Now that he has undeniable experience of the Second Noble Truth (that suffering is caused by craving), it is time for the Young Monk to begin to understand the Third Noble Truth, namely that there is an end to suffering for individuals who learn to govern their mind and passions.

However, Noble Truths do not one whit concern the detectives pursuing the young felon; they have nothing in mind other than to capture their man. Disembarking on the raft with pistols drawn, they look more like gangsters than police. The Young Monk, jolted out of his fragile self-control, threatens them with his bloody knife. The cops are shadow figures incarnate – like split-off parts of the young man's personality. They too have their priorities back to front, a factor implicit in the old man rowing his boat backwards when he brings them to the raft. They live life in a manner far removed from the meditative calm of the Master. Bored by the prevailing quiet of the monastery, they blast their pistols at an empty can they have dropped into the perfect lake, repeatedly missing it. Whereupon the old man interrupts his painting, cradles the cat, casually tosses a single pebble – and hits the can. The gesture sums up his response to the intrusion of these coarse figures from the outside world: they must wait until he is ready to authorise the arrest. The Master brooks no interruption to the Young Monk's work because the intense and drawn-out focus demanded to carve the sutra requires of the younger man both labour and meditation. Having commenced perforce and in rage, by degrees the latter finds the discipline of the work draws him toward emulating the Master's observance of the Middle Way requiring the cultivation of Morality, Meditation and Wisdom (see Keown, 1996: 57–8).

The characters of this sutra do not evaporate, because the Young Monk has great need of learning them. As day passes into evening, the detectives watch the murderer they have come to arrest carve the sutra that should teach him how to govern his passions. The calm of the moonlit lake and its nocturnal bird life soften their attitudes. When they awaken in the misty morning, the exhausted young man, his labour ended before dawn, sleeps on the hard boards. They cover him with a jacket and help the Old Monk paint the sutra. What has been carved in pain becomes beautiful in its truth, signifying the work of self-knowledge and love, which is to hold the tension between opposites until a new perspective emerges. Yet the sutra is not quite complete – the path has been started but not followed to its end.

The Young Monk awakens to wonderment over the painted sutra and takes leave of his Master with a deep bow. As the latter watches the cops row their prisoner to shore, he raises his hand in farewell and, to the astonishment of the detective on the oars, stops the boat for a moment to show his novice the power that a monk practised in deep meditation can command. After the party land, the cat – which has travelled with them – is free to roam again. The little creature disappears into the forest, implying metaphorically that the younger man's primitive characteristics no longer oppress him. At last he has allowed his ego to submit to the Self, a practice the Old Monk has long since mastered.

The cat's disappearance also coincides with the ending of the old man's animal vitality, a decline that occasions a number of mystical signs. Before the novice's departure, the floating monastery, rather than turn gently as usual in response to wind and water currents, had swerved in a dramatic arc across the lake, sweeping close to the tree-lined shore. Yet at the moment of leave-taking, it stands in its original, unchanged position. After the novice has gone, leaving the Old Monk terminally exhausted, it swings away from the trees back to its usual station. The disjunction (taken in combination with the Master's command over the boat, which he wills back to the raft after the cops abandon it) is not an editor's continuity error. Instead it nicely troubles our acceptance of a hard-edged divide between outer and inner worlds. It does this in synchronicity with the great changes of life overtaking both men. The symbolic values that have accumulated around the image of the monastery have long overlapped with the idea of a temple redolent not only of Buddhist ideals but also the being of the old man. In short, it conveys the idea of the Self, both personal and archetypal. His impending death will momentarily disturb the temple, but as we shall see, like the temple, the archetypal Self will soon resume its station, paradoxically changed but recognisably the same.

Nowhere more evidently than in the manner in which the Old Master takes leave of life does fantasy bridge from the inner world of archetypal structures to external reality (Samuels *et al.*, 1986: 59). Having written on strips of paper the character that the English subtitles translate as 'Closed', he seals his eyes, ears, nose and mouth with them. He arranges wood on the dinghy and, placing a candle to ignite it, climbs onto his pyre, removing the bung so the boat will scuttle after the flames have done their work. In perfect tranquillity he exhales for the last time and fire consumes his body. His death, by no means an act of high drama, expresses a simple and moving ritual in which flames separate the soul from the detritus of the body which itself sinks into the water to transform and nourish future life. As if to embody that observation, a snake swims away from the funeral vessel, and makes its home in the old man's vestments, which he has placed neatly in front of the temple's Buddha, awaiting his successor.

That snake remains there until the former novice, now middle-aged (Kim Ki-Duk), returns in deep winter after his release from jail. He walks over the frozen lake to the monastery, understands from the wrecked boat that his Master had died, and performs funeral rites. He extracts fragments of bone and ash from the ice-filled vessel and wraps them in scarlet cloth. Then he inserts the little bag like an offering in the head of a Buddha. This he has carved from a frozen waterfall in the very ponds where he had played in childhood and seduced the girl in adolescence, a metaphor readily understood. Leaving the ice image of the Buddha to melt as the spring resumes its flow, the successor Monk has, like his Master before him, conveyed power over death and life.

The snake, which has intermittently been present since spring when it first surprised the boy, has a complex symbolic function that comes in part from shedding its skin. Thus, appearing reborn and immortal, it symbolises the death and rebirth motif. Other associations arise from its threat to human life, its 'sudden and unexpected manifestations' (as when the snake in question swims from the funeral vessel to the monastery) 'its painful and dangerous interventions in our affairs and its frightening effects' (Jung, 1956: §580). The Garden of Eden was put at risk by a serpent, and this exquisite lake with its monastery has snakes too. Yet although they doubtless could harm the monks, these ones do not behave as the enemies of humankind. To the contrary, a snake has been thoughtlessly killed by a child. In fact the snake that takes up residence in the monastery in the very hour of the Old Master's death now attends the returning monk as he prays. The snake's presence invokes 'a form of the ancestral spirit, guide to the Land of the Dead and Mediator of hidden processes of transformation and return' (Ronnberg, 2010: 196). Nevertheless, in this role it still carries the resonance of terror that snakes arouse in humanity. Read symbolically, the snake delivers sudden strikes from the unconscious, from which new consciousness may emerge, equally fecund of enrichment or calamity.

The present Monk's grief when he injured small creatures as a child overwhelmed him when he saw the fatal damage done to the snake. Now an adult, rather than drive the snake out, he shares the monastery with it, even drawing the reptile down toward him when he drums to express his devotions. Nor is it driven away when a mother brings her baby to the temple; and the Monk's acceptance contrasts with circumstances when the old Master cared for the present incumbent, at which time no snake was seen to enter the monastery. Being in relation with the shadow — the snake as the source of creative life with all its dangers — is necessary to healing unconscious damage, in this case the negative anima complex.

As the former prisoner restores the monastery, he discovers a manual demonstrating the moves of kung fu and starts practising the exercise sequences with great masculine intensity. Having finally accepted the consequences of his action by submitting to imprisonment, he is receptive to change, living with the shadow in service to his growth. Now, with the routines of kung fu available to him, he goes beyond the physical and mental development that sprang from his self-control in prison. This discipline serves the integration of Yin and Yang into a single Ultimate, being the nearest Buddhist equivalent to the Jungian archetype of the divine hermaphrodite mentioned below. The disciplined meditative movements of kung fu focus the Monk's internal power, in contrast with his use solely of external power (the ego position) when he killed his wife.

A desperate lone woman (Ji-a Park) approaches through the gates which, for the sole time in the film, are only open on one side. Her head and face, completely wrapped in a purple scarf, suggest that she may be a widow mourning her husband, but she never discloses who she is. She brings a wailing infant in her arms and the Monk deals with her kindly. Although he touches her scarf, he does not force her to show her face when she gently restrains his hand. The contrast cannot be missed with his adolescent behaviour toward the sick girl that lacked the kindness evident here, for the mother's grief and silent communion with the Monk leave no doubt that she means to abandon her son. After soothing the child and resting awhile, she departs in the night, her face still concealed.[3] The obscuring of her visual features implies she is *a no self*, having neither persona nor ego strength to face the future alone. Her image embodies the wounded feminine. Instead she looks back while hurrying away, which proves fatal when she loses her footing and falls through a hole the Monk has cut in the ice to draw water. The cold water symbolically amplifies her frozen grief as she drowns in the primal darkness of her psyche.

After the Monk has made her infant son secure in the monastery, he lifts down the statue of a female Buddha previously hidden in an overhead locker. With this, he symbolically liberates the anima from his own early loss, freeing the psychic energy attached to the mother-son relationship. Thereby he discovers his authentic anima function as the bridge to the Self, connecting to the inner component of the psyche that is necessary for wholeness. As we have already seen in interpreting a number of films, anima can be a guide and a mediator, leading a man to his transformation. She can be a messenger and personification of supreme wisdom, and function as a catalyst in the process of integration. Radmila Moacanin writes that in Tibetan Buddhism Tara is revered as the feminine aspect of the Buddha and mother of all divinities.

> Tara, in her essence, symbolizes the totally developed wisdom that transcends reason. She is the buddha of enlightened activity, the liberator who, by releasing one from the bondage of egocentric passions, leads from the shores of profane worldly involvement (samsara) to the other shore of illumination (nirvana).
>
> (Moacanin, 2010: 63)

In Jungian terms, Tara symbolises the highest form of the feminine archetype, the Great Goddess (Ibid.). The journey of individuation and connection to the Self leads to the archetype of the divine hermaphrodite, signifying integration of feminine and masculine.

The Monk's compassion for the mother and acceptance of the guardian's role has readied him at last to accept the feminine principle in himself and in nature at large. It confirms his healing and readiness to transcend his personal suffering. He sets out on an arduous pilgrimage ascending the steep flank of Kumgang, the sacred mountain that rises high above the lake. As he climbs, an incantation fills the soundtrack, telling of the devout passion of someone who undertook just such a harsh journey across the mountains in the hope of illumination.

In accord with both Buddhist and Jungian principles, the Monk does not follow a path prescribed by dogma, but searches out his own route. The statue of Tara that he carries is an awkward but not impossible burden for a man of his impressive physique. However, replicating the suffering he first inflicted on small creatures and the Old Master then forced him to endure, he now handicaps himself by dragging a millstone on the entire journey as he crosses snow and ice, tears a way through thorny scrub and labours over boulders, his heels bloodied by chafing clogs. His arduous but resolute progress expresses the hard work required if he is to avoid wrong paths and find his own way to freedom. As he struggles forward he sees in fantasy the small creatures he had killed as a child. All three are alive and moving but still tied to their stones. His fantasy indicates that reparation has occurred in his psyche.

Authentic in his entire being, he moves forward although he must continue to carry the weight of his trauma history behind him as he strives toward his destination. At the summit he sets the stone disc as a base for the statue and faces this figure of the feminine archetype toward the lake that can be seen thousands of feet below. As the sun sets over the mountains, he prays, setting down the heavy burden he has carried since childhood. Here, on the solid ground where the symbol of transcendence and grace now sits, he adopts a perspective made new to him by the goddess's presence. As he does so, the sun is setting, a cooling image that symbolically accompanies the onset of the second half of life. The business of that second part of life as Jung often said, is to attend to the inner world and prepare for death – just as the Monk is now doing. The traumas induced by his appetite to possess are cleared and he has attained spiritual completeness – nirvana.

At this, the climax of the Monk's journey, Buddhist philosophy and Jung's theories diverge from each other in one crucial factor. As J. J. Clarke observes, they are closely aligned in recognising a direct parallel between the Buddhist path toward enlightenment and the Jungian concept of individuation. However, Jung emphasised 'the fact that Buddhism held out the possibility of *complete* emancipation and enlightenment – a goal which he himself deemed to be impossible' (Clarke, 1994: 121).

Spring returns with the infant now grown into a sturdy child just the age the Monk had been when we first saw him; but the new Master has a much less austere demeanour than his predecessor and occupies himself in painting an empathic portrait of the smiling youngster. When the boy plays with a turtle and torments it by banging on the top and then the bottom of its shell so that the creature pulls in its head and limbs, the Monk does not interrupt his play. Myths and legends depict the turtle's dome-like upper and flattened lower shell as comprising the totality of the cosmos (Ronnberg, 2010: 192). It also has mythic associations with the fertility and wisdom of the great goddess, the lunar qualities of yin, and the primeval waters in which all things have their beginning (Ibid.). As the child rows across the lake to the landing stage, we cut to the distant shot from the perspective of the goddess's statue, high on Kumgang mountain. Under her auspices, this child, notwithstanding the harm inflicted by the loss of his mother, can be expected to suffer less than the Monk did at the hands of his stern Master. The Monk's healing journey has made him a gentler man who has integrated the feminine with the masculine.

Notes

1 The English subtitles for the Region 1 and Region 2 editions differ slightly. We use the Region 2 DVD which, unlike the North American version, translates the song.

2 'We resolve the Oedipus Complex by working through the depressive position, and the depressive position by working through the Oedipus Complex; [so] that neither [is] ever finished and both have to be reworked in each new life situation, at each stage of development and with each major addition to experience' (Britton, 1998: 32). The concept of the depressive position was developed by Klein. It posits that a child's greater knowledge of the object (the primary caretaker) includes awareness of the latter's continuity of existence in time and space. An essential element in this position is the growth of the sense of distinction between self and object, and between the real and the ideal object. With this, the idea of permanent possession has to be given up, with the effect that the ideal of one's sole possession of the desired parent has to be relinquished (Ibid.: 34).

3 Coverage in the DVD supplementary footage 'Behind the Scenes' shows the actress Ji-a Park (and the dummy of her character's corpse) made up with a fresh facial scar. Had it been visible to the audience, this disfigurement would have restricted the range of possible causes for her abandoning her son. In the finished film spectators are not limited to imagining that a man has attacked her.

10

MORVERN CALLAR (2002)

Morvern Callar is the only film among those we analyse that focuses on one character's lone journey. Furthermore, it communicates its narrative primarily through images and music: the sparse dialogue rarely expresses what weighs most heavily on Morvern's mind. Edward F. Edinger's *Anatomy of the Psyche* (1985) informs our writing of this chapter because, by focusing on the symbolic value of alchemy to psychotherapy, he enables us to use this late mediaeval, quasi-scientific form of inquiry to track individuation. He does this by developing Jung's argument that what makes alchemy so useful in the present day is that its images concretise the experiences of transformation that the individual undergoes in psychotherapy (Edinger, 1985: 2).

While historians of science perceive alchemy as proto-scientific research into the chemistry of matter, psychotherapists consider it to be 'one of the precursors of modern study of the unconscious and, in particular, of analytical interest in the transformation of personality' (Samuels *et al.*, 1986: 12). Alchemists themselves did not accept that there was an unbridgeable divide between the material and spiritual worlds. Instead they saw them 'linked by hidden connections and identities.' (Edinger, 1985: 3). Jung explained in *Mysterium Coniunctionis* why alchemy fits the study of an individual's progress toward individuation.

> Alchemy, with its wealth of symbols, gives us an insight into an endeavour of the human mind which could be compared with a religious rite, an *opus divinum*. The difference between them is that the alchemical opus was not a collective activity rigorously defined as to its form and content, but rather, despite the similarity of their fundamental principles, an individual undertaking on which the adept staked his whole soul for the transcendental purpose of producing a *unity*.
>
> *(Jung, 1954b: §790)*

Edinger identifies among the alchemists' 'tangled mass of overlapping images' (1985: 14) seven major operations that feature recurrently in the Opus – although they are not inevitably used in every case. They are *calcinatio, solutio, coagulatio, sublimatio, mortificatio, separatio,* culminating in *coniunctio.* 'Many images from myth, religion, and folklore also gather around these symbolic operations, since they all come from the same source – the archetypal psyche' (Ibid.). Morvern, governed by the Orphan Archetype, has neither knowledge nor experience of therapy. Nevertheless, she will lead the viewer to understand how each person who goes through individuation enters its depths alone. Morvern, unlike the Buddhist monks will not follow a spiritual discipline to attain transformation; nor is Giovanni Sermonti's self-reflection a route open to her; her journey is solely directed by experience, with music functioning as the doorway into her emotional life.

Alan Warner's 1995 novel *Morvern Callar* was the source for the film. Lynne Ramsay and Liana Dognini wrote the screenplay; Ramsay directed and Samantha Morton played the lead. Although both novel and film are set in a town on the west coast of Scotland, the film inevitably differs from Warner's novel because the book depends for much of its effect on a young woman's stream of consciousness after she finds her boyfriend dead. At first in shock, she cannot speak to anyone about what has happened. Nor can she find adequate language in her mind to help her process the trauma. Ramsay's film deploys devices other than language alone to express Morvern's intense subjective experience; and thus it keeps faith with its source.

The film opens with an extreme close-up on Morvern's face. A woman in her twenties, she is seen briefly in a dim pool of light then plunged into darkness. Light returns then cuts off and on intermittently. Extreme close-ups accumulate: she is lying on the floor, caressing a man's body. Her fingers traverse deep cuts across his wrist, heavy with congealed blood: her boyfriend has taken his life.[1] The Christmas tree lights flash. Time passes. Then the sound of a small motor draws Morvern's eye to a computer screen displaying the instruction 'Read Me'. She scrolls down to find a message: 'Sorry Morvern. Don't try to understand, it just felt like the right thing to do.' She skips some lines about his novel and scrolls down to the last words: 'I love you. Be brave.'

Aldo Carotenuto notes that 'the silence that follows abandonment is opaque, empty, without resonance… we must have the courage to admit there is nothing we can do (1989: 84). Gradually this realisation comes over Morvern. The night is freezing when she walks out to the public telephone on the station. She cannot bring herself to dial and sits awhile on the empty platform. Then bizarrely the phone starts to ring. When she surrenders to the relentless noise she finds herself talking to a person worried about someone who might be missing. Morvern reassures the caller sympathetically, a brief conversation that shows her warmth of personality but with the synchronistic twist that her own missing person will never return. Back in the flat, she opens the presents he left for her under the blinking tree – a leather jacket, a cigarette lighter and a Walkman with a cassette of music dubbed for her.

Her haunted face reveals the trauma as she takes a bath and turns under the water in a foetal curl. To bathe, according to Edinger is, like other images of immersion in water, the symbolic equivalent for the alchemical operation of *Solutio*. Water was thought of as the womb of life and *Solutio* as a return to the womb for rebirth. For alchemists the significance of *Solutio* lay in their belief that the process turned a solid into liquid; and they identified this as the return of differentiated matter to its original undifferentiated state. That was called the *prima materia* (literally 'first matter'). It consisted of the primary psychic ingredients that influence how lives unfold.

The relevance of the *prima materia* runs deep when considering Morvern's state in facing her man's suicide. As a foster child she can be identified with the orphan archetype. This archetype has arcane connections with *Solutio*, which alchemists regarded as the essential first step in a series of processes that would transform matter into the Philosopher's Stone. Adepts used the term 'orphan' for this Stone because it represented for them the totality, or the 'one', a metaphor for the psychological idea of the Self and the individuated person. In one text the Philosopher's Stone is known as the homeless orphan slain at the beginning of the alchemical process for purposes of transformation (Rothenberg, 2001: 47). As we shall see, the idea of the archetypal orphan has the characteristic ambivalence of all archetypal images. It embodies opposites: feelings of worthlessness and being precious.

As one alchemical text cited by Edinger asserted, bodies cannot be changed except by reduction into their first matter. In this respect alchemical procedure corresponds to what takes place in psychotherapy: where static aspects of the personality permit no change, they must be dissolved to allow transformation to proceed (1985: 47–8). Alchemical and Christian symbolism converged here too in that for both, baptism signified cleansing and rejuvenation, a ritual to bring about the creation of a new personality (Edinger, 1985: 58). Interpreted psychologically, the purifying power of water conveys the idea that whoever desires real change must enter the deep waters of the unconscious.

This is the psychological exigency in which Morvern finds herself when she turns under the bath water, perhaps testing whether the emptiness that her boy-friend's suicide has forced on her may suck her too into the same scoured, suicidal void. But it doesn't, so, a stranger to the woman in her mirror, she emerges from the water and gets ready methodically for her Christmas night out: black dress, scarlet nails painted on fingers rigid with tension, and heavy black eyeliner (which, until she adjusts it, produces a sad clown's face). Morvern's dressing up is not a sign of rebirth – it's too soon for that. The time-honoured topos, the arming of the hero before she goes into battle, is more to the point.

One clue to her state of mind is her necklace flaunting the name 'Jackie'. Her best friend Lanna (Kathleen McDermott) notices it as something new and Morvern admits she found it: clearly her unconscious now already supports renewal, know-ing she will need a different persona – what Michael Meade refers to as her intended personality – in order to face her fate and find the thread toward her destiny.

Meade says that fate refers to one's deepest sense of subjectivity and can be seen as whatever limits, restricts or even imprisons the individual (2010: 2), for example, Tsotsi. (Refer also to the Three Colours Trilogy). Destiny, in his account, entails finding a way through exactly those constraints on the vitality of our lives. Thus, fate places us in a specific context where meaning and purpose can be explored. Wherever we brush against the limits of our fate we also stand near the doors of our destiny (2010: 4). Morvern is already initiating a move into a new life rather than succumb to living in the neurotic repetition that goes with unending trauma.

The girls take a tab of E (which Marion Woodman finds symbolic of a longing for the light [2004: 64]) before joining the close-knit community in the pub. When her foster father asks after 'Dostoyevsky', Morvern mutters that he is at home in the kitchen. The calculated half-truth adds to the signs we see that, now in denial, she sidelines thoughts about the body in the kitchen.

Gradually booze, the tabs and exhilarating dance music spin the night. A hard cut takes us from the pub into a car pulsing through the dark. Morvern, head stuck out the window, whoops with excitement, streaming hair lit by a following car, her ears filled by Can's 'I Want More'. Another hard cut – the elisions allow us to experience those moments only that impress her consciousness – and we're in a house party, immersed trance-like in the engulfing womb of Holger Czukay's 'Fragrance', camera surging with dancers under rosy lights. Then we're outside in the yard where the rave continues around a bonfire with folk stripping off and leaping through the flames. Later, pulled out from exhilaration by the trauma that refuses to release her, Morvern stands alone by the loch at the bottom of the yard. The rave barely audible behind her, she watches a boat chug past through black water. The bargee, khaki-clad with black goggles (like a subhuman figure from a Czech animated film), turns his floodlight full on her. With 'Fragrance' still heard in the distance, she hoists the black dress above her waist and stares back. Time passes. Is she gripped by feelings of guilt and responsibility and seeking a numbing sexual adventure to mask her emptiness? Is she asking herself what should she have done to save her man? Or is she still nosing after an encounter with death? The light goes out, the boatman goes on his way.

> Only in being left do we have the sense of failure. When I am abandoned I imagine I have not given enough or been everything I should have been to the other... This is the moment when one wants to die or hopes for some fatal disease or accident because the idea that one's own inadequacy caused the separation is unbearable. This is difficult to live with.
>
> *(Carotenuto, 1989: 83)*

Back in the house it swiftly becomes evident that music organises not only our reception of the film, but Morvern's re-engagement with life and the grieving process. Gilbert Rose, advocating the idea that music is the temporal art form par excellence, proposes that one of its functions is to support the illusion that time flows (2004: 78). Yet he also perceives the converse, that 'music has the power to destroy the sense of time's passage' (2004: xviii). So too does pain, and both warp Morvern's (and our) perceptions when the rhythm changes and gamelan drumming mixes through into 'Goon Gumpas' (Aphex Twin). The party absorbs her once more and the lock that ties language and sense to self loosens. Under warm lights the camera swirls among the drugged and drunk. The tabs and booze free Morvern to shout nonsense into the blasts of noise and music (mouth and words out of synch). Some fragments of speech – hard to tell whether it's her voice or someone overheard – cut to the bone: 'Has anyone seen my boyfriend? I've lost my boyfriend?' She dances madly, deely boppers spring like crazed antennae on her head and a girl's voice (it could be hers) threads through the uproar: 'How d'you know when you've lost somebody? When you sit on your own and not really say anything.' Morvern's verbal dislocation intrigues all the more because it echoes her history of loss that has no language and thus no consciousness.

In the grey light of a winter dawn, Morvern leaves Lanna and another friend in the bed where, entwined in sensual drunkenness, they had all crashed. She gathers her stuff from the party wreckage, lights a cigarette, then repeatedly sparks the flame of her Christmas lighter and smothers it, sparks the flame and smothers it, sparks flame and smothers... Morvern smokes habitually, her sucking on cigarettes suggesting a yearning for the nurturing and containing mother: she has introjected the latter's absence. So the little flame of her new lighter has significant associations drawn out by Clarissa Pinkola Estes (1990) who casts the orphan's internal mother in the role of keeper of the flame. While an unmothered child thus has an internal light that will never go out, surviving is not enough. To thrive, orphans must grow a fully developed inner mother by adopting self-love and self-respect. Edinger encourages us to relate this to the alchemical operation *calcinatio*. This operation is symbolically evoked by any image that contains fire and affects the substances that it burns. By association *calcinatio* invokes the psyche's dealing with the shadow side (1985: 18). Edinger's illustrations centre on powerful, often consuming conflagrations; but Morvern's lighter produces a tiny flame that she controls (as if trying to manage her fate). Eventually, in the desert, it expires. Far from cleansing (which is the archetypal power of fire at the root of *calcinatio*), Morvern has used her boyfriend's gift to light cigarettes and breathe in smoke. Thus, metaphorically she has been inhaling the very contamination that *calcinatio* would purify. After the lighter fails, however, we do not see her smoking again. It implies that she has matured and no longer needs cigarettes as a substitute for her missing inner mother. Rather she has begun living by the guidance of an orphan's strongest aspect, intuition, which Estes (1990) calls 'the light of consciousness'.

In the cold dawn of Christmas Day she thinks of her boyfriend who gave her the lighter and tears start. Time passes. Lanna finds her outdoors gazing down the length of the chilly loch and comforts her without knowing what is wrong. Morvern conceals her immediate affliction behind another sorrow: an island just visible in the mist is her foster mother's burial place. Although a displacement of her latest grief, Morvern's words are no deception. We now understand that the loss of her birth mother created a deep early wound requiring considerable healing in her life. She has mixed the loss of one mother with longing for the other. Edinger reminds us that,

> the death of a loved one is an aspect of individuation. The death of a parent, a sibling, a child, a lover, or a spouse is an individuation crisis that challenges elementary states of identification and *participation mystique*. The ego's unconscious connection with the Self is embedded in these primary identifications, and therefore the occasion of such a death is crucial. Either it will lead to an increased realization of the Self, or if the potential for consciousness is aborted, then negative, regressive, and even fatal effects may follow.
>
> *(Edinger, 1985: 202–3)*

Rose-Emily Rothenberg adds, 'The orphan begins life in solitude or abandonment and then like the archetypal hero, must undertake the tasks that will lead to the discovery of her real identity' (2001: 21). This, like all initiation rites, offers a form of rebirth that has a more conscious and psychological nature than one's first birth. This second birth must be a conscious choice of life made in the face of a threat of the death of one's spirit and one's reason for being alive (Meade, 2010: 67).

Morvern, the lost orphan, needs to project her absent parent onto another object in her futile search for love. Thus, the suicide forces her to face her fate as an orphan: it has created the specific context as a way to enter parts of her unborn psyche by confronting the original heartbreak with new meaning. One side of the orphan feels loss and abandonment but the other side is tough, independent and resourceful (Meade, 2010: 18). Now she will need to draw on great courage fulfilling to the utmost her boyfriend's last words 'Be brave'. And her destiny will involve finding her way through.

Neither girl wants to go home yet, so they call on Lanna's granny. Couris Jean (Ruby Milton) welcomes them with tea, affection and understanding. At her suggestion, the girls take a bath to repair the night's ravages and in the warm intimacy of the tub, Morvern tries to share with Lanna that something bad has happened. Unable to open up completely, she cannot deal with Lanna's prying questions and says only that her man has left forever – muttering implausibly that he has gone to another country. Lanna says that doesn't make sense, but then responds in an equally disconnected way, 'Is it something he's given me?' This goes unnoticed because Morvern is focussed on his death and we are focussed on her. Only later can we appreciate that Lanna too was trying to say something difficult.

Denial, splitting and repression enfold Morvern once again when she returns home. The Christmas lights still flash and her boyfriend's corpse still occupies the floor. She takes refuge in cigarettes and cheerful music, finding 'Spoon' on the gift tape, another funky track by Holger Czukay and Can.

Morvern returns to her supermarket work. Ramsay covers the dreary necessity in an unexpected, sarcastic parody of Hollywood romance. Gossipy Lanna has already told their workmates that Morvern's man has gone. When Morvern enters the supermarket, Lee Hazlewood fills her ears with 'Some Velvet Morning' in the manner of Johnny Cash at his moodiest, while Alwin Kuchler's camera glides around the floor and leads her along the aisles. It's another bizarrely disconnected moment: the lyrics refer to Phaedra whose illicit love for her stepson led to her tragic death. There is no evident link to the circumstances of Morvern's life. Yet the combination of these oddly assorted elements makes the scene a waking nightmare from which she cannot escape. In that regard she is indeed like Phaedra who, while tormented by devouring love, the victim of 'Venus in her might seizing her prey', pretends to the world that nothing has ripped her heart out (Racine, 1677: Act 1, Scene 3).

Something, superficially the peace she experiences in the old woman's house, draws her back to Lanna's granny. Morvern heats soup for her and they sit in companionable silence with snow falling outside the window. But a need deeper than tranquillity brings Morvern here. In Couris Jean, Morvern has found someone she can feel safe and connected to – a woman so old that she fits the archetypal image of the wise old woman. As Jean Shinoda Bolen helps us see (2003: 7), the 'crone's-eye view' is a potential that Morvern needs to recognise and develop. The old woman lifts a frail arm to draw Morvern's attention upward. The scene ends with this richly ambiguous but unexplained gesture. Couris Jean could be pointing at a vigorous lily on her window ledge which has burst into flowers to herald spring-time rebirth. Alternatively she could be inviting Morvern to look up to the hills and seek a broader perspective by acting upon her perceptions and intuitions as a means of finding 'soul rather than ego' (Bolen, 2003: 7–8). For the ciné-literate audience there's a third, inescapable association. The distinctive way Couris Jean points is so rare it must pay homage to *2001: A Space Odyssey*. Near the end of Kubrick's film, the astronaut Dave, now an ancient traveller breathing his last, calls attention in just this way to the Star Child and the new life that will succeed him in the cycle of death and rebirth. The resonances flood into Ramsay's film like an omen yet to be worked through.

Wordlessly and probably not fully conscious of what she has witnessed, Morvern nonetheless responds to the sign. Returning home with renewed energy, she sits at the computer for a second time and reads her man's message in full. She discovers that he wrote his novel for her and wanted it sent to publishers. Envy, the characteristic shadow material of the orphan, kicks in. 'Looking out from the interior window of the psyche, the orphan longs for what others have, from literal objects to their creative endeavours' (Rothenberg, 2001: 50). Hesitantly searching for the right keys, she deletes his name and laboriously substitutes hers before printing the novel, never so much as glancing at the typescript. In plain language this is theft, but stealing is an archetypal action that can be tricksterish and in that mode exposes the shadow side of the Self, a phenomenon authenticated by myth. Jung reminds us that Hermes, in one aspect god of thieves and cheats, was, in another, a god of revelation who gave his name to a whole philosophy (1948a: §281). And Meade recalls that Jesus made a distinction between the kind of thief who was merely a common crook stealing to satisfy personal greed, and another capable of awakening and becoming something worthy of heaven (2010: 73). Meade asserts that a greater need and purpose is hidden in each individual. It knows best how he or she must live and is worth stealing, dying and living for. 'Thus, rules must be broken and penalties must be risked in order that choosing to fully live becomes a truly conscious act' (2010: 67).

While the novel prints, Morvern lugs her boyfriend's corpse into the bath and scrubs the kitchen floor clean of blood. His message also said that his bank had enough money for the funeral, but when she checks the ATM she finds the account has far more than she imagined. She promptly buys two tickets for a resort holiday in Spain and gives one to Lanna.

A number of hints accumulate that illuminate facets of the relationship between Morvern and her boyfriend. His last message to her starts 'Sorry Morvern'; and 'Sorry' is what she says to his body as she goes out on Christmas Eve having taken £20 from his back pocket. She also mumbles 'Sorry' when her foster dad says he thought she would have visited them – hinting that her orphan self feels overly guilty and responsible for causing many of the events that happen around her.

> Guilt is primary in this psychological profile. The orphan feels a fundamental guilt as if condemned by the Self. She feels that the Self (as the mother and as the hostile betrayer) has turned away and that this is a higher judgement for which the orphan must carry the guilt. If guilt continues to fill her existence, it leaves little room for the Self to come into being. This is an archaic guilt not to be confused with the more conscious guilt one feels when leaving a familiar container (such as religious belief or the personal family), but more closely akin to the guilt for becoming more conscious and for being alive.
>
> *(Rothenberg, 2001: 48)*

Deep though it once was, the open affections between Morvern and her man, as in all relationships, had differences and limitations. He was an intensely private, thinking introvert; she an extravert sensing type who appears to have been his main link to the town's community. They came together in the music that he introduced her to – and this, as we hear, still continues for her as a deep, formative communion. However, she has no interest in his work, which will have redoubled for him the usual isolation of a writer. Although Morvern knows his PIN code, she does not know how much his bank account holds – which implies both of them were of independent mind. Morvern receives no inquiry from family about his absence, making us wonder about his own familial relationships, which, according to W. R. D. Fairbairn, form the context for each person's growth (1952: ix). Nor does anybody seriously question her assertion that he has left her and gone away. Thus, the abandoned child, the core motif of the orphan archetype is fully represented in their relationship.

> Difficulty in accepting adult life and the creative force that accompanies it is a common problem for an orphan. He or she is tempted to stay in an unborn state, as if wrapped in a protective cloak where everything is safe. The dictate

of the orphan complex in its negative aspect insists that one must not move forward into new life.

(Rothenberg, 2001: 90)

For Morvern's boyfriend, finishing the book appears to have resonated cruelly with his own wounded inner life and consequent refusal to grow. On one side he seems to have over-identified with his as yet unborn novel in bonded *participation mystique.*

> The main set of opposites the orphan has to carry is, on the one hand, being abandoned and alienated from the source of nourishment and thus inferior, not worthy of a rightful place in life, yet the orphan carries the autonomous life force inherent in the psyche.
>
> *(Rothenberg, 2001: 48)*

In another aspect, though he unconsciously identified with abandonment in the orphan archetype, Morvern's man, as a writer of fiction, belonged in a different frame from her, for his business was to create a new world. To judge by the publishers' keen response, he succeeded all too well. In mythic terms, therefore, the writer plays god. Gods have no parents in the ordinary sense, but that does not make them orphans of the mortal kind. Since playing a god is not the same as being one, the writer may be guilty of hubris if overly cathected with his work in *participation mystique* when creating a fictional world. He cannot be ignorant of this crime. Just as the task was his own invention, so too must be the punishment payable when the writing ends. It is, Rothenberg notes, a great error when the ego takes personally what belongs to the gods (2001: 112).

Jung observed the danger of dissolution (destructive Solutio) when an individual identifies with the creative powers. He said that these,

> have you on the string and you dance to their whistling, to their melody. But in as much as you say these creative forces are in Nietzsche or in me or anywhere else, you cause an inflation, because man does not possess creative powers, he is possessed by them. That is the truth. If he allows himself to be thoroughly possessed by them without questioning, without looking at them, there is no inflation, but the moment he splits off, when he thinks, I am the fellow, an inflation follows...
>
> But if you know you are creative and enjoy being creative, you will be crucified afterwards because anybody identified with God will be dismembered.
>
> *(Jung, Zarathustra Seminar 1, 67 cited by Edinger, 1985: 64)*

Tensions between abandonment and inflation were evidently manic in her boyfriend's last hours. In one respect his choice of Christmas presents has been made carefully to please her. The jacket has obvious associations with warmth and protection; the lighter with the inner flame that she must develop; and the music for her new Walkman reinforces the emotional connection between them. Contrast this with his death, not an attempted suicide crying out for help but coldly planned to take account of the shifts Morvern worked on Christmas Eve to ensure she would come home to find him dead. Whatever his motivation, the timing and method of his self-slaughter show brutality, the most favourable account of which might be that he turned the suicide's indifferent blind eye on the living. His accounting for his action betrays the same tensions. On the surface there is a gentle element in his writing, 'Don't try to understand, it just felt like the right thing to do.' But his controlled affective tone confirms that he was indeed caught in the grips of inflation well contained in his self-delusion of complete independence. This is in complete opposition to the gradual maturational path from total dependence in infancy to the mature dependence of the adult personality. Development is unattainable in isolation so, according to Fairbairn, the individual is necessarily dependent upon relationships with other individuals in the external world. Fairbairn describes mature dependence as 'a capacity on the part of the differentiated individual for cooperative relationships with differentiated objects' (1952: 145). This psychological understanding emphasises the necessity for adults to do the emotional work that helps them separate from issues inherited from their families of origin.

Robert Johnson comments on the difference between feeling (one's ability to value) and mood (one's being overtaken or possessed by an inner feminine content).

> If a man has a good relationship to his anima, his inner femininity, he is able to feel, to value, and thus to find meaning in his life. If a man is not related to his anima, then he can find no meaning and has no capacity for valuation. As soon as a man gets into a mood, he has no capacity for relationship, no power to feel, and therefore no capacity for valuation.
>
> (Johnson, 1991: 38)

The dead boyfriend wrote: 'it just *felt* like the right thing to do'. His referring in the past tense to an idea that at the time of writing was current and concerned an act he had yet to perform amounts to striking a pose. Despite his use of 'felt', he was clearly, in Johnson's terminology, locked into a mood. It implies that he saw himself post mortem still controlling Morvern's perceptions, an impossible inflation! Now that he has opted out of her life she must proceed without him. It falls to her to defy the dictate of the orphan complex and move both the novel and her own life forward.

When we first saw her, blackness swallowed Morvern each time the Christmas tree lights pulsed off. When she went out to call help, the dark night's chill engulfed her; and, joining Lanna for the party, she wore black. Edinger described *mortificatio* as the most negative operation in the alchemical process, but one from which the psyche can rebound into new growth. The symbolic encounter with death and *putrefactio* therefore have great weight in the individuation process.

> [They have] to do with darkness, defeat, torture, mutilation, death and rotting. However, these dark images often lead over to highly positive ones – growth, resurrection, rebirth – but the hallmark of *mortificatio* is the color black.
>
> (Edinger, 1985: 148)

As we saw, shock froze Morvern's responses after she found her boyfriend's body. She could not, in her trauma, understand and absorb into consciousness the shadow side of what confronted her. But now, with the corpse decaying and tainting the air in her flat, Morvern cannot escape *putrefactio* and *mortificatio* in a form no less grisly than the emblems picturing them in alchemical texts (see Edinger, 1985: 147–80).

Energised by the sign she took from Couris Jean, rather than continuing to deny the horrific consequences of her lover's death, Morvern deals with them. She strips to her knickers, straps the Walkman to her waist and gulps whiskey. Not lacking rebarbative irony, she chooses The Velvet Underground's ditty 'I'm sticking with you' and sets about the bloody business of cutting up her man's body. Edinger shows that the dismemberment of which Jung spoke belongs to the symbolic cluster that expresses *separatio*, an operation intended to separate out the confused mixture of undifferentiated and confused components in the *prima materia*. A number of methods, including evaporation, filtration, sedimentation and the severing of part from part were available to the alchemist (1985: 183–9). The last of these could be expressed in visual emblems of death-dealing swords, knives and sharp cutting edges of all kinds. Their action was held to symbolise Logos, 'the great agent of *separatio* that brings consciousness and power over nature – both within and without – by its capacity to divide, name and categorize' (1985: 191). Psychologically, 'the elemental *separatio* that ushers in conscious existence is the separation of subject from object, the I from the not-I. This is the first pair of opposites' (1985: 187). If, as the opening images of Morvern caressing her boyfriend's body suggest, she had been linked to him symbiotically in *participation mystique*, then he, by cutting his wrist, brought about his severance both from her and what the relationship symbolised to him. Now, in dismembering his body, she enacts her severance from him, psychologically as well as physically, in a second, opposing death. It signals Morvern's progress in the mourning process as she begins to die away from her old life and adhere to new forms. The goal of *separatio* is to reach the indivisible, that is, the individual within her (see Edinger, 1985: 203). Success in this journey will be assured only by her continual reconciliation of the opposites that live within her and her own willingness to die a little in order to grow into a bigger life.

Later, the gory work done, she struggles up the braes bearing a massive rucksack to gain a lonely high point with views to the surrounding mountains. She gives him an unconventional funeral, but it does not lack the honour and solemnity due in final leave taking. Her face puffy with grief, she spins a private ritual dance, divines the proper place and labours at opening the turf with a hand trowel (the largest tool she could have carried secretly). The body disposed of, she gallops down the hill, free of a great burden, then halts in a spinney to stroke the early buds and wonder at worms and wood lice. As they stir in peaty water, she cannot miss that these creatures are cousins of the insects that will soon go to work on the corpse. Edinger cites Paracelsus appositely.

> Putrefaction is of so great efficacy that it blots out the old nature and transmutes everything into another new nature, and bears another new fruit. All living things die in it, all dead things decay, and then all these dead things regain life.
> *(Paracelsus, 1967: 1: 153)*

The whirling motions of her funeral dance imply that psychic movement is underway, promoting the necessary ego development to solidify her new personality. In the language of alchemy, *coagulatio* is commencing, the process which, allegorically translated, means that a content of the psyche 'has been concretized in a particular localized form; that is, *it has become attached to an ego*' (Edinger, 1985: 83 – original emphasis). The cycle of life and death moves Morvern forward in ways that Greg Mogenson, arguing that mourning is an intensely active, creative process, would endorse (1992: xi).

Lanna moves into Morvern's flat eager to explore the stuff Morvern's man has left and to look into his computer. Both girls are high, but Morvern refuses access to anything except his music and chooses 'You Can Fall' by Broadcast. Its overtones of electronically processed and off-kilter gamelan chimes make it 'weird' to Lanna's ears while its strangeness delights the bereaved girl. They decide to bake and joyfully shower each other and the kitchen with flour: for Morvern, this wildness cleanses the room that his suicide defiled, easing terrible memories. Her regression toward childish pleasure-seeking confirms that she needs to find *coagulatio* in a balanced relationship to desire (neither anaemic nor excessive) to integrate her autonomous spirit with the heavy reality of her boyfriend's suicide (Edinger, 1985: 90–1). This conflict will continue to play out.

Morvern's reprieve is brief because that night, occupying the empty side of the bed where he had lain, Lanna can no longer keep it secret that she had been his lover. Her confession is a blow that Morvern feels painfully, deepening the earlier reference to Phaedra's betrayal; nevertheless she does not spurn her repentant friend. The unwelcome knowledge cannot rip out her heart as it would if he had still been alive, such has been her progress in the grieving and separation process.

Morvern lets nothing get in the way of her holiday – not the betrayal nor a letter from publishers inviting her to visit them in London and discuss 'her' typescript. Nor does it deter her that that from the moment of touchdown in Spain, Lanna is on a chemical high. In the taxi to their hotel Morvern lovingly cradles her crashed-out friend who misses the brilliant sunshine, strange sights and sounds in which Morvern revels. But once again her freedom proves fleeting.

The two friends find themselves in a multi-storey tower with hundreds of young British holidaymakers. The coastal resort is set up to gratify every sensual desire of the visitors while isolating them from the country and its people. At first the two young women enjoy everything together – the bars, the beach, teasing and flirting with the boys. But Morvern draws back, and sometimes sits alone on her balcony while her peers riot drunkenly through the hotel. Her discomfort grows when tour guides organise games where, to titillate the onlookers, a guy and a girl have to get into a voluminous bag and exchange swimsuits – the girl inevitably being left with bare breasts. Lanna, eager for sexual adventure and careless of humiliation, takes part and is soon deliriously topless in boxer shorts beside a sheepish fellow, his manhood strangled by her bikini. Later two guys invade the women's toilets to pull Lanna and Morvern, indifferent to the fate of another girl having a dangerous trip. One web commentator wrote that '*Morvern Callar* is an intense but quiet reflection on the consequences and morality of carelessness' (Factory Girl, 2002). The scenes in the resort show this not only in relationships within Morvern's intimate circle but also between young Britons at large.

That night Morvern, weary of booze, pills and techno racket, quits a nightclub and returns alone to her room. She clears her head and sits on the balcony, out of the scene. At Christmas, only when trauma took hold of her had she briefly dropped out of her friends' party. But now the relentless, organised hedonism of the holiday resort repels her – the way it hurls people into a seething crowd of sensation seekers yet isolates them. Few vestiges of feelings (let alone grieving) survive in an atmosphere calculated to wreck caring or meaningful connections between individuals.

Morvern's reaction to the mindless craving that surrounds her provides further evidence that *coagulatio* is in effect: she uses restraint while discovering a psychic secret: in order to grow one must be decent and good to oneself (Estes, 1990). Edinger writes that 'the alchemical operation of *coagulatio*, together with the imagery that clusters around this idea, constitutes an elaborate symbol system that expresses the archetypal process of ego formation' (1985: 115). Adopting his insights on Morvern's behalf, we can now anticipate that 'When the ego's relation to the Self is being realized – that is, when the ego is approaching the *coagulatio* of the psyche in its totality – then the symbolism of ego development becomes identical with that of individuation' (Ibid.).

If further evidence were needed that *Morvern Callar* foregrounds the inner life of its heroine, it arrives at this glum hour. As she gazes around disconsolately, a beetle catches her attention crossing the floor and going under the door into the corridor. Sprung out of her emotional blockage, Morvern acts on impulse and follows it. No sooner in the corridor, than her door slams, locking her out. As in legend, she has reacted to the summons of a mysterious messenger who leads her across a threshold from one world to another. And as in the frame of analytical psychology, the beetle acts as a psychopomp, an image in the fantasy that arrives synchronously at the very moment it is needed and leads her psyche from one stuck complex to a new state of mind.[2] And so it proves when Morvern follows the insect until, outside another closed door, she hears a guy (Raife Patrick Burchell) crying out. She knocks to check whether he is all right, but he has just heard that his mother has died. He asks her to stay and talk to him and she, touched by this unexpected contact that allows her for the first time to reveal her own feelings, softly offers (since she cannot speak about her late boyfriend's interment) to describe her foster mother's funeral. We cut hard through the night hours to Morvern and this lad making love. Theirs is not the Ecstasy-fuelled, pleasure-seeking shag that meets the needs of Lanna and the Cat in the Hat (Paul Popplewell) who did indeed pull her in the toilets. But Morvern and the boy explore a spectrum of passions together. They taste freedom and joy in release from their grieving isolation, yet their flirtation and Morvern's gleeful seduction of him do not override their care of each other. The boy's tears return and she sees that he must hold back for a while to let grief out. When later they do couple, ecstatic wildness leads to tenderness (see Carotenuto, 1989: 71). Then they lie together in perfect silence until he has to leave for the airport. Morvern gazes and gazes, feasting in wonder and sadness on his eyes, imprinting the memory of his face and of their intimate connection. And although this is exactly what an infant does, the image of a mature woman whose psychological rebirth we now witness can only be incarnated through a loving relationship. She will carry with her this silent secret – for once her mind running deeper even than music to the crystalline, sacred reaffirmation of her life.

In the intimate encounter with this young man she senses his vulnerability. Trust floods in as she surrenders her own defences and by giving and receiving love experiences herself as body and soul. The orphaned Morvern is now actively engaged with the Archetypal Mother and, giving all of herself to this blissful encounter, she participates in the necessary corrective experience the orphan desperately needs. Integrating the split in her psyche between dependency and independency, she is healing her maternal wound and thereby feeding her psyche. Having opened to this new psychological perspective, Morvern can truly embrace the feminine principle of relatedness and perhaps begin to connect to the transpersonal dimension of the psyche. Our perception of the couple's lovemaking, its shifts of mood and rhythm, is given joyful confidence by the constant beat of Lee (Scratch) Perry's appropriately named reggae 'Hold of Death'. The fact that this track is non-diegetic does not negate Ramsay's practice in earlier scenes but, in a familiar manner, lets the music play on us – its confidence reassuring us that Morvern has, so to speak, got into her stride.

According to Paul Ashton, participants in experiments about emotional arousal by music become moved to much the same degree and at the same times. Under experimental conditions where music is the only stimulus, what they actually feel differs from person to person (2010: 133–4). However, in a feature film such as *Morvern Callar*, audience members' emotional responses will be formed by the *entire* narrative setting – music plus visual imagery, plot and character development. We already have remarked that music hooks Morvern in a way language cannot. She neither plays an instrument nor sings; she has no analytical knowledge of musical forms. But none of that matters one jot. What does matter is that certain functions of music bear directly on the emotions that she feels, as we do with her. Oliver Sacks writes,

> Music, uniquely among the arts, is both completely abstract and profoundly emotional. It has no power to represent anything particular or external, but it has a unique power to express inner states or feelings... Music makes one experience pain and grief more intensely, [but] it brings solace and consolation at the same time.
>
> *(Sacks, 2007: 138)*

Lawrence Wetzler could have had in mind Morvern (unable to speak of her own abandonment trauma) when he argues that music has power to recover us from that exile to which the symbolic order (frequently, language) banishes us, namely the exile from ourselves (2010: 148–9). As Michel Hazanavicius has remarked, 'There are times when language reduces communication, when you feel you are losing something when you start talking' (in Turan, 2011). For Wetzler, music can restore the lack and invite us into a place beyond words: 'An attempt to reach for and encounter the real, music can be heard as a questing, an exploring, an infinite longing' (2010: 155).

Emma Jung asserted that there is a sense in which music is spirit.

> For music can be understood as an objectification of the spirit; it does not express knowledge in the usual logical intellectual sense, nor does it shape matter; instead it gives sensuous representation to our deepest associations and most immutable laws. In this sense music is spirit, spirit leading into obscure distances beyond the reach of consciousness; its content can hardly be grasped with words – but strange to say, more easily with numbers – although simultaneously, and before all else, with feeling and sensation. Apparently paradoxical facts like these show that music admits us to the depths where spirit and nature are still one – or have again become one.
>
> *(1957: 36)*

The music therapist Helen Anderson uses Emma Jung's words as a springboard to account for the way in which one of her own analysands was helped in the individuation process. Anderson's client experienced a powerful emotional reaction to Beethoven's Piano Sonata No. 31 and brought these experiences into therapy sessions where they helped her draw previously hidden material into consciousness (Anderson, 2010: 45–66).

For her part, Morvern goes it alone, seemingly with no thought of seeking help. She reveals the independent side of the orphan and simply follows her highly developed intuitive side with vigour. Her feelings grow and transform, urged by music and the events that befall her. As her psyche expands under their combined influence a genuine vitality unfolds from within. For Patricia Skar, active engagement of this kind is the key. She notes that in music just as in analysis active engagement creates the ground for the emergent properties of meaning, spirit and soul to appear. Whether played or listened to, the music that is right for individuals at a given time in their life can provide a pathway that leads to the self's coherence – and may even furnish them with a link to the infinite (2010: 90).

Music can be destructive as well as constructive. In the public realm, for example, the Nazis used it programmatically to cajole people to hatred, as Michael Eigen notes (2010a: 164). He recognises too that destruction is an inescapable part of music's contribution to spiritual and psychological rebirth in the personal sphere (2010a: 170).

> 'I die, I die' is a common saying when one is under the sway of deep feeling, erotic or sheer poetic musical beauty. One feels one will go under, under the impact of unbearable beauty…
>
> It is… true that music can function as a toxin. But it is also true that its power or beauty can destroy your usual way of organizing experience,

destroy your own cliché, or habitual style, a radical revision of the psyche just by hearing a few notes.

(Eigen, 2010a: 165–6)

Eigen reports his own experience as a young man hearing Bartok for the first time:

My approach to sensitivity underwent radical reworking in an instant. What I was moments before no longer existed, except perhaps as a dull shell that would haunt me like a ghost, skin that can't ever quite be shed but that was already dead, gone.

(Eigen, 2010a: 166)

This too touches on the kind of transition that Morvern experiences as music draws her into soundscapes with which she actively engages: they reshape her psyche, her state of being. So it is to the combination of actions and music that we should look in accounting for her individuation.

Her night as the bereaved boy's lover changes Morvern forever. She has found a deep validation of self with someone whose vulnerability she shared – a reparative experience that supercharged her. Trusting intuition, she now flows with the waves of emotion that formerly pulled her hither and yon when mourning, but now embody for her a vital, life-giving affirmation.

At the start we noted Edinger's statement that the alchemists' Opus culminated in *coniunctio* or union of the opposites. It so happens that sexual intercourse between man and woman (Sol and Luna) is a traditional and recurrent emblem of *coniunctio*. Love is fundamental to its phenomenology, being both its cause and effect. Its inward turning aspect promotes nothing less than connection with the Self and the unity of the individual psyche (Edinger, 1985: 223). We find further evidence of Morvern's achieving this state of being as the film ends. Meanwhile action declares her new confidence. Returning to the room she shares with Lanna, Morvern's fingers dance against the wall like an insect preparing for flight. She barges in and announces to an astonished Lanna (who is in bed enjoying a post-coital Ecstasy pill with the Cat in the Hat) that they are leaving. Before her friend knows what is happening, Morvern has pulled her half-naked into a taxi and away.

The cheerfully manic driver (El Carrette) whirls them through avenues of palms and up into desert mountains. His in-car system blasts out pulsating gipsy dance music by the Romanian group Taraf de Haïdouks. Its strangeness, frenzied beat and irrepressible exhilaration soon boost the girls into uninhibited enjoyment of the adventure. So when their driver stops at a high viewing point and asks where they are headed, Morvern surveys all that lies before her and borrows Couris Jean's gesture to point upward into the mountains. They come then into the narrow lanes of a hilltop village, suddenly jammed by the entire population. Realising it is a parade, the girls clamber out of the car. Morvern, aroused by the elemental nature of the event, finds a vantage point to watch as men run a bull through the streets leading the ritual parade of holy icons. But Lanna, still tripping, treats the event as a rave, offending local people with her lack of respect for the sacred images.

Come late afternoon, with the festivities and her head trip over, the dejected Lanna (her suitcase lost) wants to return to the resort. But Morvern, dragging her own bag and amazed by the evening beauty of the place, leads her out of the village and along a cactus-lined track, ignoring her friend's protestations. Night overtakes them and Lanna's grumbling escalates. She accuses Morvern of hating her because she once – only once, she insists – fucked her boyfriend. To silence the tirade Morvern admits that he is dead, but Lanna treats this as another weird fantasy. She does not understand a pal who has paid for two weeks of wild partying and walks away from it to get lost in the desert: 'What planet are you on?' she asks and stomps away down the road. They spend the night apart – the turning point in their relationship.

The moonlight frightens Lanna, but delights Morvern. The moon (one side always invisible from Earth) is an emblem for human beings unconscious of their dark side. Lanna has no interest in looking into her own shadow or ever changing. But for alchemists, the task was to navigate this uncharted territory of the soul and bring it, so far as possible, to light. The adept could emerge from the far side of the psyche initiated into self-knowledge, or become irretrievably lost in darkness. Morvern has taken the shadow on and developed a relationship with it which has urged her forward into the light of consciousness. Since her night with the bereaved lad, she has taken on some of the characteristics of the moon goddess. Although not sexually a virgin, her swiftly evolving mindset associates her with the type. Bolen writes, 'In moonlight, a person in touch with Artemis becomes an unselfconscious part of nature, in it and one-with-it for a time' (1985: 52). And, 'The archetype she represents enables a woman to seek her own goals on terrain of her own choosing' (Ibid.: 49). By the film's end, Morvern's kinship with nature, her determination to make a new life for herself, and her sisterly feelings for Lanna (another mark of Artemis) are all recognised.

Next morning, Morvern gathers the few things she needs, leaves the sleeping Lanna and strides forward with 'Spoon' on the Walkman giving her confidence. A local family take her into their car and the mother strives to make conversation across the language barrier. She notices Morvern's Jackie necklace and compliments her on having the name of a popular Spanish singer's daughter. The family start on the singer's hit and Morvern joins them quietly, humming her own contentment. For the first time she is making her own song, drifting into bliss.

In a small coastal town she takes a bright and airy room with a window open to the beach, buys a vivid summer dress and prepares to meet her publishers. Tom Boddington (James Wilson) and Vanessa (Linda McGuire) are barely able to conceal beneath sophisticated chat their avidity to sign this fresh talent. The expectation of profit and cultural kudos lamps their eyes, but the conversation with Morvern is deliciously surreal. They ask her to talk about herself, hoping she will give them material for publicity. Out of her depth, Morvern relates the things she recalls envying in her boyfriend's writing day – time to take a coffee, look out the window or have a shower. The Londoners misread Morvern's gloss as an obvious spoof. They treat her words as the smartass backchat of writers hiding their insecurities.

During the afternoon the editors offer Morvern what they describe as a fair deal for an unknown writer's first novel – a hundred. When she realises this is shorthand for a hundred thousand pounds she leaves the table briefly to hide her shock – then promptly accepts the deal. By the time a couple of bottles of Cava have eased day into night, Tom and Vanessa ask about her next book, but Morvern (her contract secured) now has the measure of their games. She hesitates before admitting that she works in a supermarket. The others laugh, certain she is telling them the identity of her next heroine. Morvern gazes at them drunkenly, holding her face in a ruthless mask which she suddenly switches to register wry conspiracy: she knows how things stand, plain and clear, and now has another pressing use for them.

At dawn, before the townspeople stir and at the end of the trio's all-night party, she leads Vanessa and Tom to a secret enclosure, hushing their exuberant chatter and drawing them into a cemetery. There, as is the Spanish custom, the dead are buried within flower-decked wall niches. The filmmakers make this a moment of cinematic magic. While birds sing in the blossoming light, Morvern contemplates a well-tended niche and lifts a scarlet chrysanthemum from its vase. The camera leaves her and tracks along the wall of graves until, violating normal spatio-temporal conventions, it picks her up at the end of its movement where she is organising a less tidy niche. She adorns it with the neighbour's flower to honour the forgotten person in the grave. Meanwhile her publishers watch their strange new author play an inexplicable game, unaware that Morvern has led them on a pilgrimage of her own devising. Here in utter tranquillity, accompanied by witnesses whom she requires to see what only she can understand, she makes peace symbolically with the man who stole his life from her. By stealing his novel she has created a new life for herself. Moving now into the last stage of her grieving process, acceptance has led Morvern safely away from the plight of orphans – that of living incompletely.

As ever, Morvern shows innate wisdom in trusting her feelings wherever they lead her. Contentedly alone once again, she phones to check that Lanna has found her way back to the resort (to her amusement, her irrepressible friend has gone to Aqualand). Then she suns herself in a parched field near the coast where goats nose around her for grass and an ant treks to and fro across her dusty hand, the Artemis whose contact with elemental life delights her.

The sunlit image fades to black and reopens on a dank night. Another transformation: Morvern has returned to Scotland with an empty suitcase to collect her man's CDs and the publisher's cheque – nothing else. She comes back looking stylish as any young Spanish woman, embodying the feminine through her increase in self worth. Her oiled hair is woven into a pigtail; she has replaced her heavy black leather jacket with a fashionable olive one cut for style rather than warmth. In casting off the jacket that had been her man's present to her, she makes the point that she can generate her own warmth. She will feel no chill because she will not tarry in her old home. Like the moon goddess, she knows her true nature and in the light of that deity she is instigating her own new odyssey.

Having found the things she came for she leaves, drops her keys through the letterbox and goes to the pub. As she comes through the door, she looks at the familiar scene, the inevitable sadness of the self-exiled individual marking her face. She steels herself and ignores her foster father from whom she accepts a drink with only mumbled thanks. Her mission is with Lanna alone, but her friend is full of chatter about guys she met in the resort who still want to see her. So when Morvern invites her to move back to Spain, Lanna refuses because everyone she knows lives around her. 'Nothing wrong with here, Morvern – it's just the same crap as everywhere. Stop dreaming!' Lanna has no desire to risk change and perhaps fears the unknown. She lives unconsciously and has no understanding that big dreams may bring the light back in. 'They are experiences of grace, of a heavenly containment. They lift our spirits because they come from beyond the ego, from something far greater that opens us to a deeper level of the psyche' (Rothenberg, 2001: 193).

The two girls cleave to distinct attitudes that will shape them for life. As a foster child, not born a Scot, Morvern lacks the deep roots that tie Lanna to the place, its community and culture. Those roots that she did put down have been cut by the deaths of her foster mother and her boyfriend. Perhaps it was one of his attractions that he was a nomad in his head just as she is a traveller now. Although the want of deep roots had caused her emotional suffering, Morvern has now connected to her true companion, the Self. That achievement will sustain her relationship to her inner world. On her journey, to reiterate, she has reached the *coniunctio*, the culmination of the *Opus* produced by combining the opposites and rectifying her one-sidedness, which has led to conscious understanding. As Edinger says, the experience of bitterness, properly understood, brings wisdom (1985: 214).

The final scene bears careful attention, set as it is in a nightclub crammed with dancers and lit by momentary flashes of light (a piquant variation of the lighting set-up in the opening scene). Morvern at first sight seems to have gone back to the very life which she had left behind. Is she truly once again trying to numb herself with Ecstasy, techno music and sex? Not at all, for now she is plugged into her Walkman rather than the club's speaker system. Wearing the Jackie necklace, she drifts through the dancers as if in slow-motion, living through her new self, alert, serene, curious and searching. It is not the nightclub's techno but The Mamas and The Papas' 'Dedicated to the One I Love' – a gentle ballad for an absent love – that fills her head.

Michael Eigen makes an observation about the mind's limitations that pinpoints Morvern's state on discovering her boyfriend's suicide – her inability to report the death and resorting to cutting up his body before disposing of it herself. 'The psyche lacks the equipment to bear what it produces' (2010b: 262). However, he argues, music is one creative means of trying to process the deep emotional material that the psyche produces and ensure that it does not overwhelm (2010a: 173–4). Meanwhile dance, a comparable means of processing emotional experience, 'creates experience and catalyzes body processing of it at the same time. One might say dance is part of music or music grows out of dance or is dance' (2010a: 174).

Some of Eigen's insights come from his experience as a former jazz musician. It ensures that he understands the emotional potency of surprise, a factor that students of classical music do not always value.

> The music of the psyche, the rhythm of the psyche, can be a rhythm of surprise, a rhythm that plays against and breaks rhythm – that opens new rhythmic possibilities.
>
> *(Eigen, 2010a: 167)*

Thus rhythm is not necessarily a homeostatic thing – not necessarily restricted to reinforcing the static internal state of the individual: 'There are rhythms that destroy homeostasis, break new experiential grounds' (Ibid.). Referring to jazz drumming (but his words describe Morvern's constantly surprising choice of music) Eigen adds, 'Something keeps varying in thrilling ways, sometimes tone or emphasis or texture, but often sequence and pulse...' (Ibid.).

> My sense now is that this is what psychic processing is like, ...an ever-changing rhythm, the depths and scope of which we scarcely can imagine. It is part of emotional life that we can express or narrate or convey only a bit of what we feel. We do not know the whole of it. There is always some frustration built in. It is like swimming in the ocean. We can never take in the whole ocean all at once. But we do swim in part of it, and the water we swim in, while not the whole ocean, is real water.
>
> *(Eigen, 2010a: 168)*

And there, swimming in just such an ocean of music where cross rhythms from two entirely distinct musical forms destroy homeostasis, we take leave of Morvern. She glides too through an ocean of people, alone but safe in the mêlée of dancers. The extraverted aspect of individuation is transpersonal love that we see Morvern has discovered, which lies at the root of all group and social loyalties such as allegiance to humanity itself (Edinger, 1985: 223). Now at peace, dedicating herself to herself, she gazes around, searching Artemis-like, dreaming in the uncharted territory of the moon's as yet dark side for a new goal, perhaps having in mind her future with a lover yet to be found. In the final flash of light on the dance floor, she withdraws from the frame, like the offspring of Kubrick's Star Child, reborn into her new universe.

Notes

1 Although the title page of the boyfriend's typescript has a name on it, we follow the characters' example in not using his name.
2 C. G. Jung described as a rebirth symbol the arrival of a scarab beetle at his consulting room window while he was treating a patient (1952: §843–5).

11

APPROACHING *THE TREE OF LIFE*

By necessity, stories impose more order into a telling than there is in real life. That's why we tell and listen to them in the first place. Filmmakers can, and most do, choose to feed audiences weaned on mainstream storytelling with obvious plot points linked by the script in a familiar cause and effect chain that ensures narrative thrust is undisturbed. But so doing, they risk discouraging spectators from looking beyond the plot arc and lead them to expect that the obvious entry level pleasures will satiate their appetite. All plot conundrums solved, a resolution to that motivating desire to know basic answers to basic questions attained, filmgoers interested exclusively in entertainment may indeed look no further – and many fine films deliver manifold pleasures in just that way. However, this dominant conventional pattern breeds audience dependency on easily recognised generic markers to show the way through a movie. When the story is difficult to make out, it causes some spectators unease. As Jana Branch says, *The Tree of Life* does not *blatantly* work to seduce the audience (hoping for their love) so much as open a sensual door inviting their experience (2013). However, having opened (like the adult Jack) that surreal door into the unknown, Malick invites spectators to abandon resistance and succumb to the brilliant light that exposes memory's dark places to view.

Some people did leave each of the cinema screenings of *The Tree of Life* that we attended. That said, even sardonic reviewers (like J. Hoberman (2011) deriding Malick and his admirers' seriousness) did not miss that this is a film of high purpose. Rather than give priority to a narrative arc centred on character development, it tempts audiences to revel in spellbinding images and sumptuous music. Gilbey writes of its commonest currency being images that drift free of narrative context and montages that convey mood alone, as when the three O'Brien brothers race round the house in elation knowing that their father is away on business (2011).

The film's register seeks to govern the responses of audiences such that, in succumbing to sensual suffusion, they cannot focus on steadily taking hold of obliquely indicated plot points. Jana Branch remarks, 'It's a body film before it's a head film' (2011), and her observation implies a broader context for the present authors' excitement, which can be found in Vivian Sobchack's theorising about embodiment as,

> a radically material condition of human being that necessarily entails both the body and consciousness, objectivity and subjectivity, in an *irreducible ensemble*. Thus we matter and we mean through processes and logics of sense-making that owe as much to our carnal existence as they do to our conscious thought.
>
> *(Sobchack, 2004: 4)*

> In sum, the film experience is meaningful *not to the side of our bodies but because of our bodies*. Which is to say that movies provoke in us the 'carnal thoughts' that ground and inform more conscious analysis.
>
> *(Sobchack, 2004: 60)*

In considering embodied experience, Jennifer M. Barker describes the nature of tactility and emphasises the reciprocal intimacy between touching and touched. In effect she endorses Roland Barthes's celebration, 'The pleasure of the text is that moment when my body pursues its own ideas – for my body does not have the same ideas I do' (Barthes, 1973).

> Tactility is a mode of perception and expression wherein all parts of the body commit themselves to, or are drawn into, a relationship with the world that is at once a mutual and intimate relation of contact.
>
> *(Barker, 2009: 3)*

> ...Cinematic tactility, then, is a general attitude toward the cinema that the human body enacts in particular ways: haptically, at the tender surface of the body; kinaesthetically and muscularly, in the middle dimension of muscles, tendons, and bones that reach toward and through cinematic space; and viscerally, in the murky recesses of the body, where heart, lungs, pulsing fluids, and firing synapses receive, respond to, and reenact the rhythms of cinema. The film's body also adopts toward the world a tactile attitude of intimacy and reciprocity that is played out across its nonhuman body... kinaesthetically, through the contours of on- and off-screen space and of the bodies, both human and mechanical, that inhabit or escape those spaces....
>
> *(Ibid.)*

Awareness of this kind permits a radical development in the way cinema can be understood.

> ... what keeps us separate from the film isn't a 'thing' at all, but our bodies' own surfaces and contours... the material contact between viewer and

viewed is less a hard edge or a solid barrier placed between us – a mirror, a door – than a liminal space in which film and viewer can emerge as co-constituted, individualized but related, embodied entities.

Watching a film, we are certainly not *in* the film, but we are not entirely *outside* it, either. We exist and move and feel in that space of contact where our surfaces mingle and our musculatures entangle... This sense of fleshy, muscular, visceral contact seriously undermines the rigidity of the opposition between viewer and film, inviting us to think of them as intimately related but not identical, caught up in a relationship of intersubjectivity and co-constitution, rather than as subject and object positioned on opposite sides of the screen.

(Barker, 2009: 12–13)

As Raymond Bellour expresses it, each change of shot, each movement in the camera is a mini-shock and the body and nervous system of every spectator adapt to the rhythm, affecting his or her bodily sense of time (2012). We would add, developing an implication of Barker's work, that such mini-shocks must affect the experience of emotion. She borrows Jennifer Deger's phrase the 'transformative space of betweenness' (2007: 89) to characterise the experience of contact between image, imaged, and viewer. This transformative space has significance for our understanding of emotions. Barker argues that meaning and emotion do not reside in either films or viewers, but emerge in the intimate, tactile encounter between them. They 'are not pre-existing emotions brought into *contact*; rather, they are brought into *being* and given shape by the contact itself' (2009: 15–16).

Love isn't something a lover 'has' for a loved one; but something that emerges in the encounter between lover and loved, just as 'fear' isn't 'in' someone fearful, but emerges in the contact between two entities, in which they take up a certain temporal and physical orientation toward one another.

(Ibid.)

Thus for Barker emotions are not simply something that one has. Rather, she agrees with Ahmed, it is through emotions, or how one responds to objects and others that surfaces and boundaries are made. 'The "I" and the "we" are shaped by, and even take the shape of, contact with others' (Ahmed, 2004: 4). These two writers stress that consciousness is always consciousness of something: one must attend not only to the object itself but also to the conscious act through which it is perceived, and do both together, with the understanding that they cannot exist separately (Barker, 2009: 17). In this way existential phenomenology recognises 'the role of subjective experience in co-constituting objects in the world' (Ahmed, 2004: 5).

Barker's model appreciates the interactive, theatrical attributes of cinema in a way that invites us to extend her hypothesis and make room for the unconscious.

She develops some of the concepts that we mooted in Chapter 1, in order to relate embodiment to the impact on audiences of cinema screenings.

> The film experience is conducive to this kind of mutual absorption, perhaps even more so than the experience of a painting or landscape, because of the circumstances that surround it (and surround us): the darkness of the theater enshrouds us; the screen stretches bigger than life before our eyes and bathes us in light; and carefully placed speakers throw voices, music, and ambient sound around our shoulders… We take in the film's vitality and the style of its experience of the world, and we adopt and express those things back to it. We in-spire in both directions at once… We *cause* the film to erupt in sound and music in a given moment in the same way that we inspire a close-up with our desire for a closer look or provoke an action film's aggressive tracking shot with our desire to catch up to the fleeing villain.
>
> *(Barker, 2009: 147–8)*

Barker recalls Mikel Dufrenne's point, that 'aesthetic objects… call for a certain attitude and use on the part of the body – witness… the cathedral that regulates the step and gait, the painting that guides the eye, that poem that disciplines the voice' (Dufrenne, 1973: 461). 'The artwork's ways of being in the world resonate meaningfully with its beholder's ways of moving, looking, listening, and speaking' (Barker, 2009: 11). We do not need to imagine cathedrals to recognise this effect. The architecture of houses and offices shapes the movements of those who live in them – and hence impact on family life. As we shall see, one of Malick's characters, Jack, becomes a successful architect and property developer: his work contributes to shaping people's embodied lives. In his buildings, people walk, talk and dress in certain uniform ways. His architecture also reveals him as his father's son. Just as his father instructed him, he has sought and found power. While he is not his own boss, he has as much power as massively capitalised corporations grant their creative people – and as much power as his father complex can possibly grant him. His buildings express it, puritanical in design like his beautiful but barren house, diamond precise like his searing office towers. But *The Tree of Life* sets off the razor-edged prism of his cityscapes against the centre-ground churn of cosmic space and time. Do Jack's towers mock or yearn for the heavens they reach up to?

Barker's account of the embodied cinema experience is not of itself enough to account for the sensation of breathless exultation that seized Izod, although it is undoubtedly helpful. Happily it complements Ira Konigsberg's explanation, itself an expansion of what we wrote in Chapter 1. Konigsberg explains the process of emotional investment as involving fantasy and the experience of energies the source of which is not always registered in complete consciousness by viewers or filmmakers.

> In the silent, darkened theater, removed from a direct confrontation with reality, and perceiving images that seem half-real and transitional we slip into

a state of half-wakefulness, into a reverie that weakens our defenses and sets loose our own fantasies and wishes to interact and fuse with the characters and even the landscape that we see on the screen. I do not have to describe for you the way in which we loosen hold of ourselves at times and become fastened to what we see on the screen, but not completely fastened – a merging takes place, a sense of the characters as me and not-me, as part of my subjective world and part of objective reality. What actually transpires is a process of introjection followed by projection, a process by which we… take in the images and then project ourselves into them as they appear before us – a process of introjection and projective identification…

In the dynamics I am describing, the introjection of the film images triggers an internal process by which we invest these images with our own psychic and emotional overlays and then project them back out, along with our own involvement, onto their imprints on the screen – a process that continues, back and forth, as we watch the film. I need only remind you of the sudden jolt we feel, of our sense of loneliness and incompleteness as we are forced to pull back into ourselves, as our ties with the images on the screen are suddenly severed when the film ends.

(Konigsberg, 1996: 885–6)

Although Konigsberg's project was the development of post-Freudian and Lacanian theoretical perspectives on film, his observations harmonise sweetly with the Jungian recognition that the spectating subject makes an emotional investment in the film (Izod, 2006: 17). We may now take Barker and Konigsberg together, adding Jung's reminder that, while we think we possess emotions, our emotions control us. In short, our unconscious complexes and the operation of archetypal images will complement the conscious experience of the cinema.

We believe – and mean our work to demonstrate the conviction – that any attempt at film analysis will negate Jungian principles and produce no better than a mechanical account if it fails to weave the affect experienced by its writers into their reading. That said, as authors we must not fail to respect the film's text by allowing our own thoughts and passions to rewrite it. Our stance certainly does not require us to present ourselves as figures of interest to our readers. Thus, like most academic post-Jungians, the two of us have tried to make contact with our readers through the vigour of our observations and the feeling-toned strength of our depth analysis, while remaining committed to what Jung calls the instinct for self-reflection. Furthermore, with one of us extravert and the other introvert, the former a feeling type, the latter a thinking type, the give and take in our union of opposites creates the necessary tension to give the film its psychological body.

Relating reflection to activity, Jung wrote,

There is another instinct, different from the drive to activity and so far as we know specifically human, which might be called the *reflective instinct*. Ordinarily we do not think of 'reflection' as ever having been instinctive, but associate it with a conscious state of mind. *Reflexio* means 'bending back' and, used psychologically, would denote the fact that the reflex which carries the stimulus over into its instinctive discharge is interfered with by psychization. Owing to this interference, the psychic processes exert an attraction on the impulse to act excited by the stimulus. Therefore, before having discharged itself into the external world, the impulse is deflected into an endopsychic activity. *Reflexio*, is a turning inwards, with the result that, instead of an instinctive action, there ensues a succession of derivative contents or states which may be termed reflection or deliberation. Thus in place of the compulsive act there appears a certain degree of freedom, and in place of predictability a relative unpredictability as to the effect of the impulse.

(1937: §241)

Through the reflective instinct, the stimulus is more or less wholly transformed into a psychic content, that is, it becomes an experience: a natural process is transformed into a conscious content.

(1937: §243)

As Jungian writing partners, we are committed to the hard inner work necessary to break the aforementioned stimulus-response link. As we send our developing drafts back and forth between Scotland and California we create the opportunity to see the film as consciously as possible in the intervals that arise. By reflecting on the film throughout this extended process we mean to have transformed it into a psychological experience for both our readers and ourselves.

The Tree of Life, however, has exerted such pressure on engaged restraint that it seems (in the spirit of the film) time to break with self-discipline and speak frankly about our experience. Izod was overwhelmed by his first viewing and subsequent screenings, far from diminishing, intensified the response. For him, *The Tree of Life* gloriously demonstrates Walter Pater's dictum that all art constantly aspires to the condition of music. To experience the film in its entirety is like listening to music so powerful that the vortex of conflicting emotions aroused assails the conscious mind with such force that joy and terror contend for dominance. In early viewings, none of the passions comprising this *coniunctio oppositorum* gained ascendancy over the other. However, the beauty of the film provides the aesthetics of transformation in Perez's sense of beauty as an agent that sways and moves us with a manifold capacity for persuasion (see Chapter 9).

Dovalis felt stunned by her first viewing, held in a state of aesthetic arrest throughout the film. In the absence of dialogue to anchor her experience, the powerful images and accompanying music immersed her into liminality, the realm where Hermes resides. The psychic movement Dovalis experienced led her intuitively to Murray Stein's *Solar Conscience/Lunar Conscience* and *In Midlife*, which provide skeins with which we thread the film's labyrinth. For her, the film embodied Thomas Aquinas's three things which must be present for a work of art to attain the sort of transcendent beauty that leads to revelation: *integritas* (wholeness) *consonantia* (harmony) and *claritas* (radiance). Expressing all three of these exquisite qualities, *The Tree of Life* carries the Jungian critic through a journey happily conducive to depth interpretations and, ultimately, epiphany.

Inevitably, despite our continuing excitation, successive screenings revealed information not apprehended at first. It soon became evident from more than our own reactions that spectators need to see *The Tree of Life* more than once before they can grasp plot details. Malick tells the story of the young O'Brien family in high-key images, but those bright visuals actually represent a journey through the dark woods of memory (Branch, 2013). This helps explain errors of fact incorporated by some reviewers in early-day reports concerning, for example, the number and names of the O'Brien sons, which of them died, when and how. Similar omissions and errors became apparent in discussions with friends who had just seen the film for the first time. Some could not name all three sons, or distinguish one from another; others speculated that the dead boy had committed suicide or that Jack does so in his sixties.

The inability after a single screening to identify narrative facts with confidence is a consequence of the film's design. For example, characters whisper at certain key moments: it is often hard to know who is speaking and what they are saying. One sometimes cannot tell whether the speaker is among those in shot, or even a living character, 'the voice-over slipping from one actor to another with the fluidity of water passing along a riverbed' (Gilbey, 2011). Do these whispers reveal characters' inner thoughts? Is an unseen chorus uttering ideas 'in the air'? Or are they voices of the ancients? Is there an overlap between all these possibilities? As John Bleasdale notes, 'The voice-over… triumphs as a mixture of meditation, introspection and prayer – whispered, sighing, internal mutterings – [and] almost entirely does away with the traditional dialogue-rich scene' (2011).

As it happens, the concept of the inner voice of conscience has long been familiar to Jungians through the writing of Erich Neumann (1954: 403; 1969: 105). Stein elaborates on it, using the adjectives solar and lunar to denote the poles of conscience, which he sees as a complex psychological unity. For him conscience is an archetype, and as such inevitably bipolar in structure with Sol on one side and Luna at the other.

> The main goal of conscience is to create an attitude that transcends a narrowly egoistic standpoint, and it does this by proposing ideals and images of harmony and beauty on the one hand and coercing the disinclined ego by inflicting on it guilt, remorse, conflict, depression, illness, and even madness on the other.
>
> *(1993: 21)*

'Conscience is a daimon, a mighty force that the ego cannot monopolize, and it determines a person's fate far beyond what is usually understood by free will' (Stein, 1993: 6). The paradox is that conscience gives voice to both the instinctual and spiritual sides of the self (Stein, 1993: 21). All of this has its place in the narrative of *The Tree of Life*.

12

THE TREE OF LIFE (2011)

Nel mezzo del cammin di nostra vita
mi ritrovai per una selva oscura
ché la diritta via era smarrita.
                    Dante Alighieri, *Inferno*

Narrative minimalism

As we indicated in Chapter 11, the film has a structure and register that make it hard
to tie story knots on first viewing. Although narrative connections can be discerned
in subsequent viewings via hints, signs and gestures everywhere present, the film
does not privilege the what and why. Ryan Gilbey has noted how few complete
scenes there are, most being foreshortened or distilled: 'a court case, for example, is
reduced to shots of the jury's vacated chairs and a lawyer's comforting hand' (2011).
Bernard Aspe describes Malick's process of deduction from cinematic continuity so
that only the minimal elements are retained to render it possible to understand the
action (2011: 20). We have to search for signs before we can assemble a storyline.
This is all the more true because the O'Brien family story is dispersed like a mol-
ecule splitting across the Universe's history.

The following outline of the film's opening five minutes (though the merest
sketch) supports our claim that the film absorbs audience members into co-creating
its feeling, meanings and emotional impact before they comprehend the storyline.
The film begins with a title, an epigraph, God's answer to Job insisting the man
recognise the terrible majesty of numinous power compared with the sufferings of
put-upon humanity.

OPENING TITLE
'Where were you when I laid the foundation of the earth?... When the morning stars sang together, and all the sons of God shouted for joy?' (*Job* 38: 4, 7).

At incalculable distance, solar winds stir.
VOICE OVER, a man whispers: 'Brother. Mother. It was they who led me to your door.'
FADE OUT

FADE IN
A peaceful and measured CANTICLE, a constant presence in the following sequences, enriches them with a sense of the benign, even sacred nature of existence.

A ten-year old girl with long reddish-brown locks gazes from a stable door across farmland. Her wonderment is plain. Cattle look at the girl who cradles a baby goat. A field exults, dressed in glowing sunflowers. The girl considers her hand, turning it in the daylight. A man puts an arm round her shoulders and cradles her, a warm father embracing the feminine child.

VOICE OVER, a woman, softly: 'In man's house there are two ways through life – the way of nature and the way of grace. You have to choose which one you'll follow. Grace doesn't try to please itself, accepts being divided, forgotten, disliked, accepts insults and injury.'

THE 1950s.
STEADICAM MONTAGE of three boys and their parents at dinner – the father (Brad Pitt) says grace over the food. Then, fragments from many occasions, the kids play in the yard, sometimes with their father, often with their russet-haired mother (Jessica Chastain). We swing among them racing happily along the quiet suburban street they live in. A tilt shot from beneath the majestic live oak in the yard reveals the boys climbing joyfully.

VOICE OVER, the woman (continues): 'Nature only wants to please itself and others to please it too, likes to lord it over them, to have its own way. It finds reasons to be unhappy when all the world is shining around it and love is smiling on all things.'
[Pause]
'You told us that no one who loves the way of grace ever comes to a bad end.'

HIGH ANGLE FULL-FRAME SHOT a waterfall in blue spate. CUT BACK to the great oak.

VOICE OVER, the woman (continues): 'I will be true to you, whatever comes.'

CUT TO BLACK
RESUME ON A MORE MODERN HOUSE. A messenger delivers a telegram to the mother and, with a bleak smile, turns away purposefully. The mother, ten years older now, walks through her home reading the message.

SLOW FADE OUT OF CANTICLE to silence broken only by her footsteps. She sits and rises again. The camera backs away from her and she falls with a cry.

CUT TO AN AIRFIELD
Her husband answers a wall phone. A Dakota moves off its stand obeying his signals. Its engines deafen him and us. His face at last registers that he hears. Although he continues despatching aircraft, his legs too suddenly give way. At day's end, his eyes like ours are drawn to the sun falling beneath the horizon beyond the airfield.
A GREAT BELL TOLLS ONCE.

It's worth taking stock of what understanding an audience can and cannot receive from these opening sequences. To revert to Aspe (Ibid.), narrative information is minimal. We have heard none of the characters' names. There is no dialogue other than some of the father's prayer of thanks for the meal and if we attribute the male voiceover to him we shall discover our mistake later. On the other hand, we can make connections with the woman's voiceover. Although the long reddish hair of both girl and woman does hint that they are the same character at different ages, it is their movements that identify them. At both ages she is imbued with the effulgent grace (embodied joy and beauty) that her voiced thoughts invoke.

In these early scenes, the actors' movements blend with fluent Steadicam coverage and the Canticle's sweet calmness, endowing spectators with a sense of flow that embellishes the grace and beauty of the universe. The beauty of sound and image draws us into sharing the feelings that the characters experience. Already in these first minutes, grace entices spectators' imagination to flower. Bliss suffuses our senses until the telegram extinguishes it. Yet an intense paradox that will sustain the film's thematic riches is quietly slipped beneath these joyful scenes. The music that accompanies them is John Tavener's *Funeral Canticle* (1996) written for the interment of the composer's father. And indeed, we no sooner hear the woman vowing fidelity to grace than she is struck down by rending torment. Yet in that calamitous moment we can infer that a family death has occurred but cannot tell who has gone. Only in retrospect can we perceive that the nervous telegraph boy knew he was carrying a death notice.

The O'Briens have lost their second, 19-year-old son RL (by inference killed on military service in Vietnam). After the funeral, the sun falls beneath the horizon again, the great bell tolls once more as neighbouring women come by to console Mrs O'Brien. Their simple gesture reminds us, firstly, that the anguish of the bereaved parents is not unknown to others and, secondly, that loss of this magnitude carries the potential for the mourner's transformation. An individual can experience grace through either joy or suffering (Dass, 2002: 34). Even at that darkling moment, the film deals with the numinous.

Two aspects of conscience

Bleasdale notes that one thematic strand running through the film is an attempt to understand life through the lens of absence, loss and death (2011). The suffering that bereavement causes can enrich consciousness. However, Mr and Mrs O'Brien have radically different ways of dealing with pain. Mr O'Brien (Brad Pitt) can admit neither his grief nor the guilt aroused by memories of treating RL harshly to anyone other than his wife. He pushes the neighbours away and rebuffs their consolation, governed by what Murray Stein identifies as solar conscience.

The better-known aspect of conscience, *solar conscience* comprises the introjected values and moral norms of society (1993: 10). As the equivalent of Freud's superego, it presses the ego into 'the service of collective norms, ideals and values'; these norms, together with the actions to which they give rise, appear on the surface to be steadfast and permanent (1993: 13). Solar conscience, which emphasises the patriarchal, is not particularly creative; but it is 'more or less fully available to consciousness, and… exists in the light, so to speak' (Ibid.). It plays an important role in helping individuals conform to societal values, but is also a negative force in repressing instinct and impulse (1993: 17–18).

Mrs O'Brien's opening voiceover describes nature as only wanting to please itself, liking to lord it over others and have its own way: 'It finds reasons to be unhappy when all the world is shining around it and love is smiling on all things.' We argue that the way of nature exhibits the marks of solar conscience.

Jung identified the second aspect of conscience as arising from moral pressure exerted by the archetypes. Rather than being a consequence of societal pressures, it resembles an inner voice, like the voice of a god (1958b: §839–41, 845). Stein describes this as *lunar conscience*, 'the oracular voice of nature' which introduces the counterbalancing presence of the mother. 'It speaks for an intuition of cosmic order that permeates the natural world… [doing so] out of and for instinct, body, and *materia*' (1993: 19). It is 'based more on the unknown factors of the collective unconscious than on a contemporary society's rules and customs' (1993: 13). Since it arises from the dark of the unconscious archetypal aspects of human nature, it has symbolic links with the matriarchal (1993: 56). Aspects of lunar conscience are analogous to Freud's id, the prime reservoir of psychical energy. As Stein says, lunar conscience aims to destroy the narrowing rigidities and exclusiveness induced by solar conscience and insists on giving the archetypes their due (1993: 100). Healing, as Marie-Louise von Franz affirmed, always comes from archetypal experience (1999: 9). In its positive aspect, lunar conscience is 'a kind of conscience that would coerce the ego not onto a narrow trail of moral perfectionism but onto the way toward wholeness and completeness' (Stein, 1993: 56).

Mrs O'Brien's description of the way of grace lists qualities that on the surface seem passive: 'Grace doesn't try to please itself, accepts being divided, forgotten, disliked, accepts insults and injury.' However, in her dichotomy it provides the sole (or soul) positive alternative to the aggression of the way of nature. Read with insight, the way of grace infers freedom, and we think it equivalent to the positive aspect of lunar conscience. One further point: the idea that a choice must be made between the way of nature and the way of grace is an instance of a solar norm.

The O'Brien family – developmental patterns

Actors by definition embody characters: their capabilities for so doing being a main consideration in casting them in any role. Malick encouraged Jessica Chastain to adopt unusual methods in her preparation to signal Mrs O'Brien's state of grace and wholeness of body and spirit,

> studying the hands of Raphael's Madonnas in the Metropolitan Museum of Art, reading, watching old Lauren Bacall films (to learn about grace). Not to mention learning reams of Malick's lines, which he'd then ask her to say *in her head*.
>
> *(Rose, 2011)*

Gilbey, in line with his notes on the film's aesthetic pattern, says that with many shots of Mrs O'Brien, her arms and hands slip swiftly into and out of frame (2011). Such ecstatic, free movements respond as much to the currents running through her soul as the breezes passing across the yard and the light held in net curtains.[1]

The Tree of Life touches on embodiment of the soul in a sequence covering the O'Briens's courtship and marriage and her first pregnancy. Blithesome in the glancing, minimalist style that Gilbey and Aspe note, these lustrous scenes are saturated by a gorgeous, exquisitely Mozartian andante. Its delicate formality culminates in and blesses a vision: approaching full term, Mrs O'Brien treads gently along a river's edge summoning infant souls luminous in white linen. Marie-Louise von Franz notes that, for its transparency and delicacy, this fabric has a long history in myths as a textile belonging to the realm of the spirits. 'Linen has to do with fate, with destiny, with the feminine' (1999: 68). In the film, the mother-to-be opens a minute book of life to one of the souls, preparing his entry through the iron gates that open on embodied life. The new arrival will pass through the gaping maw of a hellish ogre, its menacing inscription warning that all thoughts fly from those who take this journey.[2] The infant soul rises up through the river from his underwater home. Mrs O'Brien gives birth to her first son, Jack.

Alexandre Desplat's subtle chamber pieces help characterise the mother and her young family. His pieces delay melodic resolution but evolve quietly and thereby deliver a sense of waiting, of slow change. With 'Childhood' a piano stitches a delicate, vital energy in a simple, one-handed motif with open-ended notes lifting over the quiet hum of strings – innocence in a garden. It links the infants' tender threads of life with their mother and reaches out from the cycle of their individual lives to weave them into universal time. The music also enriches the images of Mrs O'Brien (arms/house/legs/grass/hands aloft/trees and radiant sky) and communicates her grace to those around her. The combined effect draws listeners toward empathy with her spiritual ease, her oneness with the infants. In Jennifer Barker's terms, as we sense in ourselves that same virtual grace, the kinaesthetic qualities of Chastain's performance and the light and music of the filmic moments when she occupies the screen arouse in us a corresponding, embodied response, 'not *in* the film, but… not entirely *outside* it, either' (2009: 12).

As Bleasdale recognises,

> Malick is always grounded. This might seem like an odd claim, when viewing the visual poetry that at times is almost overwhelming, but his films can only get to the spiritual via the intensely physical... The ordinary is elevated, tinged though it is with the elegiac.
>
> *(Bleasdale, 2011)*

Gilbey complements this thought with the observation that 'the repeated positioning of the camera at knee level, tilting upwards, makes even the tiniest children in the film as ennobled and imposing as Easter Island statues' (2011). So Chastain's Mrs O'Brien is not the only character whose body and soul are indivisible: each of the sons when newly born is bonded in uroboric unity. Later, the simplicity of Desplat's 'Childhood' grows slowly in his 'Circles' toward something by degrees more substantial, stronger and darker, just like every individual's life. Then, as the three lads pass beyond infancy into vigorous boyhood, Smetana's *Ma Vlast* colours the imagery of their wild and joyful summer games with the gathering energy of his River Moldau as the children race around neighbouring streets and meadows, moving into the broadening currents of life around them. The children's experiences during the early years of attachment will live on inside them as a deep well they will have access to, but inevitably the passing years nudge them into boyhood, adolescence and on toward adulthood. Emerging differences between first-born Jack (Hunter McCracken) and his younger brothers RL (Laramie Eppler) and Steve (Tye Sheridan) reveal this starkly.

The human story in *The Tree of Life* is strapped across four main time frames. These are intercut forward and back with each other and a vision that fuses the mysterious present with the pre-history of the universe. A key thematic device is, as Jana Branch notes, the presentation of particular, vivid moments in the boys' lives within the overarching vagueness of what is actually happening and why (2011). Paradoxically it provides the starting point for exploration into the psyche's depths but only when Jack is in the throes of a midlife crisis.

In the family history, the chronologically earliest period starts, as we have seen, with brief glimpses of the future Mrs O'Brien's childhood with her sisters and parents. The second begins with the O'Briens's courtship, the birth of their children and ensuing lives through the 1950s until the family moves away from Waco as Jack reaches puberty. In the third time frame (circa 1972) all the sons have left home and the parents receive word of RL's death. The last period engages with the present and Jack's life as a man in his sixties. Issues of separation and loss that arose during his adolescence recur in his mid-life crisis. He has edgy exchanges with his father by phone; but concerning his mother we hear nothing.

From our brief sight of the future Mrs O'Brien aged ten, the fragments of family history to which we are party cover about seventy-five years – a nanosecond in the full chronological extent of the narrative. The vast swathe of cosmic time cradles the human storyline; but although the major representation of the Universe unfolding comes relatively early in the plot, we shall discuss it only after analysing the O'Briens because it reveals an epiphany witnessed by Jack in his late-middle years.

As a family unit, the O'Briens display dynamics typical of many mid-twentieth century Western societies. The third son Steve is least noticeable. Has he, as the youngest, observed his mother's and his siblings' relationships with his father and become compliant, making no attempt to find his own voice? Is his the compliance, like Karol's in *Trois Couleurs: Blanc*, that Winnicott associates with the false self? That is, connected with despair rather than hope, does it bring immediate rewards so that adults too easily mistake the child's compliance for growth (1971: 102)? Alternatively, do few problems weigh him down because, as the last-born child (albeit protected by his mother when his father rages against all his sons) he has a greater capacity to get along with people and interact within the family (Kluger, 2011: 72)? Has he learned, in Winnicott's countervailing term, both compromise and appreciation for the shared nature of reality (1960: 149–50)? Either way, as a cheerful lad, he blends so evenly into the crowd of kids as to be barely noticeable. The O'Briens (like the audience) seem to find their last born unobtrusive too: we neither see nor hear of him after the family leave Waco.

Far from Steve's anonymity, RL's vivacious but gentle nature makes him his mother's child.[3] He lives in harmony with other people and his environs. This is characteristic of children who have an older sibling and learn insight earlier and faster. The less powerful can find it advantageous to anticipate what's going on in the other's mind (Kluger, 2011: 73). And indeed RL takes his elder brother as a role model and follows when Jack leads him into new adventures and scrapes. When his father silences him at the dinner table, RL makes an attempt to find his voice by in return telling his father to be quiet. This enrages Mr O'Brien and RL has to retreat. On another occasion Jack bullies RL into trusting him, but when the younger boy puts his finger over the muzzle of their airgun, Jack fires into it. Worse than the physical injury, RL suffers from Jack threatening the fraternal bond. Nevertheless the younger lad, a clear soul endowed with his mother's grace, soon gets over feeling betrayed and forgives Jack. RL has developed beyond unquestioning admiration, discovering a compassionate love that lets him accept his troubled brother not as a cynosure, but as he is.

Stein cites Robert Scholl in *Das Gewissen des Kindes* (1970) arguing that the roots of conscience lie in a child's relationship to his parents. The development of conscience commences with attachment to the mother, where feelings of security and protection need to be experienced. As the ego develops and the child successfully separates from his primary dependence on her, the father takes over as principal carrier of the projection of conscience (Stein, 1993: 27–8). The necessity to move from pre-Oedipal to the Oedipal stage of development creates a deep divide within conscience. Stein argues that one pole is identified with the father, while the other stays behind with the mother. The former develops into solar conscience, the latter into lunar conscience (1993: 29–30).

Jack as the eldest son carries the heaviest parental burden. In part this is because, like many firstborn, he enters the world as a miracle and receives the devotion of both parents. First children have therefore an incentive to accept their parents' worldview and excel in endeavours the latter deem important (Kluger, 2011: 69). Jack soon becomes the prime focus of his father who passionately desires the boy should achieve the success which, as the years pass, the pained man accepts has eluded him. In his dealings with Jack, Mr O'Brien thus unconsciously requires the lad to carry the burden of his shadow. And although solar conscience, 'the way of Nature' does not wholly define Mr O'Brien, it does dominate his personality. He lords it over all three sons, but governs Jack with special severity; he charges his eldest (unlike the others) with domestic duties and demands his obedience and love.

With the onset of puberty, Jack becomes aware of the wider world beyond the home. Very occasionally he sees African Americans, a disadvantaged people unknown to the white kids. The white youngsters see the others only when the latter venture into affluent suburbs to sell produce. In town the O'Brien boys encounter poor whites, drunks, convicts and disabled individuals. Their presence does not disturb RL, but they cause Jack anxiety when he becomes aware (as childhood boundaries break) that some people live a troubled life apparently not protected by a benign deity. He witnesses a drowning. His friend Robert is injured in a house fire. Facing the collective shadow for the first time brings the need to penetrate mysteries about the godhead: 'Where were you?' Jack whispers. Yet at one point while he puzzles at these things, we cut to the schoolyard where the kids play during a break from classes. The O'Brien lads are indistinguishable in the crowd, ordinary lads whose delight is as unconstrained as the running piano arpeggio that accompanies the scene. Jack's search to find answers to these questions does not get satisfied in his youth but will resurge in midlife. Both in his anguish and his relish for life, he is everyman.

Meanwhile he begins to feel stirrings of sexual interest. First aroused by gazing at his mother, he soon projects erotic feelings onto other women her age as he meanders in neighbouring avenues to spy on them. Observing a young wife leaving her house, he gains entry to explore furtively. It is grander than the O'Brien bungalow, air-conditioned, spacious, furnished with reproduction antiques. All this Jack remarks; but it is the woman's lingerie, a powerful symbol for adolescent Jack's mother complex, which fascinates. Stein notes that 'Mother provides the experience of mutuality and intimacy, and she creates a personal world of attachment and emotional bonds' (1993: 35), yet it is a developmental necessity for the lad whose sexuality is maturing to separate from his dependency on her. Jack unpacks a drawer, steals a slip like one his mother wears and runs panicking to the river. A musical crescendo mixes with the roar of a powerboat that hurtles past, an overpowering racket the pitch of which stoops menacingly as solar guilt overwhelms him, preying on the lunar conscience to which he is now in thrall – a conflict embedded in his ambivalent relationship to his parents. He drops the slip into the water and gazes in acute anxiety as the current whips it clean away.

Solar conscience triumphs after this initial traumatic conflict. Evacuating his guilt onto his mother as he struggles with the psychic pressure to separate from her, Jack angrily accuses her of letting his father-cum-rival 'run all over her'. He also engages his father in increasingly fierce Oedipal battle: 'It's your house. You can kick me out any time.' And, to the older man's astonishment, 'You'd like to kill me.' But Jack's truth runs the other way. The sight of his father servicing the car tempts the youngster to kick out the prop and drop it on him; but he can't quite manage patricide and calls in aid a higher power: 'Please God, kill him.' Later, prowling round the whole family, he yells furiously at his father, 'She only loves me!' To paraphrase Mitchell, the vulnerability of dependency on his parents makes him feel endangered and, as a consequence, angry. He wants to seize control from them and perhaps eliminate his father, the other (2003: 138).

Freud's anthropological theory about a primal horde with a brutal and overbearing father and his subservient, rebellious son may partially explain Jack's actions. But a Jungian explanation of the father-child relationship gives deeper insight into his conflicted impasse. Stein finds extreme oppositions in the father-child relationship depicted in myths, religion and fairy tales. One set represents the father and child who enjoy a benevolent relationship of mutual respect; the contrary shows the father and child in a relationship tormented by tyranny, victimisation, and rebellion. In general, matters lie somewhere between these extremes (1993: 36). The hostile O'Brien encounter between father and son reveals Jack's negative father complex creating tension between solar conscience and his ego.

Stein draws from Greek mythology an image of fatherhood that amplifies our idea of Mr O'Brien as a type. Kronos suppressed his children by swallowing them whole and holding them captive in his stomach – the father who devours his children's lives by robbing them of psychological and spiritual independence (1993: 37, 42–43). Jack appears to be the son of a Kronos father: 'In an individual, this situation is spelled out psychologically in the picture of placid obedience to the canons of collective morality within consciousness while dreaming and fantasizing about rebellion' (1993: 41). And Jack exemplifies a further phase of Kronos development when,

> Frustration, conflict, and anger quietly build up inside and gather around a still deeply unconscious but potentially heroic determination to change. The explosive elevation of Kronos has a revolutionary transformative effect upon ego-consciousness. There is a dramatic reversal of attitude within consciousness. The formerly placid child becomes a rebellious teenager...
>
> *(Ibid.)*

The contrary, positive aspect of solar conscience in Kronos power shows when Mr O'Brien's demanding presence in Jack's life creates an environment that supports the necessary separation from the mother: 'Kronos frees a person from the mother, from concrete identification with the body and unity with instincts, and puts up a barrier against automatic and unreflective gratification of impulses' (1993: 46). Thus solar conscience plays a part in ongoing development of the differentiating function of conscious, adding the moral element (1993: 47).

In his adolescent explorations of Self, Jack discovers another key feeling – something perhaps learnt from RL's kindness to him. Unlike a boy in his gang who lords it over Robert, the boy who bears scars from a house fire, Jack shows compassion, reaching out to touch and help him. So too when Mr O'Brien loses his job, his father's deep dejection affects Jack. Although the boy's inner voice tells him, 'Always you wrestle inside me. Always will', shared confession dissolves their hostility for a few moments. O'Brien admits he is not proud of being tough on his son and Jack responds from a deep place revealing that, as children tend to, he identifies with the parent of his own sex: 'I'm as bad as you are. I'm more like you than her.' O'Brien, on the edge of tears, tells his boy, 'You're all I have.' Steadicam close shots reveal the boy's face relinquishing its haunted uncertainty, while shame and agony ease their grip on his father. They hold each other close. A major crisis has brought about this emotional nakedness; but it does not endure. Before the family leave Waco to move to his new job, Mr O'Brien has resumed his tough patriarchal demeanour.

Ultimately the rage born from his father's suffocating love burdens Jack with what Jung said is the greatest price a child may have to pay: living the unlived life of the parent. Troubled by his desire to defy the paternal Logos, the boy's libido is disorganised; but in his adulthood it forces an outlet in his embodiment of the very imago that dominates him. Stein offers a pertinent gloss on libido and heroism that enables us to anticipate ways in which Jack will eventually turn his midlife crisis into the depths of a midlife transition.

> …The 'hero' represents a specific configuration and movement of [psychic energy], *libido*, moving dynamically forward – into sometimes adaptive and often defensive directions – but essentially in an expansive motion outward and forward. Even in defense the hero is expansionistic and offensive: taking the initiative, catching the enemy by surprise, overwhelming him with superior force and aggressive strategy. The heroic pattern is the 'progression of libido'… in a phallic, expansionistic modality, taking charge and winning glory.
>
> *(Stein, 1983: 33)*

When Mr O'Brien fails in both his first passion to be a great musician and his second ambition, to bring a patented engineering design to market, he vents his frustrations only on the family. By contrast, Jack hones anger into an implement of will, something that helps him achieve success. First seen in leadership of his ragtag gang of neighbourhood boys, his matured will does not wholly ease his embattled inner life but is a factor driving the sophisticated architect. We expand later on the psychology motivating his professional achievements.

It is tempting, as we have revealed, to fixate on Mrs O'Brien as the embodiment of a grace so pure that she seems directed by the spirit. Malick emphasises her numinous existence in ways more subtle than the simple and attractive dresses she wears.[4] In one moment, unrestrained by gravity, she dances joyously in the air beneath the great oak. In another she sleeps in a crystal casket, a fairytale princess waiting to be awakened by young Jack. On another, less dramatic occasion, she sits on the front steps and the family cat snuggles into her lap. All these images (which we begin to perceive as memories and fantasies visited on Jack in adulthood) show there are psychological mysteries, and possible archetypal realisations connected with the inner journey of our emerging hero.

Von Franz reports that historically the cat was worshipped as lunar. It was believed that during the hours of darkness, when the rays of the sun were invisible to humans, they were reflected in the phosphorescent eyes of the cat, as the light of the sun is reflected in the moon. The cat is also closely linked with consciousness and all creative processes (1999: 55–6). Jack's powerful visions of his anima invest key memories (whether joyous or painful) in effulgent light, steeping them in Edenic fantasy (Aspe, 2011: 20–1). They arise from the unconscious as archetypal experience, an act of grace which carries the healing factor. Our hero Jack must do something for his transformation and redemption. Something doesn't function with his anima; he doesn't have the right contact with her, blocking the way to his unconscious.

Nevertheless, although Mrs O'Brien has the wholeness of a person with integral body and soul, the film stops us from idealising the state of grace. A vicious row bursts out when, seated in majesty at the dinner table as we have mentioned, Mr O'Brien is tweaked by RL. He rages against the impertinence and drives all the boys to their room, scattering furniture in his delirium. His wife rescues Steve from the onslaught but, returning to the kitchen, her fury explodes when her husband charges her with turning his kids against him. The only woman in an all male household, she punches the tyrant before weeping tears of anger. Stein says that 'Lunar conscience tells us when [a] word or act does not match up, when it oversteps or violates… [in order] to remind the ego it cannot do whatever it pleases' (1993: 66). Mrs O'Brien's fury springs from the archetypal urge to heal. She challenges the old solar principle to overcome it (see von Franz, 1999: 117). Grace, the incident implies, is not beyond human attainment, but must come from healing the feminine. Mrs O'Brien, no less than her husband, is in the grip of an old patriarchal attitude that needs integration.

As we ourselves experienced, thanks to the several components of cinema that create the character, spectators' kinaesthetic response to Mrs O'Brien can be intense. Playing Mr O'Brien, Brad Pitt moves in less striking ways, as befits a character whose attitudes and behaviour typify a generation and class ruled by solar conscience. Except when anger breaks out, his emotions and physical movements are those of a stolid man who walks four-square upon his yard but resents having to observe the boundaries (topographical and cultural) that separate him from richer neighbours. His hyper focus on limits and boundaries arises from a one-sided masculine identity and repressed anima. Whereas the feminine is concerned with relationship and connection, Mr O'Brien (under the influence of the shadow) separates and feels separate from others. A deeper connected relationship can only open up when the sacrosanct boundary between 'mine' and 'yours' (key to intra-psychic as well as interpersonal distance) is dissolved. As we shall see with Jack, this can only come from the integration work with anima and shadow during the midlife transition in which he recovers a sense of authority in himself.

Employed as a lower-middle manager, Mr O'Brien works a tough six-day week in an industrial plant and comes to believe that those who command power and wealth have not granted him his due. His inability to cross this borderline eventually brings awareness of his limitations, with envy swiftly following. He tries to advance by designing new equipment; but his application to file patents fails and a world trip to sell his ideas leads to nothing. His grudge deepens over the years and forms the basis for life lessons he inculcates in his boys; but in teaching them to fight their way to the top, he inadvertently replicates the hierarchy he has internalised from his own father complex (reinforced by the power structures at his place of work). He subordinates his sons to his commands.

One day Mr O'Brien finds himself facing a brick wall, both literally and metaphorically. The plant is closing and he must choose a job nobody wants and uproot the family or face unemployment. Loss and defeat drop him into midlife crisis and the annihilation of his persona opens him to an elusive, confessional moment of grace. 'I wanted to be loved until I was great, a big man. Now I'm nothing.' In the agony of failure he experiences a moment of revelation, noticing, as if for the first time, 'The glory around us, trees, birds. I lived in shame. I dishonoured it all and didn't notice the glory.' The sacramental overtones of his words link to the numinous glory of the cosmos in *The Tree of Life*. And they emphasise the symbolic weight attaching to the live oak that stands at the family's door. Adding to the poignancy, Malick mixes through this sequence a reduced version of the sweet Mozartian theme that accompanied O'Brien's courting days. Stripped of its honeyed orchestra, a lone piano now tentatively carries the theme, steadying only when O'Brien brings the bad news home and his wife comforts him. Her compassion hints at the possibility of renewal through their loss. Jack too, as we saw, feels his father's humiliation and suffers for him as they share a rare moment of empathic love.

The conflicts in Mr O'Brien's personality sometimes make him a sacred monster to Emmanuel Lubezki's camera. Music animates his passion and occasionally draws him nearer to the lunar state of grace enjoyed by his wife. On one occasion Jack watches his father play Bach's Organ Toccata and Fugue in church. The boy stands beneath the great pipes afraid, curious and finally drawn in by his father's absorption, the meticulous movement of his fingers. (Just this once, Jack compares his hands with his father's.) Yet Bach's ascending harmonic progressions are mixed through Mr O'Brien lecturing his eldest son on how to live without, like him, getting sidetracked. In truth, it was not abandoning his ambitions that sidetracked him, but what he repressed, in Jungian terms his shadow. O'Brien is stuck and does not know how to guide his son further than he has himself gone.

Meanwhile, over his father's rendition of the Toccata and Fugue (as if Malick were dovetailing the two lectures), another hard lesson is taught, the priest's sermon on Job. According to the clergyman, Job thought that his virtuous life would save him from misfortune.

But no. Misfortune befalls the good as well. We can't protect ourselves against it. We can't protect our children… We vanish as a cloud. We wither as the autumn grass and like a tree are rooted up... Is there some fraud in the scheme of the Universe? Is there nothing which... does not pass away? We cannot stay where we are. We must journey forth. We must find that which is greater than fortune or faith. Nothing can bring us peace but that... There is no hiding place in all the world that trouble may not find you.

The boy is about to glimpse through the fate of other people the painful truth of the lesson with which the priest concludes; and the O'Briens's understanding of suffering will be dreadfully amplified by the death of RL. However, Catholic dogma renders it unthinkable for the clergyman to give an account of humanity's relation to the numen that embraces Jack and his mother's (let alone the audience's) experiences of the divine as *The Tree of Life* reveals it. We shall return to this topic with the help of Jung's *Answer to Job*; but for now we must continue with Mr O'Brien's influence on the development of his eldest son.

According to Stein, developing the ideas we touched on briefly in Chapter 3, successful navigation through the mid life transition involves making a crucial three-stage shift from a persona orientation to a Self orientation. Taking an intra-psychic view, the first phase is separation from an earlier identity, the persona. The ego needs to let go of this attachment before it can float through the necessary second stage of liminality. This is a period preliminary to the third stage, deeper discovery of the Self. To do this thoroughly and decisively, a person needs to identify the source of pain and put the past to rest by grieving, mourning, and burying it. But the nature of the loss needs to be understood and worked through before a person can go on (Stein, 1983: 27–8). Becoming stuck psychologically is significant because it defends against something deeper and larger. Something more must be asked of the Self, which is not going to come from ramping up the will. It has to come from withdrawing one's projections (such as Mr O'Brien's on his boys) in order to assimilate shadow into consciousness.

The boy standing by the organ listens to his father and the priest but cannot connect with the stern words of either man, although in years to come his mag-nificent buildings will direct toward the heavens their precise structural complex-ity, reminiscent of Bach's architectonics. Meanwhile, still in childhood, Jack's jealousy is aroused when RL hesitantly but sweetly plays a François Couperin duet with his father. RL has found connection with his father where their shared interest in music touches the feminine in their personalities. As a boy, Jack (in the masculine, solar way) is stuck in an impersonal world, finding it difficult to feel a warm connection to his father. His inner voice echoes his old man, then rebels: "'Don't put your elbows on the table!" He does. Insults people. Doesn't care.' But as these thoughts run in Jack's head, his father (now a loving monster dad) plays bedtime games with the three lads and recalls their births. In an evocation of Jack's father complex, his surreal recurring fantasy, an etiolated giant worthy of David Lynch stoops glumly in a secret attic, leaning over a small boy who spins his tricycle in empty circles. The father figure wields his Bible and points the way forward. The boy points in another direction. The dream, Jung noted, 'is a spontaneous self-portrayal, in symbolic form, of the actual situation in the unconscious' (1948b: §505).

According to Stein, 'it is necessary to go *through* an encounter with the anima at midlife if the individuation journey is to continue' (1983: 99). Mr O'Brien does not have direct access to his soul because of his lack of relationship with his anima, so music must serve as a medium of communication, his mid-life transition aborted by this lack of connection to his inner feminine. Nor does music help him connect with his boys when he forces them to listen to Brahms and leaves them with bowed heads. No wonder that their father's solar obsessions reverberate in RL's and Jack's lives as an inescapable, discordant obbligato. In childhood, RL demurred timidly when his father tried training him to fight. In late teens, unlike many other young Americans of peace-loving disposition, RL did not defy the *senex* ideology of his father's generation but, accepting conscription into a war he must have abhorred, paid with his life.

A private grief endured

Malick's organisation of the plot twice draws the audience into sharing the irruption of unconscious contents into Jack's adult psyche. We first plunge into the cosmic cauldron as it rips into form, a cinematic experience so immense that it suffuses the senses, leaving us staggered, seeking out understanding. The second encounter with this archetypal turmoil occurs after the family history has been covered, a context giving us better hope of comprehending the visionary experience.

In the former instance we cut to the adult Jack (Sean Penn) from his parents grieving RL's death via a smeary sequence of hectic urban neon (a hint of lunar conscience). The forty-year flash-forward brings us (with solar wind providing a mysterious aural setting) to Jack, loath to face the anniversary of that fatal day. Reluctantly he leaves his bed and, like his wife, silently dresses for work in dark business wear. He has achieved glittering success at heights his father could not but approve, yet cuts a morose figure in his late middle years. Kent Jones notes the 'evasive body language between Jack and his wife, choreographed within and perhaps brought into being by the pathways in their own glass box' (2011). Jack does indeed close out the silent woman as, in cool morning light, they trace separate orbits through their elegant house. Yet she shows compassion for both brothers (lunar conscience ignored by Jack) and honours RL by bringing a fresh-cut sprig into the house; meanwhile Jack lights a candle for his brother, first spark of the illumination to come.

The anniversary plunges Jack into suffering that he has neither worked through nor escaped. It halts his tongue and deadens his soul. Stein, reminding us that Jung called the midlife transition a 'confrontation with the unconscious' (Jung, 1961: 194–225), describes what Jack seems to be experiencing as follows.

> As the midlife transition begins, whether it begins gradually or abruptly, persons generally feel gripped by a sense of loss and all of its emotional attendants... The fundamental cause of this distress is separation, and the anxiety about it

is a type of separation anxiety. What has been released is two repressed and otherwise unconscious elements of the personality: the rejected and inferior person one has always fought becoming, the Shadow and behind that the contrasexual 'other,' [the anima] whose power one has always, for good reason, denied and evaded.

(Stein, 1983: 24–6)

Jack's mind loses focus on diurnal time and hosts long-repressed questions, too powerful to silence: 'How did you come to me? In what shape, what disguise?' Bewildering images break in on him: memories from his personal unconscious – 'I see the chap that I was. I see my brother, true, kind' – juxtaposed with archetypal images whose surreal nature signals that his psyche teeters on the cusp of a split between madness and numinous revelation. There come unbidden crazy glimpses of himself in his fine suit walking hesitantly through gullies and over sand toward an old doorway. Standing on the beach, it connects to nothing, surreal in its apparent lack of function.

Intermittently Jack returns to consciousness of his office, a niche suspended among blue steel and glass shards where his colleagues wear black, grey, navy blue or white to synchronise with décor as rigorously minimal as his home. Edits defying continuity fragment these monuments to human ingenuity as Jack scales breathtaking heights in glass lifts – fragmentation, precision and immensity all characteristic of his designs. Disconsolate, the architect cum high-end property developer prowls the elegant ring of transparent pathways and steel boxes making up glittering, hard-edged towers. Desplat's 'City of Glass' on the soundtrack echoes poignantly in its hanging chords the same composer's 'Childhood'. It underlines the loss of infant joys in a man tangled in the complex, beautiful but relentless geometry of his professional and inner life. His recollections of long lost infant years as the iridescent cynosure of his parents' love conflict with his apathetic muttering with business colleagues. However, the inrush of memories and fantasies also hints, while he teeters above a mental vortex, that recovery of soul is not impossible.

Further recollections of childhood break in on Jack together with intimations of something visionary and other. We have remarked on his anger, but he has benefited from a loving mother who was always present to him; and although his father is difficult, Jack knows that he means much to the old man too. He calls his father to apologise for an earlier ill-tempered conversation and admits to thinking about RL every day. Notwithstanding the typically marginal quality of this brief, muttered exchange, the conversation is key to the developmental theme. On one level *The Tree of Life* is about what must be healed between father and son as they mourn the loss of RL, a shining life extinguished by war. Yet the conversation (its tone dictated – since Jack is mending fences with him – by Mr O'Brien) also invokes the culture of a patriarchal society: significantly, the two men do not mention Jack's mother, the first hint that she may be dead. As the film will eventually confirm, there is no healing of ourselves, our families, communities or the planet without integrating lunar conscience: the feminine in both men and women needs healing.

Stein, in words that describe Jack's state of mind, helps us see that so great a loss can destroy an individual's heroic defence against change, drawing the psyche into liminal space coloured by grief for a vanished past.

> Liminality is created whenever the ego is unable any longer to identify fully with a former self-image, which it had formed by selective attachments to specific internal imagos and embodied in certain roles accepted and performed. While the ego hangs in suspension, still it remembers the ghost of a former self, whose home had been furnished with the presence of persons and objects now absent and had been placed in a psychological landscape now bare and uninhabitable without them.
>
> *(Stein, 1983: 11)*

The unconscious aids the ego in coming to terms with deep-going, transformative change, and does so teleologically, that is, as a goal-oriented activity (Stein, 1983: 13). When Jack is thrown into midlife transition, he is led by unconscious purpose to move further downward into the roots of his grief. Entering into a state of liminality will allow him to deepen his connection to his personal, and the archetypal mother, enriching the feminine presence in his psyche that his creative life affirms.

With Jack in the grips of angst, the geometry of the towers takes on jagged edges; but the imagery is not exclusively bleak. We cut to a plaza under construction where young trees promising hope and new life are being planted in a plaza reminiscent of New York's Ground Zero. Visionary images force into Jack's mind again: still in business suit and tie, he explores a passage through rock-walled desert and finds a jetty tipped up to the sky.[5] Memories of his mother return him to the Waco days: she shrouds RL in a lace curtain and kisses him a long, tender farewell. Impossibly present as a 60-year-old at his parents' side while they grieve their teenage son's death, Jack asks himself how she could have borne the loss before reaching across the decades to stroke her hair. Through all this, long chords slow the rhythm as strings and woodwind move into the foreground and we cut away to a murmuration of starlings massed in their millions over drab city housing where they sculpt the air in a breathtakingly lovely sky dance. A mezzo-soprano lifts her voice over suspended chords and the grieving mother cries out in agony as she wanders in woods.[6] Like Dante's pilgrim, her limbs not fully hers to command, she loses herself, directionless as her anguished son who forty years later is imagining this scene. Only the relentlessly cheerful birdsong from the branches overhead implies the prospect of relief from trauma. Hard for us to anticipate that this disoriented man will become our hesitant guide and psychopomp, our Hermes searching for answers denied him in adolescence, asking questions that bring to mind those he asked almost fifty years earlier. We cut to black, Jack's questions: 'How? Why? Where were you?' not yet answered.

The twenty-first century rebirth of the universe

His questions cue a vision of the Universe's birth, the efflorescence of light and energy as great clouds of supernovas and plasma erupt. In rending ecstasy, thunderous galaxies rumble into existence and die; a glorious soprano (Elzbieta Towarnicka) sings Zbigniew Preisner's searing *Lacrimosa*; music and light soar in a rip tide of saturated colours as, in a seamless circle, we celebrate *and* grieve for the birth and destruction of countless forms of existence, evanescent across the fleeting aeons. Jack's whispered queries, 'Did you know? What are we to you? Answer me!' stitch his – humanity's – bewildered suffering into the immeasurable paroxysms of a myriad worlds as they form and re-form, sometimes like lacy fabric evolving beautifully in opening blossoms, sometimes evocative of cancerous tumours, hideously elephantine.

The scene shifts from the universal to our galaxy, thence to this dark rumbustious planet in flaming meltdown and eventually the present century's volcanic eruptions, so furious they silence other music. But Mrs O'Brien's whispers come through a lull in the plasma tempest, 'We cry to you, my soul, my son. Hear us.' A prayer to a numinous trinity: universe, soul and child – three in one. We cut to the waterfall in spate seen in the opening scenes, thence to a desert passage and a sandy wet estuary reminiscent of Jack's earlier visionary glimpses. The first microcosmic cells unite, triggering a light show as animate life forms evolve – echoing the star forms, some being lovely, others hideous. Appositely, the film honours Kubrick's *2001: A Space Odyssey* with its journey beyond Jupiter powered by music that stoops to the curvature of space-time. Malick does not at this moment explore outer space, however, but voyages undersea implying his interest in the depths of the inner life. There jellyfish, corkscrew worms and a variety of marine creatures begin to take recognisable form. Then, the lovely and the abhorrent holding fast to each other, a beached marine dinosaur awaits its death from wounds gouged by a predator. Blood feathers the sea. The dinosaurs move on land and for the first time compassion figures when a carnivorous creature decides to reprieve an injured herbivore on which it had meant to breakfast. It pre-echoes young Jack's intuitively caring gesture toward his scarred pal Robert.

As Branch observes, *The Tree of Life* doesn't privilege the what and the why. Instead it dips below that surface order into the visceral sense-making of personal memory – surely disorienting and disturbing for a lot of people. 'That's as close a visual as I've ever seen depicting grief – that feeling of being torn open and tossed back into the primordial soup… Words suddenly seem paltry' (2011). The suffering and joys of humanity lodge in the arc of universal time and change, the amoral numen in all its glory *and* horror.

Jack's unsteady psyche is, of course, not the only vantage point available, Malick having the primary authorial claim to the vision. However, the nature of the cosmic perspective demands that something more, in terms of its socio-cultural dimension, cannot be ignored. *The Tree of Life* is mythmaking and, even when it draws on stories cherished by the ancients, renders myth for and of our time. What we see is knowable only through astrophysics, the related sciences and digital technologies. That said, much scientific knowledge is provisional, liable to change and based on what we can see (solar, the light) rather on what cannot be seen (lunar, the dark). Scientific knowledge, not least our understanding of the cosmos, actually re-enters the realm of popular, mythically vital consciousness from which it evolved; but it returns refashioned to accommodate new theories, knowledge and expectations. This mythologising cycle is not new. Jung traced collective excitement with the idea of unidentified flying objects to the sixteenth century (1959: §757–63). Arthur C. Clarke reported before the moon-landings of the late 1960s on the long dream of humanity yearning for space exploration, regarding it as the leap of imagination essentially prerequisite to the technological achievement (1968). Subsequent robotic exploration has further refined understanding of our galaxy but for many people, it has not demystified the wonder of the cosmos and the ineluctably curious phenomenon of humanity. In *The Tree of Life* those scientists, technicians, other specialists *and* artists who recorded, generated, wrote plots and composed sounds, images and music were essential co-creators and myth-makers who rendered the knowledge of 2011 into truth as best they could tell it (albeit provisionally) in story form. The audience too (as members of a complex, technologically oriented culture) co-create with Jack O'Brien and Malick what they take from the film. Alan Mack (2011) wrote that the film is deeply personal to Malick and feels 'torn from the heart'. That, scarcely less elementally, is true for the engaged audience too.

Evolution of sacred myths

As the title *The Tree of Life* insists (and we say more about that specific image later), the coming of new life and joy – even the recovery of joy after bereavement – are integral to its majestic spread. Although the film draws heavily on Christian values and imagery, it does so because they inform the characters' culturally specific, Texan understanding of the nature of life. As we have argued, their 1950s patriarchal culture suppresses the anima in Mr O'Brien and his eldest son. Only via Jack's eventual exposure to liminality is the repressed feminine recovered. So we agree with Mack that *The Tree of Life* is neither obligated to nor proselytises any church or organised faith. In the O'Briens's world, 'The politics, the sentiments, the ideology – all are theirs' (Mack, 2011). In this, through links deeper than Douglas Trumbull's vivid animations for both films, it resembles Kubrick's *2001: A Space Odyssey*. Both centre on quests to discover and share understanding of what we can humanly know of our place in the always-evolving time and space of the Universe.[7] In this respect, both deal with the sacred, the numinous. But while Dave in Kubrick's film purposely journeys further than any other human, Jack O'Brien has not set out on a conscious quest. Buffeted by emotional forces that he cannot reconcile, his character metamorphoses *in extremis* into a type of Hermes – an unconscious hero of the family on the dangerous journey of individuation. In bringing together the ways of nature and of grace in his hard-won recognition of the Self, he becomes a messenger of the gods.

As his memories reach the moment when the family leave Waco forever, and summon again the wish-fulfilling scene of visiting his greying, bereaved mother, Jack's imagination thrusts him for the second time into the surreal wind-carved desert. As the Steadicam glides around him, Jack (still accoutred in his incongruous suit) approaches the empty doorway a second time, now drawn forward by a comely woman. She is neither his wife nor mother, but (understood mythically) both a messenger who will become Jack's guide and the counterpart to the telegraph boy who brought news of RL's death. As an anima figure, she offers access to the soul. The calm spiritual welcome she brings affirms that she offers Jack the gift of relationship.

After hesitating, Jack goes through the gate, crossing the threshold (in Latin, the *limen*). With this step he aligns himself with Hermes, the god who violates boundaries, an archetypal figure representing a consciousness that exists within transitional time and space (here, the midlife transition). Thus, Hermes guides the groping ego on the path to deeper liminality (Stein, 1983: 13). The high significance of movement from one liminal state of consciousness to another is marked by Jack's voice now heard for the first time as if in prayer and acceptance: 'Keep us, guide us to the end of time.' We cut to black, then a planet crosses the sun's face, volcanic lava swells, and bleak landscapes spread under moonlight. Hector Berlioz's 'Agnus Dei' from *La Grande Messe des Morts* exalts the following scenes as a choir of women's tender voices pull against the brassy terror of funereal trombones.

In a closed room the anima–messenger lights candles (promising Jack further illumination) before opening a door back into the desert. As in a dream, Jack is led by his adolescent self over the rocks and up the wooden jetty, not at first onto the beach but to a field outside a distant town where two corpses lie wrapped in linen shrouds for burial. We can recall with von Franz that in myths linen often belongs to the realm of the spirits (1999: 68). And for Stein, Hermes, the soul's guide to the underworld, leads to the place of the corpse (1983: 36). Here the corpse, an image representing Jack's awareness of past grief, will be faced and buried. The anima, seen from within an open grave, now touches a hand mysteriously reaching up toward her: Jack's mother. Next Jack sees Mrs O'Brien lying dead in her wedding dress, then ready to walk into the open as the bride.

These mysteries release meaning when read as interlinked metaphors. As we have said, whatever is left incomplete in adolescence (the petticoat sucked away down river, emblem for what Jack did not finish) will surface in mid life. That later period of development offers the chance to recapture parts of the self left behind and lost, the positive shadow. The bride's rebirth will, when Mrs O'Brien's strange scene plays out, present itself not as Oedipal wish-fulfilment but as a teleological, or goal-oriented variant of a familiar *topos*. In this the soul finds its home in the inner marriage (a metaphor reiterating the erotic charge of *The Song of Songs* where the groom is read allegorically as the godhead). To hold back for a moment from the archetypal and revert to Jack, the anima's emergence from the grave implies the recovery of his long-buried soul.

The Song of Songs, like other image clusters in this film that have strong roots in myth and Christianity, make it worth pausing here. For, to reiterate our earlier claim, although Christian readings are relevant, they do not release fully the metaphoric and mythic implications that lie latent here. This is our cue to turn to the Tree of Life. Malick's film focuses on family life blossoming beneath and in the live oak's branches, but it links the emblem with death too: when the O'Briens leave Waco, a tearful RL buries his pet fish at its roots. In Christian exegeses the tree has a place in an allegorical cycle that commences with the illicit fruit of the tree in Eden, site of a crucial decision for the first humans who learnt through the calamity of losing their immortality the moral necessity of consciously distinguishing good from evil (see von Franz, 1999: 46). That first tree had its New Testament successor in the crucifix which reverses the symbolism by delivering Christ to death and restoring humanity to eternal life. The imagery had associations so powerful that St Bonaventure wrote his thirteenth-century *Tree of Life* as a meditative aid to devotion, furnishing the faithful with a formal exegesis of the twelve fruits of the crucifix as the salvific tree of life (1978: 119–21). Malick's tree, however, has equally strong resemblances to one described by Michael Meade as deriving from Norse mythology. The cosmos formed around an eternal tree that supported the entire universe and everything in it. This world tree connected the underworld, the middle earth and the heavens above, serving as a mystical axis that kept things in place. It linked all living things and represented all phases of existence from birth to death to renewal (2010: 31).

Finally we must include the long-established emblematic equivalences that trees furnish for human life both physical and psychological. They draw sustenance through their leaves and roots, flourishing in the light of day through photosynthesis while the roots weave a network through the dark underworld to anchor them and supply nutrients. The surface area of trees is much the same above as below ground. By analogy, human consciousness thrives in sunlight only when it recognises its reliance on the unseen (but not wholly undetectable) nourishment springing from roots in the unconscious.

Another marker that shows Christian readings to be insufficient aids in analysing Malick's film is Jack's cry from the heart, 'Keep us, guide us to the end of time.' It sounds like a prayer steeped in biblical language but, in fact, was written for the script. Despite the illusion of familiarity arising from its choice of language, rhythm and direct appeal to a greater power, it does not originate in the book of prayer directed at the Christian God. Though it is indeed an appeal to a powerful and mysterious root source, it voices hope for oneness with the Cosmos and its numinous energy – unity of the outer and inner worlds. Once again, thematic links are evident between *The Tree of Life* and *2001: A Space Odyssey*, both films seeking, as we have mentioned, to share such understanding as humans can know of our place in the always-evolving time and space of the Universe. Both evoke the sacred through intense beauty and grace, and both endow those in their audiences who have embarked on similar quests with a sense of their embodiment of the same high passion.

Valediction

To return to the beach: the adult Jack led by his young self is resuming the search he had long ago forgotten. It is a classic instance of the adult finding wisdom in his own abandoned child, the child who in the beginning of the film whispered in voiceover, 'Find me'. This reading is confirmed when, walking on the beach, he again sights his young self on a strand and falls to his knees recognising that in boyhood he had been nearer the mysterious sea than now. His anima guide returns to the water's edge and Jack embraces her muddy feet in a humble gesture of devotion.[8]

Gulls fly, and the people on the beach become a crowd, most of them unknown to us. Their movements do not correspond to the focused linear journey of pilgrims at the end of their hard road. These walkers flow this way and that across the beach as if drawn by tides in the affairs of humanity. The gathering parade across the sea front recalls another great cinematic moment of reconciliation, the finale of Fellini's *8½*. But while Fellini (as Nino Rota's circus music announces) celebrates life, Malick in this valedictory scene is concerned with bereavement, mourning, acceptance *and* life.

Discovered among the crowd, Steve happily gazes at his eldest brother and relishes his connection with the sea, waving his arms at the birds. Now comes Jack's mother, like the rest of his original family locked in the years of his boyhood. The young woman dressed in green and the son now much older than her embrace tenderly. A cut, out of temporal order, shows us a lunar eclipse in a night sky, a hint that Jack is no longer solar dominant. Still in his suit, Jack greets his young father and they stroll together quite comfortably. Now RL, the shining boy, comes forward, embracing Jack and his parents lovingly. For a moment all the O'Briens are gathered on the beach cherishing each other.

A beautiful mask (emblematic of the discarded persona) sinks through the water, a dying to the old self. Acceptance of this transformation is marked by the almost unbearable sweetness of Berlioz's 'Agnus Dei' as Mrs O'Brien, attended by hand-maidens, prepares to give her son to the Universe. Lest we sentimentalise the moment, the brassy growl of menacing trombones again refuses to let us ignore the horror of death. As Mrs O'Brien leads RL to a final door that opens in evening light onto salt flats, she makes her valediction while adult Jack strokes her hair, a timely reminder that it is he who needs to release his phantoms. RL, at first loath to depart (indicating Jack's reluctance to let him do so), slowly disappears from sight. Thus, the phantom Mrs O'Brien symbolically releases the wounded masculine. Then she too passes through that door and walks directly toward the setting sun which will soon absorb her – symbolic liberation of the feminine and the heart.

Like her handmaidens, the fluent camera caresses her ritually (low angle, high key lighting, back lit by the sun, the camera following her hands raised to the heavens). Berlioz's sumptuous Mass concludes with the Amen through which Mrs O'Brien whispers, 'I give him to you. I give you my son.' In the manner of Christian icons of the Virgin (and reminiscent too of Venus, goddess of love who was also accompanied by the dove), her hands open as if releasing a bird. The sun at her head brings to mind a halo; but her loving gesture prepares for the release of soul – a gift for Jack and recognition of the divine nature of his inner anima and the Universe. Jack releases both RL and his dead mother to complete his personal transformation, his discovery of the Self.

In three shots Malick, our all-seeing Hermes, offers his audience three transpersonal emblems so that, to paraphrase Stein, the gradual stabilisation of the Self's felt presence and its guidance in conscious life can become the foundation for us too of a new experience of identity and integrity where the Self becomes the internal centre (1983: 27). The camera tilts down from the heavens to a field where, in majestic blossom, sunflowers pack the screen. Each stands, a beautiful and fertile mandala, distinct from yet tight with its fellows. Separately their flowering harmonises with the blossoming of soul. Taken as a whole, the field makes a striking emblem for individuation within the collectivity, the one world soul, the *anima mundi*.

We return to the personal as Jack descends from his office, walks out onto the plaza beneath the towers and looks up at his work. With the start of a smile a sense of acceptance, integrity and wholeness comes over his face. In releasing his mother he has neither abandoned the anima, nor has the anima abandoned him. His final reconciliation, now he accepts and is completed by the feminine, may also embrace his wife. There has been no rage between them, but a disconnection based on one-sidedness. United in peace and love, Jack represents a new form of masculine consciousness. The peaceful union of lunar and solar, nature and grace is his achievement of individuation. Now he is free to become emotionally present to his wife, open to the vulnerability that necessarily comes with love. As von Franz writes, 'In a man, the positive anima is the magic of life… I have even defined the anima as the stimulus to life' (1999: 116).

We cut back to the transpersonal with the second emblem, a steel bridge across dark waters. Immediately, this crossing between two shores reaffirms Jack's mid-life transition; but its broad and robust way (built to carry people in their thousands) signals nothing if not an image of archetypal majesty. It implies the inevitable transition of all creatures from life to death, their going beforehand now known on the very pulse of Jack's being.

The image fades to black and the third emblem, the film's final shot, encourages us to infer that the road onward is also the road back to rediscovering our origins: in this last shot we resume on the beginning of the Universe with the stirring of light and solar winds. And thus we are led full circle back to the film's first words, the adult Jack's voiceover: 'Brother. Mother. It was they who led me to your door.'

Answer to Job

The Tree of Life opens on God's curt inquiry to Job: 'Where were you when I laid the foundation of the earth? … When the morning stars sang together, and all the sons of God shouted for joy?' (*Job* 38: 4, 7). As an epigraph it invites attention in its own right not least because, as we have seen, when the O'Briens's priest delivers a sermon based on the Book of Job, its theme is the inevitability of human suffering. For us, this epigraph has the additional pertinence that Jung in *Answer to Job* sought to understand the mystery of Yahweh and the meaning of the omnipotent Old Testament deity brutally afflicting the wretched Job, a creature of his own making, with sicknesses and woes.

Paul Bishop argues that in this book Jung laboured to re-animate myth. Rather than conventional theological dogmatics, his feeling for symbol and myth governed his investigations of the biblical Job (2002: 23). In this, Jung echoed Nietzsche who

had asserted in *The Birth of Tragedy* (1872, §10) that the suppression of myth represented nothing less than the death of religion (Bishop, 2002: 15).

> For this is the way in which religions are wont to die out: under the stern
> intelligent eyes of an orthodox dogmatism, the mythical premises of a reli-
> gion are systematized as a sum total of historical events...
>
> *(Bishop, 2002)*

As it is our conviction that Malick's *The Tree of Life* engages with myths conveying
sacred mysteries, the relevance of *Answer to Job* is inescapable. Jung's reading of the
biblical text as myth rather than religious dogma produces an account of Yahweh's
self-discovery through the agency of Job.

Jung notes (not without sarcasm) that Yahweh thunders at Job for seventy-one
verses to convince himself of his unassailable power; but the tormented man,
although cowed, remains loyal. For Jung, this makes Yahweh's relentless attempts
at intimidation incongruous, something that the deity (despite his omniscience)
completely misses seeing. God's tremendous emphasis on his omnipotence only
becomes intelligible when seen as 'the outward occasion for an inward process of
dialectic in God' (1954e: §587). Yahweh's brutal treatment of Job has revealed his
dual nature (1954e: §607–8); and the encounter with the creature changes the
creator (1954e: §686).

Concerning the New Testament God, Jung argues that, though he was in some
measure reformed by the increased self-awareness that Job had raised in Yahweh, he
too should not only be loved but also feared. He has reformed to the extent that 'He
has not lost his wrath and can still mete out punishment, but he does it with justice.
Cases like the Job tragedy are apparently no longer to be expected. He proves himself benevolent and gracious' (1954e: §651). However, from a wholly good and
loving omnipotent deity, one would expect understanding and forgiveness. One
would not expect that such grace must be bought through appeasement by the
human sacrifice of his son (1954e: §689). Nor could one anticipate that a loving God
would have filled humanity with evil as well as good (1954e: §747). Jung's thesis is
that the paradoxical nature of God tears humanity asunder into opposites and delivers them over to a seemingly insoluble conflict (1954e: §738). The powerful symbol
of the crucifixion conveys the conflict that humanity and the deity share as between
light and dark, good and evil. As Jung wrote in *Aion*, 'the progressive development
and differentiation of consciousness leads to an ever more menacing awareness of
the conflict and involves nothing less than a crucifixion of the ego, in agonizing
suspension between irreconcilable opposites' (Jung, 1950: §79).

Bishop identifies the profoundly moving significance of reading *Answer to Job* as
an account of the development of the God-concept. It centres on,

> the idea that, as the God-archetype constellates itself in the collective uncon-
> scious, so it impinges upon, interacts with, and involves humanity. The devel-
> opment of human consciousness – our progress towards the Self, as individuals

and as members of a species – is thus bound up with, and intimately related to, the development of the archetype of God in the collective unconscious.

(Bishop, 2002: 84)

In a letter to Elined Kotschnig dated 30 June 1956, Jung wrote,

> The significance of man is enhanced by the incarnation. We have become participants of the divine life and we have to assume a new responsibility, viz. the continuation of the divine self-realization, which expresses itself in the task of our individuation.
>
> *(Jung, Letters 2, 316 in Bishop, 2002: 84)*

Bishop comments that the cosmic dimension of Jung's thought was never more literal or so inspiring.

> Human consciousness and the collective unconscious have, in this vision, two mutually interdependent histories, stretching out along two time-lines that intersect and intertwine. … For Jung, the story of Yahweh and Job marks the entrance to a dynamic moving from the unconscious to consciousness.
>
> *(Bishop, 2002: 84–5)*

Jung, of course, saw humanity's task as 'to become conscious of the contents that press upwards from the unconscious' (1961: 358). Contemplating both personal and collective approaches to wholeness, he associates the metaphysical process of bringing the God-image further into consciousness with the individuation process wherein symbols, produced spontaneously by the unconscious, are amplified by the conscious mind (1954e: §751–757). 'The encounter between conscious and unconscious has to ensure that the light which shines in the darkness is not only comprehended by the darkness, but comprehends it' (1954e: §756).

The requirement that one knows darkness speaks to an essential aspect of the individuation process. The present authors are both able to speak of confrontations with the Self which came uninvited (emerging from the unconscious) when each of us encountered a life event that was emotionally, psychologically and physically disruptive.[9] Going through intense suffering requires courage, leaving one with no alternative but surrender to it. One must take a religious attitude toward a symptom, Jung insists, and find meaning in it in order to heal. Then one learns what it means to let go of all that is unessential and live in present time. One understands that there is another, higher power moving through one's life, namely the unconscious. This becomes increasingly significant as one ages and, with physical energies weakening, needs to draw on resources arising from the spiritual.

In *Answer to Job* Jung reiterates his thesis that the psyche is real as an autonomous world of experience and has an authentic religious function. God he observed was an obvious fact since there is plenty of evidence for the existence of God, not as a physical phenomenon, but a psychic one (1954e: §554–5). Crucially the God-image cannot empirically be distinguished from the archetype of the Self: 'It is only through the psyche that we can establish that God acts upon us, but we are unable to distinguish whether these actions emanate from God or from the unconscious' (1954e: §757).

> Faith is certainly right when it impresses on man's mind and heart how infinitely far away and inaccessible God is; but it also teaches his nearness, his immediate presence, and it is just this nearness which has to be empirically real if it is not to lose all significance. … The religious need longs for wholeness, and therefore lays hold of the images of wholeness offered by the unconscious, which, independently of the conscious mind, rise up from the depths of our psychic nature.
>
> *(Ibid.)*

Bishop shows that in *Answer to Job* Jung ultimately attempted to develop his work on the individuation process beyond the personal experience of those individuals who in the cycle of life experience regression into the collective unconscious, the contents of which are then integrated into consciousness. Jung extended his thinking to contemplate individuation as a phylogenetic process running across many aeons of history (Bishop, 2002: 160). It is in thus contemplating humanity's interaction through history with the numinous collective unconscious that *Answer to Job* prepares the way for Malick's *The Tree of Life*.

The embodiment of psyche

Aspe argues that the root origin of things in *The Tree of Life* is not the story. Language comes later and the whispering voices over are structurally retrospective. They do not so much express what a character is thinking as let us understand what he or she ought to have thought but does not realise until much later. The device demonstrates the prerequisite imperative to becoming a psychological being: reflection. In the opening nothing can be seen but light and the manner in which it sculpts the space in which beings exist, the amplitude that this life can have, the weave of existence. Only after that comes the creation of the world forged in our modern myths: the big bang, emergence of the elements of life and of animals. Thanks to Malick's method of reducing shots to the minimum possible, like recollected bursts of happiness, grace and beauty saturate the entire film. But the fact that these retrospective voices are sometimes associated with moments in the images that they ought to have accompanied permits a kind of reparation. It is as if the grace that has not really been experienced can nevertheless return provided there is a conjunction between the voices arriving late and the present tense of the light (Aspe, 2011: 20–1). If this is true for Jack, then it is potentially equally true for the audience, which sees and understands retrospectively with him, their man-god messenger. As Jung wrote in 'On the Nature of the Psyche',

> Image and meaning are identical; and as the first takes shape, so the latter becomes clear. Actually the pattern needs no interpretation: it portrays its own meaning.
>
> *(Jung, 1947/1954: §402)*

Translated into Jungian terms, Aspe perceives the process of individuation not only in the characters but the very weave of the film. In *Answer to Job*, Jung reworks the story of Job into the story of God's self-discovery through the agency of man. We experience a comparable urge toward reforming the numen as the organising drive expressed throughout *The Tree of Life*. Half a century after Jung chose Job to challenge an angry but ossified deity as humanity's agent, Terrence Malick and his creative team use Jack as their agent, creating in him an unexceptional man (though a leading professional member of his society) for whom the Church's stern orthodox dogmatism has killed religion (as Nietzsche foretold). Through Jack – his body that goes tremulously walkabout, his intelligence that grasps so well the elegant dynamics of physical structures, his emotions (so hauntingly needful of release), and his discovery of a creation mythology fitting for the twenty-first century and consonant with every facet of his existence – through Jack's whole being, then, we experience nothing less than the necessary re-creation of the numen.

The numinous in *The Tree of Life* takes a form that no longer mirrors humankind's face back at itself, but it integrates humanity into the universal order – an order, which, unlike the rigid medieval structures of so many of the world's orthodox religions, assures us not of stasis but unending metamorphosis.

Jung wrote to a clergyman 'God is light *and* darkness, the *auctor rerum* is love *and* wrath' (*Letters* 2, 1975, letter dated 17 December 1958). Light and darkness in *The Tree of Life* reach into the theatre. To cite Jung again, 'the light which shines in the darkness is not only comprehended by the darkness, but comprehends it' (1954e: §756). Light and music involve our reciprocal embodiment – grace experienced in the cinema stalls. Just as music performed is embodied first by singers and instrumentalists, so (as we noted earlier) acting is embodied first in the players' performances. But audiences respond in an embodied way to the playing, albeit constrained by socially acceptable forms of conduct. Yet, for example, they flinch and gasp confronted by fearsome attack (whether in 3D or not), stretch the muscles in moments of relief and share too the pleasure of laughing out loud in the unseen community of their fellows. Likewise, listening to *The Tree of Life* many will feel music sway moving feet, hands or head – a physical expression of the dancing, soaring heart.

For the psyche to approach completion in its movement toward individuation, the hardships of transition and release into wellbeing must be felt in the emotions, and also affect the body of the engaged spectator. Psyche and world, the material and spiritual are inseparable. For Romanyshyn 'the body is a hinge around which consciousness and unconsciousness revolve' (1982: 150). And Jung wrote concerning his own life at Bollingen, where he felt most deeply himself,

> At times I feel as if I am spread out over the landscape and inside things, and am myself living in every tree, in the splashing of the waves, in the clouds and the animals that come and go, in the procession of the seasons.
>
> *(Jung, 1961: 252)*

Jung's words, published half a century before the release of Malick's film, capture what it is fully to experience *The Tree of Life*.

Notes

1 Radmila Moacanin's description of *mudras* in Tibetan Buddhism bears on this. *Mudras* are symbolic gestures of hands and fingers reminiscent, in their elegant and expressive manner, of Balinese dancing. They aid meditation as physical, outward expressions of inner states of being. Like mantras, they help when used in the proper context to incite higher states of consciousness (2010: 56). Although Chastain's movements are not *mudras*, because not ritually codified, her physical gestures and movements do express her personal state of grace.

2 The image is of a sculpture in the Sacred Wood at Bomarzo, Italy – an ogre with the legend around its mouth, 'Ogni Pensiero Vola' (All thought flies).

3 RL appears to be a childhood nickname that stuck. In her mourning for him, Mrs O'Brien whispers 'Michael', a name that has ancient associations that liken the holder to God.

4 Anthony Lane wrote of Mrs O'Brien that 'somehow, though the O'Briens are not well off, she never wears the same dress twice' (2011). In the 1950s many women made their own fashionable and inexpensive dresses with the help of pattern books. Lane also misses what Aspe perceives – that we see Mrs O'Brien through Jack's inner eye.

5 Wanderings in the desert have a long history representing mystic liminality. We need look no further than the Bible.

6 The forest is especially associated with the bodily unconscious, according to Von Franz (1999: 63) who cites Jung in 'The Spirit Mercurius' as saying it has to do with the psycho-somatic realm of the psyche.

7 Von Franz recalls that, in his hypotheses concerning synchronicity, Jung presupposed that space and time become completely relative in the deeper levels of the unconscious (1999: 97).

8 Analysing the archetypal qualities of a series of dreams, Jung remarked that 'The water that the mother, the unconscious, pours into the basin of the anima is an excellent symbol for the living power of the psyche' (1953: §94).

9 For Dovalis the crisis came in an accident that left her with terrible burns to her hands and legs. In the case of Izod, the breakdown of his first marriage drew him to the edge of suicide.

13
ENVOI

As we hope the foregoing chapters have sufficiently demonstrated, the cinema has long been both a sacred place and a playground where, through its images and sounds, entertainment and high seriousness co-exist. Recalling Winnicott's theory of emotional development, Jan Abram reminds us that the ability to play is an achievement for anyone, no matter in what stage of life he or she may be. By means of engagement with transitional phenomena, play enables an individual to bridge between the outer and inner worlds. Indeed only through playing can the self be discovered and strengthened (Abram, 2007: 246). The cinema proffers its audiences transitional phenomena in abundance. Both filmmaking and film viewing are creative processes that engage with transitional space. The viewer's interpretations create an analytic relationship with the body of the film that may further his or her emotional development, nowhere more than when suffering the agonies of grief.

Jung, as we would expect, was concerned not only with the unconscious needs of the individual but also of the collective psyche. In *Psychological Types*, he remarked on the aesthetic sensibility of the German poet Friedrich Schiller, and linked the exquisitely personal with the shared sense of the numinous when he wrote,

> I am not, I think, putting it too strongly when I say that for him 'beauty' was a *religious ideal*. Beauty was his religion. His 'aesthetic mood' might equally well be called 'devoutness.' Without definitely expressing anything of that kind, and without explicitly characterizing his central problem as a religious one, Schiller's intuition none the less arrived at the religious problem.

> *(Jung, 1967: §195, original emphasis)*

No doubt somewhat unexpectedly for those who have not experienced it themselves, Jung perceives this aesthetic mood of high religious seriousness as being intimately connected to the play instinct. He recognises that,

> these two concepts are in some sort opposed, since play and seriousness are scarcely compatible.... Seriousness comes from a profound inner necessity, but play is its outward expression, the face it turns to consciousness. It is not, of course, a matter of *wanting* to play, but of *having* to play; a playful manifestation of fantasy from inner necessity, without the compulsion of circumstance, without even the compulsion of the will. *It is serious play.* And yet it is certainly play in its outward aspect, as seen from the standpoint of consciousness and collective opinion. That is the ambiguous quality that clings to everything creative.
>
> If play expires in itself without creating anything durable and vital, it is only play, but in the other case it is called creative work. Out of a playful movement of elements whose inter-relations are not immediately apparent, patterns arise which an observant and critical intellect can only evaluate afterwards. The creation of something new is not accomplished by the intellect, but by the play instinct arising from inner necessity. The creative mind plays with the object it loves.
>
> *(Ibid.: §196–7, original emphases)*

Jung's words reach deep into what we have attempted, what we have experienced and what we hope for our readers. Jung speaks to the necessarily resolute, yet playful creative process that we shared in our eight years of forging in lively debate through constant exchange of drafts (thirty-two for Chapter 12 alone) a book that neither could have written without the other.

Jung's insight into the sacred nature of beauty characterises our sense of the creativity exultant in not only those films we have discussed but the many others that light flames in our mind. And, since every film comes into existence only through the presence and participation of its audience, Jung also shapes our valedictory greeting to our reader, the hope that you too may enjoy exploratory voyages such as we have taken to discover imaginary worlds that might adorn the true Self.

GLOSSARY

acting out Action based in fantasies or wishes in which an individual is in the grips of his or her unconscious (or complex) and yields to the compulsion to repeat rather than remember. Acting out often has both an impulsive and aggressive aspect directed at either the self or others. In Freudian terms it is the return of the repressed; in Jungian terminology, shadow behaviour.

affect A psychoanalytic term that is associated with a painful *or* pleasant emotional state. According to Laplanche and Pontalis (1973: 13) affect is the qualitative expression of the quantity of instinctual energy and its fluctuations.

alchemical images As Jung studied alchemy, he found the images (largely a part of the unconscious) could be used to understand the complex contents of the psyche. The images bring into visibility certain categories of the individuation process and describe the process of depth psychotherapy. They give an objective perspective to the understanding of dreams and other unconscious material.

anima and animus The contrasexual archetypes. In Jung's formulation, the anima is experienced by men, representing the hidden feminine aspects of their personalities. The animus symbolises the concealed masculine in women.

apperception In Jungian analysis a process through which new psychic content becomes understood. Clarity is achieved through reflection, resulting from the integration between personal experience and archetypal imago. Winnicott uses the term for the infant's subjective experience of merger with the mother; seeing himself or herself through being seen by the mother. Perception comes out of apperception, which ultimately creates the ability to see whole objects and the capability to differentiate between what is Me and Not Me.

archetype The part of the psyche that is inherited, it is revealed both by patterns of psychological behaviour (such as birth and marriage) and figures from the inner psychic life (for example, anima, shadow, etc.). It is a psychosomatic concept that links the body and psyche and is invoked in the analysis of images arising from the collective unconscious. It defines the major conceptual difference between Jung and Freud since Jung did not view psychology or internal images as being mainly connected to biological drives.

attachment Self experience mutually created between an infant and his or her primary care giver. All the events that create attachment, such as touch, physical proximity and responsiveness, are regulated by the primary care giver. The development of a secure attachment leads to a healthy sense of separateness and leans toward independence and a mature sense of dependence in intimate relationships.

calcinatio A procedure in alchemy that represents the element of fire. Jung argued that it symbolised libido, a process that both purged and purified those psychic energies of the ego concerned with pleasure and power. Fire is associated with archetypal energies that transcend the ego and are experienced as numinous. The psychic energy (driven from the personal) in the unconscious complexes is ultimately transformed to the transpersonal and archetypal aspect.

cathect A substantial amount of psychic energy that has become attached to an idea or a group of ideas, to a part of the body, to an object or organisation (such as a team or political party). Freud thought of cathects as displacements of excitability in the nervous system.

chiaroscuro In painting, the conjunction of light and shade. In Jungian terminology it is the critical distinction between light and dark. Psychic life lives in the conjunction between the light of consciousness and the shadow of the unconscious.

circumambulate Literally to walk around (something). Thinking psychologically, Jung saw it as a circular movement focusing on the centre. He conceived an image of a wheel with the ego at its centre contained within the greater Self.

cisplacement A defensive function in which affect detaches itself from a particular idea. For example, a phobia may be displaced onto an object that objectifies, localises and contains anxiety.

coagulatio A procedure in alchemy that belongs to the symbolism of the element earth. Psychic content has become concretised and therefore attached to the ego. Psychologically the process creates the action and psychic movement to promote ego development. An engaging and responsive therapist can stimulate this during therapy.

collective unconscious The deeper, impersonal layer of the unconscious. Its contents are the repository of mankind's entire psychic heritage. Jung believed it was essential to differentiate oneself from the collective through individuation (q.v.).

compensation Jung regarded activity in the unconscious as a means to balance, adjust or supplement any tendency toward one-sidedness on the part of the conscious mind. Psychologically, it is a strategy where a person consciously or unconsciously covers real or imagined feelings of inadequacy or incompetence in one area of life by moving towards excellence in another area.

complex An emotionally charged cluster of ideas, images or memories organised around a core archetype arising from the personal unconscious. It is marked by great affective force, and has both a sense of urgency and compulsion attached to it. Jung saw complexes as splinter parts of the self.

compulsion to repeat An ungovernable process that originates in the unconscious. As a result of its action, a person returns to a familiar distressing situation but does not recall where or when it originated. In fact the person thinks it is created by circumstances in the present moment.

coniunctio Alchemical symbolism for the union of opposites that has two phases. The lesser *coniunctio* is a union of elements that have not yet been thoroughly separated. The greater is a final union of purified opposites, and the goal of the opus (q.v.). Jung used the phrase *coniunctio oppositorum* to refer to the psychological goal of individuation in which one-sidedness is resolved.

container When early primary care takers contain an infant's emotional distress, the child introjects (q.v.) an object capable of holding and dealing with anxiety and develops its own container. The analyst functions as an emotional container for the patient, but anyone who listens can do so.

counter transference The therapist's unconscious reaction to the client, especially to the latter's own transference. From this perspective, transference and counter transference provoke a continual intersubjective, interpersonal enactment of a co-created relational unconscious. For example, a client becomes defensive and refuses to take in what the therapist is saying (symbolically rejecting his or her abusive parent). This in turn provokes the therapist to become frustrated and angry with the client (who has stirred feelings of rejection by a figure in the therapist's original family).

divine child archetype A symbol of transformation in the maturation process of individuation.

ego The central agency of the personality as a whole that is concerned with reality and safety. In its role as mediator it is in a dependent position in relation to the claims of the id as well as under pressure from the demands of the super ego. Therefore, it is not an autonomous structure.

ego-self axis Originally arises in an individual out of a certain quality of relationship between mother and infant. Ultimately a balance between separation and togetherness, and between outward exploration and self-reflection is attained through the individuation process. Connecting ego with Self is the fulfilment of the journey of individuation.

enactment In contrast to acting-out behaviour, the individual attempts to suffer the presence of an archetypal energy, consciously interacting with it until its symbolic meaning becomes known. While recognising the power of the unconscious pull, the person neither regresses nor gives into its pressure. Rather than the 'not remembering' that accompanies acting-out behaviour, enactment can lead to achievement of increased consciousness and awareness.

enantiodromia The tendency of every psychological extreme to contain its own opposite and move towards it. This principle is key to the essential duality of

Jungian myth, since the more extreme a position is, the more it can be expected to convert into its opposite.

entitlement   In healthy entitlement, individuals have a sense of ownership over what rightfully belongs to them. In unhealthy (or infantile) entitlement, people justify ownership although they have not earned the right to it.

envy   According to Klein, it is a destructive attack against the good object (breast). In a relationship it plays out as an aggressive projection, as in: 'I want what you have, but I need to destroy you in my mind to feel better about myself.'

false self   Described by Winnicott as a psychological structure whose function is to defend the true self. He divided false-self organisation into a spectrum from pathological to healthy, moulded by the early environment that shaped the quality of this necessary defence.

fantasy   '… more or less your own invention, [which] remains on the surface of personal things and conscious expectations' (Jung, 1935: §397). With fantasy the individual can in some circumstances control the imaginative process and intervene in the outcome (see Samuels *et al.*, 1986: 58–60). By comparison, when employing active imagination 'the images have a life and a logic of their own' (Jung, 1935: §397). Klein emphasised the power of fantasy and its underlying value to all mental processes and activity.

guilt   A painful emotional state (that may or may not be conscious) arising out of an internal conflict, particularly feelings of self worth. Freud emphasised the importance of guilt and its unconscious motivations that account for acts of failure and self punishment.

id   One of the three agencies of the self described by Freud. The id accounts for the instinctual pole of the personality and is the prime reservoir of psychic energy. Derived from the instincts, its contents are unconscious, some being innate and inherited and others repressed and adopted from childhood experience. From a dynamic perspective the id is in conflict with both ego and super ego.

idealisation   A mental process in which an individual elevates the qualities and value of an object or person.

identification   A psychological process whereby an individual assimilates certain aspects of another and is transformed. Personality development is influenced by major attachment figures.

imago   A subjectively experienced image created by the internal life and based on primary and fantasised relationships within the individual's environment. It is shaped both by personal experience and archetypal forces.

in media res   In the middle of something such as a story or a process.

individuation process   Key concept in Jungian psychology. The journey of self-discovery as a person integrates the personality and becomes increasingly authentic. Jung used the term to denote the process by which a person becomes '"in-dividual", that is, a separate indivisible unity or "whole"' (1939: §490).

inflation   A state of mind in which one has an unrealistically high sense of identity.

integration Either the recognition or the process of bringing about the interaction between conscious and unconscious, masculine and feminine (animus and anima), and other pairs of opposites in the personality such as the ego in relation to the shadow. In midlife, the capacity to hold an optimum level of tension between these opposites can potentially be attained.

introjection A psychological process opposite to projection that internalises experience. In fantasy the individual transposes objects (such as early care takers) and their inherent qualities, from outside to inside him or her self.

libido For Freud, it is the energy underlying the transformation of the sexual instinct. Jung extended the concept to mean mental or 'psychic energy'. Hence libidinal energy comes from the id (Freud) or the instincts (Jung).

liminal space Borderline psychological territory between the conscious and unconscious parts of the mind. In the mid-life transition this borderline space must be navigated.

manic defence A psychological position that protects the ego from experiencing feelings of guilt and loss. The individual develops an exaggerated sense of independence to defend against anxious feelings of dependency.

memento mori Reminder that death is inescapable.

mentalise The process by which people realise that having a mind mediates their experience of the world. It is an essential feature of emotional self-regulation and thus a core aspect of human social functioning. It allows individuals to make sense of or understand themselves and others.

mirroring In order to see the world, an individual must have had the experience of feeling seen. This process begins at the very beginning of life. The infant depends on their primary care takers' facial responses in order to establish his or her own sense of self. This imperative process continues throughout childhood, which provides a deep sense of connection to the individual's own emotional life along, potentially, with feeling understood. The premise of our book is that film is an active mirroring agent for personal growth and therefore has influence over the development of the collective conscious.

mortificatio A procedure in alchemy that refers to the experience of death. It is regarded as the most negative operation and includes dark images of torture, mutilation and rotting. It is represented by the colour black, psychologically referring to the Jungian shadow. What had become fully concretised in the alchemical process of coagulation is now ready for transformation and transcendence.

narcissism Freud originally defined two types. Primary narcissism is characterised by the absence of relationship to the external world and a lack of separation between ego and id analogous to the womb experience. Secondary narcissism concerns the formation of ego through identification with its object relations. Narcissism can also be understood structurally as a damming up of libidinal energy.

narcissistic wounds Emotional injuries suffered at the core of the individual's sense of self and self worth.

numinous, the Transcendent energy outside the control of ego, toward the power of which a person can only open up. Jung saw experience of the numinous as an attribute of a religious or magical experience which held an unknown, fateful meaning.

object Psychoanalytically a concrete entity of attachment that can be a person, thing or even a part of the body through which gratification of instincts is received. For example, the mother is an object to the infant.

obsessive compulsion Revealed by repetitive actions in response to intense persistent thoughts a person cannot let go of – for example, constant checking if the doors are locked.

Oedipus complex Emanated from Sophocles's *Oedipus Rex*. Freud identified parallels with this tragedy when he discovered the archetype of the analytic method. Posited in psychoanalytic theory as playing a fundamental role in personality formation and the development of desire, it originates from the triadic parent-child relationship and encompasses both the loving and hostile wishes the child experiences toward his or her parents.

omnipotent fantasies An early psychological system in the infant's life responsible for development of ego and self. The critical transition from infantile omnipotence to a more balanced sense of power will fail if the child is exposed to a harsh parental environment that leaves them feeling too helpless or powerless.

one-sidedness Jung spoke of the risk of neurotic disturbance associated with overdeveloping or identifying with one side of the opposites.

opposites The principle of opposites is core to understanding Jung's theory of the psyche, which argues that alternation from one side of a pair to the other is the hallmark of awakening consciousness.

opus Symbolised by the Philosopher's Stone, the central image of alchemy represents the supreme value. Considered sacred work, the alchemical process is highly individual and corresponds to psychotherapy: to undertake it an acute awareness of the psyche's transpersonal level is prerequisite. In other words, to engage in the opus an individual must first find the *prima materia* and be Self-oriented rather than ego-oriented.

participation mystique The state of mystic identity that precedes the emergence (in an individual or a collective) of reflective consciousness. An individual or a group identifies with one side of a pair of opposites and projects its opposite. In personal therapy, a typical pair of opposites are love and hate as exemplified by a parent who can only be loving and projects his or her hate on the family by becoming overly punishing when angry. This condition persists as long as the opposites remain unconscious and not separated. Key to the work involved in therapy, separating the self from the other is fundamental so a de-identification with the pairs of opposites may occur.

persona The public face or mask a person wears in order to confront his or her world in social, gender or developmental roles. Jung conceived the persona as a social archetype that manifests all the compromises a personality must make in order to live in a community. A psychological problem may develop if a person over identifies with his or her persona.

philosopher's stone Symbol of the opus. Described in alchemical terms, the purpose of the opus (i.e. the individuation process) is to create ultimately a transcendent substance, an elixir of life or universal medicine.

phylogeny Development of a group with inherited elements common to all members of the particular species.

postmodern hero Distinguished from the classical hero in being dedicated to letting go the ego-driven persona in favour of a critical dialogue with the primitive alter ego. The postmodern hero's goal is completeness (rather than the perfection sought by the classic hero) with the goal gradually to emerge as an individuated human being (Dovalis, 2003: 10).

prima materia The term, meaning 'first matter', originated from pre-Socratic philosophers. They held an archetypal image (as a projection of a psychic rather than actual fact) that the world derived from a single original substance. This first matter is a formless state of pure potentiality, and in order for transformation of the personality to occur, the individual must return to the psychological state of innocence, symbolised by the child.

projection A mechanism in which disowned feelings, wishes, qualities or internal objects are ejected from the self and targeted unto another person or thing. It is understood as a primitive defence experienced by both healthy and unhealthy people. It is a critical psychological task for a person to withdraw projections back into the self and bear the weight of their own psychic life. This process goes hand in hand with the transformation of the shadow.

psyche For Jung 'the totality of all psychic processes, conscious as well as unconscious' (1967: §797), it can be understood through the depth and intensity of human experience and incorporates many autonomous components (complexes, images, patterns and pairs of opposites) that define it as *both* a structure and a dynamic.

psychic leakage A term developed by Dovalis in her psychotherapy practice to refer to unconscious psychic material projected outward.

psychological birth Jung believed not everyone was psychologically born. Whenever we talk about birth, we are talking about the feminine and bringing things into relationship. This process requires going deep into the unconscious. The individuation process pushes a person to reach a level of differentiation where he or she has developed the capacity to reflect and tolerate the tensions created by the pairs of opposites. Mental health can thus be described as having the capacity to hold two feelings at the same time (*see also Rebirth*).

psychopomp As a case in point, the mythological character Hermes guided souls during times of transition to the underworld, being able to slip between heaven and earth, night and day and life and death. In analytical psychology, it is the function of the psychopomp (anima and animus may also adopt this role) to help bridge the space between the conscious and unconscious.

puer Latin for 'boy'. The eternal child or archetypal image representing the Peter Pan syndrome. Describing the negative aspects of the figure, Von Franz used the term to refer to men too closely identified with spirit and therefore overly optimistic, excessively risky, idealistic and stuck in a prolonged adolescence. Hillman thought that, on the positive side, the *puer* was a divine messenger, giving men a sense of meaning and direction toward their destiny.

putrefactio Overlaps with the term *mortificatio*, both referring to different aspects of the same alchemical operation – the chemical process of rotting that breaks down dead bodies. In dreams symbols such as excrement and foul odours may appear. In psychological terms the process refers to the positive consequences of becoming aware of one's shadow, thus leading to transformation of the personality. The experience has a powerful psychological impact on the individuation process.

rationalisation A common psychological process whereby an individual attempts to offer an explanation that presents a logical or acceptable attitude, idea, feeling or action, but the true motives are concealed and not obviously perceived. It occurs on a broad spectrum, anywhere from the delusional to the normal.

rebirth The birth of something new carries the theme of death and resurrection. New life is imagined as a second birth because the old has to die in order for something new to be born. In therapy that is a psychological or spiritual birth which moves away from perfection and encompasses a life that is wholly human (*see also* Psychological birth).

regression A turning back to an earlier time of emotional development. Freud thought of it as a negative or failed experience; however, Jung thought it had necessary and even therapeutic value as long as an individual did not remain stuck in a regressive position for a prolonged period of time.

repression A psychological condition whereby an individual attempts to split off and disown certain thoughts, images, and memories, delegating them to the unconscious. The concept is analogous to Jung's concept of the shadow. Freud viewed it as a defensive process that the ego makes use of when conflicted. It is a universal mental process whose representations are bound to instinct, and it lies at the root of the unconscious.

self An archetypal image that contains the full potential of an individual, encompassing the unity of the personality as a whole. Jung writes 'The self is not only the centre but also the whole circumference which embraces both conscious and unconscious; it is the centre of this totality, just as the ego is the centre of the conscious mind' (1953: §444).

senex Latin for 'old man'. An archetypal concept that refers to psychological qualities attributed to the elderly including wisdom, the vision and maturity to see far into the future, a sense of balance and a generous attitude toward others. See **wise old man**. Negatively, it can be expressed as depressive, too grounded, authoritarian and conservative, lacking a playful attitude and active imagination.

separatio In alchemy the procedure that separates the primary pair of opposites. In psychotherapy it differentiates the I from the not-I. In order to develop consciousness, space must exist between the opposites. It is impossible to develop a sense of self without engaging in this arduous process since it is the psychological work needed to separate from our original families. Thus, it is the primary work of a depth therapy.

shadow The archetype that represents the negative side of the personality or 'other person' in the dark side. It is the sum total of all the primitive qualities that makes us human, and validates the existence of evil. It is one of the great contributions of Freud to recognise the psychic split between the light and dark sides of the psyche.

solutio One of the major alchemical procedures in Alchemy, it pertains to water. For the alchemist, the process turns a solid into a liquid, which implies returning differentiated matter to its undifferentiated state called the *prima materia* or first matter. This procedure corresponds to what happens in depth psychological therapy when rigid parts of the personality are confronted in order for change to occur.

sortes virgilianae Serendipitous divination by reference to a passage of writing found by chance.

splitting A primitive defence to ward off overwhelming anxiety and ensure survival. The division in the psyche is due to its psychological structure: the conscious and unconscious and the super ego-ego-id. For both Jung and Freud, it is human nature's way of responding to a psychological or emotional conflict.

synchronicity An acausal connecting principle where inner and outer realities intersect (outside time and space), creating a link between the psychic and material worlds. In developing the concept, Jung was attempting to explain those experiences that cross the boundary between chance and causality. Synchronistic events are deeply meaningful coincidences where fate may play a part.

teleology A psychological or spiritual orientation that points to a sense of purpose and direction. Jung's concept of individuation encompasses this point of view. He believed the hidden Self gave a particular direction to people's lives. Fulfilling the process of individuation equates to realising one's potential and achieving one's destiny.

temenos A term used by the early Greeks to define a sacred space or vessel where the presence of God could be felt. In this regard a church, therapy room or cinema theatre, are potential containers for unconscious processes where transformation may occur.

topos Cluster of related themes, often with roots in tradition.

transcendent function Has a symbolic purpose to mediate and facilitate a connection between a pair of opposites. It represents a link between the real and imaginary realms therefore serving as a bridge between the conscious and unconscious. It is exactly because of its ability to transcend the destructive tendency to be too one-sided that Jung considered it the most significant factor in the psychological process of individuation.

transference During psychological treatment, earlier familial prototypes or internal imagos re-emerge and are experienced by the client with strong affective charge. In depth psychology this is regarded as the terrain on which the patient's problems play themselves out, providing an opportunity for resolution through the relationship with the therapist. See *Counter transference.*

transformation   The psychic movement involving regression in the development of consciousness. The goal of depth psychotherapy includes a deep investigation of what has been repressed or resides in the shadow in order to make it more complete. It is a lifelong natural process, a growing connection between ego and Self.

transitional object   A term developed by Winnicott. An external object that an infant or child adopts as his or her first true possession because he or she created it. It is an emblem of the journey from complete dependence on the mother to a more relative dependence, where the baby begins to see the mother not as him or herself, and therefore is able to create what he or she needs. As a symbolic representation of a child's attachment to the mother, it helps with the necessary process of separation.

transitional space   Winnicott believed people spend most of their time in an intermediate zone, a third area that is neither the observable extroverted life explained by behaviour nor the inner life in a state of contemplation. From a depth perspective, it is an intuitively created space where the imagination and creative life come alive.

transpersonal, the   An individual experience that is beyond the personal, involving non-ordinary states of consciousness and transcendence. As a collective or universal experience, transpersonal psychic contents have archetypal and symbolic meanings that cannot be explained by personal experiences alone.

trauma   An emotional event that a person is not psychologically prepared for. The reaction creates a primitive type of anxiety. A trauma occurs because the child or adult has no organised defence against what he or she has experienced and therefore falls into a state of confusion and psychic disintegration. The psychological experience can be narcissistically wounding and hit to the core of the person's self worth if it remains unintegrated.

trickster   An archetypal image. Jung conceptualised the figure psychologically as analogous to a collective shadow figure that brings the possibility of transformation by assigning meaning to the meaningless. Mythically, as an alchemical figure, the trickster (like Mercurius) displays qualities of the shape shifter and sly joker. It is the agent of the unconscious, rebelling against established order by giving voice to the truth that comes from below. With a dual nature, half-divine, half-animal, s/he resembles a saviour figure and is crucial to initiating growth and change.

unconscious   Defined by Freud and Jung as a psychic place containing mental contents that are not accessible to the ego. On the personal level, both men believed that it contains psychological material that has been split off and disowned by the ego. However, Jung thought of it not only as a personal repository for repressed primitive material, but as also having an objective component. This part included the collective instinctual side of human nature that has never been a part of consciousness and reflects archetypal processes.

unus mundus Jung's development of the relationship between alchemy and the individuation process led him to the idea of a unitary world. The focus of the concept is on the *relationship* of things rather than a literal viewpoint. For example, the body-mind connection can be understood as the psyche living in the body with the relationship between psyche and matter co-creating synchronistic events. This teleological point of view leads to a process of creating meaning from the experiences of life.

wise old man Archetypal image that represents wisdom, insight, reflection, knowledge, intuition and positive moral qualities. As a mana personality (an extraordinary supernatural power), the figure appears whenever the ego is confronted with the self. *See also Senex.*

REFERENCES

Abram, Jan (1996) *The Language of Winnicott: A Dictionary and Guide to Understanding his Use of Words* (Northvale, NJ: Jason Aronson).
___ (2007) *The Language of Winnicott: A Ddictionary and Guide to Understanding his Use of Words* (2nd edn.) (London: Karnac).

Ahmed, Sara (2004) *The Cultural Politics of Emotion* (New York: Routledge).

Anderson, Helen (2010) 'The Innate Transformational Properties of Beethoven's Passion Music,' in Ashton and Bloch, 45–66.

Armstrong, Rod (2001) '*The Son's Room*,' *Reel.com* www.reel.com/movie.asp?MID=134214 &Tab=reviews&buy=open&CID=13#tabs accessed 3 August 2007.

Ashton, Paul W. (2010) 'Music, Mind and Psyche,' in Ashton and Bloch, 121–42.

Ashton, Paul W. and Stephen Bloch (eds.) (2010) *Music and Psyche: Contemporary Psychoanalytic Explorations* (New Orleans: Spring Journal Books).

Aspe, Bernard (2011) 'De l'origine radicale des choses,' *Cahiers du Cinéma* (December) 20–3.

Barker, Jennifer M. (2009) *The Tactile Eye* (Berkeley and London: University of California Press).

Barthes, Roland (1973) *The Pleasure of the Test* (New York: Hill & Wang [1975]).

Beebe, John (1996) 'Jungian Illumination of Film,' *Psychoanalytic Review*, 83, 4 (August) 579–587.
___ (2007) 'Shadows and Healing,' Discussion list of the International Association of Jungian Scholars (17 January).

Bellour, Raymond (2012) 'The Cinema Spectator: A Special Memory,' Lecture given at the University of Edinburgh (2 May).

Bishop, Paul (2002) *Jung's Answer to Job: A Commentary* (Hove: Brunner-Routledge).

Bleasdale, John (2011) 'Review of *The Tree of Life*,' *Electric Sheep* (6 July) www. electricsheepmagazine.co.uk/features/2011/07/06/malicks-magic-hour/ accessed 18 July 2011.

Boeree, C. George (2002) 'A Bio-Social Theory of Neurosis' http://webspace.ship.edu/cgboer/genpsyneurosis.html accessed 7 June 2010.

Bolen, Jean Shinoda (1985) *Goddesses in Everywoman: A New Psychology of Women* (New York: Harper & Row).
___ (2003) *Crones Don't Whine* (San Francisco: Conari Press).

Bonaventure, Saint (1978) *The Tree of Life* (London: SPCK).

Bowlby, John (1961) 'Processes of Mourning,' *The International Journal of Psychoanalysis* 42, 317–40.

Bradshaw, Peter (2002) '*The Son's Room*,' *The Guardian* (15 February). http://film.guardian.co.uk/News_Story/Critic_Review/Guardian_Film_of_the_week/0,,650165,00.html accessed 3 August 2007.

Branch, Jana (2011, 2013) Personal communications.

Britton, Ronald (1998) *Belief and Imagination: Explorations in Psychoanalysis* (London and New York: Routledge).

Buscombe, Ed (2005) 'Million Dollar Baby,' *Sight and Sound* 15, 3 (March) 67–8.

Campbell, Joseph with Bill Moyers (1988) *The Power of Myth* (NY: Doubleday).

Carotenuto, Aldo (1989) *Eros and Pathos: Shades of Love and Suffering* (Toronto: Inner City Books).

Chaw, Walter (2004) '*Birth*' www.filmfreakcentral.net/screenreviews/psbirth.htm accessed 28 May 2007.

Chetwynd, Tom (1993) *Dictionary of Symbols* (London: Aquarian Press).

City of Johannesburg, Official Website, www.joburg.org.za/soweto/overview.stm accessed 28 April 2006.

Clarke, Arthur C. (1968) *The Promise of Space* (New York: Harper & Row).

Clarke, J. J. (1994) *Jung and Eastern Thought: A Dialogue with the Orient* (London: Routledge).

Clinical Update, California Society for Clinical Social Work (2005) (April) 8.

Coates, Paul (ed.) (1999) *Lucid Dreams: The Films of Krzysztof Kieslowski* (Trowbridge: Flicks Books).

Cooper, David E. and Simon P. James (2005) *Buddhism, Virtue and Environment* (Aldershot: Ashgate).

Cozzalio, Dennis (2006) 'The Mystery of *Birth*' in *Sergio Leone and the Infield Fly Rule* (10 February) sergioleoneifr.blogspot.com/2006/02/mystery-of-birth.html accessed 31 May 2007.

Cumbow, Robert C. (2006) 'Why Is This Film Called *Birth*? Investigating Jonathan Glazer's Mystery of the Heart' (23 January) www.24liesasecond.com/site2/index.php?page=2&task=index_onearticle.php&Column_Id=86 accessed 29 May 2007.

Dass, Ram (2002) 'Fierce Grace,' *Parabola* 27, 3 (August) 34.

Davies, Norman (1982) *God's Playground: A History of Poland* (Oxford: Oxford University Press).

Deger, Jennifer (2007) *Shimmering Screens: Making Media in an Aboriginal Community* (Minneapolis: University of Minnesota Press).

Dovalis, Joanna (2003) 'Cinema and Psyche: Individuation and the Postmodern Hero's Journey,' unpublished doctoral dissertation, Pacifica Graduate Institute.

Dufrenne, Mikel (1973), *The Phenomenology of Aesthetic Experience* (Evanston, Ill.: Northwestern University Press) 461.

Dyer, Richard (1997) *White* (London: Routledge).

Ebert, Roger (2005) 'Million Dollar Baby,' *Chicago Sun Times* (7 January) www.suntimes.com/ accessed 16 March 2005.

Edinger, Edward F. (1985) *Anatomy of the Psyche: Alchemical Symbolism in Psychotherapy* (Chicago: Open Court).

Eigen, Michael (2010a) Interviewed in Ashton and Bloch, 161–75.

_____ (2010b) cited in Stephen Bloch, 'Mercy: The Unbearable in Eigen's Writings and John Tavener's *Prayer of the Heart*' in Ashton and Bloch, 262.

Estes, Clarissa Pinkola (1990) *Warming the Stone Child* (CD) (Boulder, Colorado: Sounds True).

Factory Girl, Plot Summary for *Morvern Callar*, *IMDb* (2002). www.imdb.com/title/tt0300214/plotsummary accessed 18 February 2011.

Fairbairn, W. R. D. (1952) *Psychoanalytic Studies of the Personality* (London: Routledge).

Falkowska, Janina (1999) '*The Double Life of Véronique* and *Three Colours*: an escape from politics?' in Coates, 136–59.

Fredericksen, Don (2001) 'Jung/Sign/Symbol/Film,' in Christopher Hauke and Ian Alister (eds) *Jung and Film: Post-Jungian Takes on the Moving Image* (London: Brunner-Routledge).

French, Philip (2002) 'A Matter of Death and Life,' *The Observer* (17 February). http://film. guardian.co.uk/News_Story/Critic_Review/Observer_Film_of_the_week/0,,651369,00. html accessed 3 August 2007.

_____ (2005) 'The Lord and the Ring,' *The Observer* (January 16). http://film.guardian.co.uk/ NewsStory/CriticReview/Observer Film of the week/0,4267,1391348,00.html accessed 16 March 2005.

Friedman, Michael (1985) 'Toward a Reconceptualization of Guilt,' *Contemporary Psychoanalysis* 21 (4) (October) 501–547.

Furman, Erna (1974) *A Child's Parent Dies: Studies in Childhood Bereavement* (New Haven: Yale University Press).

Gilbey, Ryan (2011) Review of *The Tree of Life*, *New Statesman* (7 July). www.newstatesman. com/film/2011/07/1950s-america-tree-film-life accessed 18 July 2011.

Haltof, Marek (2004) *The Cinema of Krzysztof Kieslowski: Variations on Destiny and Chance* (London: Wallflower Press).

Henderson, Joseph L. (1964) 'Ancient Myths and Modern Man,' in Carl G. Jung (ed.), *Man and His Symbols*, 95–156.

Hillman, James (1983) *Healing Fiction* (Woodstock: Spring Publications).

Hoberman, J. (2011) 'The Tree of Life,' *Voice Film* (16 May) www.voicefilm.com/2011/05/ cannes_2011_the_tree_of_life.php accessed 10 April 2012.

Hopcke, Robert H., (1989) *A Guided Tour of the Collected Works of C. G. Jung* (Boston: Shambala).

_____ (1992) *A Guided Tour of the Collected Works of C. G. Jung* (Boston: Shambala).

Hughes, Darren (2006) '*Birth*' (2 June) www.longpauses.com/blog/2006/06/birth-2004. html accessed 24 May 2007.

Humphrey, Geraldine M. and David G. Zimpfer (1996) *Counselling for Grief and Bereavement* (London: Sage).

Izod, John (2006) *Screen, Culture, Psyche: A Post-Jungian Approach to Working with the Audience* (London: Routledge).

Jacoby, Mario, Verena Kast and Ingrid Riedel (1992) *Witches, Ogres, and the Devil's Daughter: Encounters with Evil in Fairy Tales* (Boston and London: Shambhala).

Johnson, Robert A. (1991) *He: Understanding Masculine Psychology* (New York: Perennial Library).

Jones, Kent (2011) 'Light Years,' *Film Comment* (15 December) www.filmlinc.com/film-comment/entry/light-years-kent-jones-tree-of-life-review accessed 13 March 2012.

Jung, C. G. (1927/1931) 'Mind and Earth,' *Civilization in Transition, The Collected Works*. Vol. 10 (London: Routledge and Kegan Paul [1964]).

_____ (1934) 'Basic Postulates of Analytical Psychology,' in *The Structure and Dynamics of the Psyche, The Collected Works*. Vol. 8, 2nd edn. (London: Routledge & Kegan Paul [1969]).

_____ (1935) *The Tavistock Lectures* in *The Collected Works*. Vol. 18 (London: Routledge & Kegan Paul [1977]).

_____ (1937) 'Psychological Factors Determining Human Behaviour,' in *The Structure and Dynamics of the Psyche, The Collected Works*. Vol. 8, 2nd edn. (London: Routledge & Kegan Paul [1969]).

_____ (1939) 'Conscious, Unconscious, and Individuation,' in *The Archetypes and the Collective Unconscious, The Collected Works*, Vol. 9, 1, 2nd edn. (London: Routledge & Kegan Paul [1968]).

_____ (1943) 'On the Psychology of the Unconscious,' *Two Essays on Analytical Psychology, The Collected Works*. Vol. 7, 2nd edn. (London: Routledge & Kegan Paul [1966]).

_____ (1946) 'The Psychology of the Transference,' in _The Practice of Psychotherapy, The Collected Works_. Vol. 16, 2nd edn. (Princeton: Princeton University Press [1985]).

_____ (1947/1954) 'On the Nature of the Psyche,' in _The Structure and Dynamics of the Psyche, The Collected Works_. Vol. 8, 2nd edn. (London: Routledge & Kegan Paul [1969]).

_____ (1948a) 'The Spirit Mercurius,' in _Alchemical Studies, The Collected Works_. Vol. 13 (London: Routledge & Kegan Paul [1967]).

_____ (1948b) 'General Aspects of Dream Psychology,' in _The Structure and Dynamics of the Psyche, The Collected Works_. Vol. 8, 2nd edn. (London: Routledge & Kegan Paul [1969]).

_____ (1950) _Aion, The Collected Works_, Vol. 9, 2, 2nd edn. (London: Routledge & Kegan Paul [1968]).

_____ (1951) 'The Psychology of the Child Archetype,' in _The Archetypes and the Collective Unconscious, The Collected Works_, Vol. 9, 1, 2nd edn. (London: Routledge & Kegan Paul [1968]).

_____ (1952) 'Synchronicity: An Acausal Connecting Principle,' in _The Structure and Dynamics of the Psyche, The Collected Works_. Vol. 8, 2nd edn. (London: Routledge & Kegan Paul [1969]).

_____ (1953) _Psychology and Alchemy, The Collected Works_, Vol. 12, 2nd edn. (London: Routledge & Kegan Paul)

_____ (1954a) 'Psychological Aspects of the Mother Archetype,' in _The Archetypes and the Collective Unconscious, The Collected Works_, Vol. 9, 1, 2nd edn. (London: Routledge & Kegan Paul [1968]).

_____ (1954b) _Mysterium Coniunctionis, The Collected Works_, Vol. 14, 2nd edn. (Princeton NJ: Princeton University Press [1970]).

_____ (1954c) 'On the Psychology of the Trickster-Figure,' in _The Archetypes and the Collective Unconscious, The Collected Works_, Vol. 9, 1, 2nd edn. (London: Routledge & Kegan Paul [1968]).

_____ (1954d) 'The Philosophical Tree,' in _Alchemical Studies, The Collected Works_, Vol. 13 (London: Routledge & Kegan Paul [1983]).

_____ (1954e) _Answer to Job_, in _The Collected Works_ Vol. 11 (London: Routledge & Kegan Paul [1958]).

_____ (1956) _Symbols of Transformation, The Collected Works_, Vol. 5, 2nd edn. (London: Routledge & Kegan Paul).

_____ (1958a) _The Practice of Psychotherapy, The Collected Works_. Vol. 16, 2nd edn. (Princeton NJ: Princeton University Press [1966]).

_____ (1958b) 'A Psychological View of Conscience,' _Civilization in Transition_ in _The Collected Works_ Vol. 10 (London: Routledge & Kegan Paul [1964]).

_____ (1959) 'Flying Saucers: A Modern Myth of Things Seen in the Skies,' in _Civilization in Transition, The Collected Works_ Vol. 10 (London: Routledge & Kegan Paul [1964]).

_____ (1961) _Memories, Dreams, Reflections_ (London: Fontana [1995]).

_____ (1964) (ed.) _Man and his Symbols_ (London: Picador [1978]).

_____ (1967) _Psychological Types_ in _The Collected Works_. Vol. 6, 2nd edn. (Princeton NJ: Princeton University Press [1971]).

_____ (1975) _Letters_, vol. 2, ed. G. Adler, and A. Jaffe (Princeton NJ: Princeton University Press).

_____ (1990) 'Dreams and Psychoanalysis,' in _Dreams_, Part 1 (Princeton NJ: Princeton University Press).

Jung, Emma (1957) _Anima and Animus_ (Dallas TX: Spring Publications [1985]).

Kenevan, Phyllis B. (1999) _Paths of Individuation in Literature and Film: A Jungian Approach_ (Lanham MD: Lexington Books).

Keown, Damien (1996) _Buddhism: A Very Short Introduction_ (Oxford: Oxford University Press).

Kieslowski, Krzysztof (1993) in Danusia Stok (ed. and trans.) _Kieslowski on Kieslowski_ (London: Faber and Faber).

_____ (1999) 'The Inner Life is the Only Thing that Interests Me,' in *Lucid Dreams: The Films of Krzysztof Kieslowski* (ed.) Paul Coates (Trowbridge, Flicks Books).

Kim Ki-duk (2004) Interview with the director, *Spring, Summer, Autumn, Winter... and Spring* (London: Tartan Video DVD).

Kluger, Jeffrey (2011) *The Sibling Effect* (New York: Riverhead Books).

Knox, Bernard M.W. (1995) 'Essay: On Looking Back To Envision the Future,' *Cosmos* www. cosmos-club.org/journals/1995/knox.html accessed 15 June 2005.

Konigsberg, Ira (1996) 'Transitional Phenomena, Transitional Space: Creativity and Spectatorship in Film,' *Psychoanalytic Review* 83, 6 (December) 865–89.

Kübler-Ross, Elisabeth (1969) *On Death and Dying* (London: Tavistock Publications).

_____ (1995) *Death is of Vital Importance* (Barrytown, NY: Station Hill Press).

Lamb, Wally (2008) *The Hour I First Believed* (New York, Harper Collins).

Lane, Anthony (2011) 'Time Trip,' *The New Yorker* (30 May) www.newyorker.com/arts/critics/cinema/2011/05/30/110530crci_cinema_lane#ixzz21YPJniOt accessed 24 July 2012.

Laplanche, Jean and J.-B. Pontalis (1973) *The Language of Psychoanalysis* (New York: W.W. Norton & Co).

Lowery, David (2004) 'Reversing the Gaze,' (7 November) www.road-dog-productions.com/reviews/archives/2004/11/birth.html accessed 28 May 2007.

Mack, Alan (2011) Review of *The Tree of Life, Little White Lies* (7 July) www.littlewhitelies. co.uk/theatrical-reviews/the-tree-of-life-15546 accessed 18 July 2011.

Main, Roderick (2004) *The Rupture of Time: Synchronicity and Jung's Critique of Modern Western Culture* (Hove: Brunner-Routledge).

Mansfield, Victor (2002) *Head and Heart: A Personal Exploration of Science and the Sacred* (Wheaton, Ill.: Quest Books).

Meade, Michael (2010) *Fate and Destiny: The Two Agreements of the Soul* (unnamed location: Greenfire Press).

Mitchell, Stephen A. (1993) *Hope and Dread in Psychoanalysis* (New York: Basic Books).

_____ (2003) *Can Love Last? The Fate of Romance over Time* (New York & London: W.W. Norton & Co).

Moacanin, Radmila (2010) *The Essence of Jung's Psychology and Tibetan Buddhism*, 3rd edn. (Boston: Wisdom Publications).

Mogenson, Greg (1992) *Greeting The Angels: An Imaginal View of the Mourning Process* (Amityville, NY: Baywood Publishing).

Mogotsi, Lebo (2005) 'Challenges Facing the South African Gold Mining Industry,' *The Alchemist* (38) 15–17, www.lbma.org.uk/publications/alchemist/alch38_safrica.pdf accessed 30 April 2006.

Neumann, Erich (1954) *The Origins and History of Consciousness* (Princeton NJ: Princeton University Press [1973]).

_____ (1969) *Depth Psychology and a New Ethic* (New York: G. P. Putnam's Sons).

Ng, Yvonne (2005) 'Fate and Choice in Kieslowski's *Blind Chance*,' *Kinema*, 24, Fall, 68–81.

O'Connor, L. E., J.W. Berry, J. Weiss, D. Schweitzer and M. Sevier (2000) 'Survivor Guilt, Submissive Behaviour, and Evolutionary Theory: the Down-Side of Winning in Social Comparison,' *British Journal of Medical Psychology* 73 (4) (December) 519–530.

Ortega y Gasset, José (1957) *In their Choice of Lovers both the Male and Female Reveal their Essential Natures* (New York: World, Meridian Books), cited in Dovalis, 250.

Paracelsus (1967) *The Hermetic and Alchemical Writings* (New Hyde Park, NY: University Books).

Pauling, Lowman and Ralph Bass (1961) Lyrics 'Dedicated to the One I Love' www. lyricsfreak.com/m/mamas+the+papas/dedicated+to+the+one+i+love_20087273.html accessed 4 April 2011.

Perez, Gilberto (2005) 'Loretta Young,' *Sight and Sound* 15, 10 (October), 38–41.

Placzkiewicz, Jerzy (2007), *Tango in Poland, 1913–1939: Todo Tango The Academy.* http://66.33.36.31/fvc/websites/todotango/www/english/biblioteca/cronicas/tango_en_polonia.asp accessed 6 February 2008.

Racine, Jean Baptiste (1677) *Phèdre* (tr.) Robert Bruce Boswell (Act 1, Scene 3). www.fullbooks.com/Phaedra.html accessed 3 March 2011.

Romanyshyn, Robert D. (1982) *Psychological Life: From Science to Metaphor* (Austin TX: University of Texas Press).

Ronnberg, Ami (ed.) (2010) *The Book of Symbols* (Cologne: Taschen).

'Ronnie' (2003), 'Patience & Prudence: One Hit Wonders of 1956,' (14 May) http://earcandy_mag.tripod.com/rrcase-patienceprud.htm accessed 17 July 2007.

Rose, Gilbert J. (2004) *Between Couch and Piano* (New York: Brunner-Routledge).

Rose, Steve (2011) 'Jessica Chastain: Ascent of a Woman,' *The Guardian* (27 September) www.guardian.co.uk/film/2011/sep/27/jessica-chastain-interview accessed 28 September 2011.

Rothenberg, Rose-Emily (2001) *The Jewel in the Wound* (Wilmette, Illinois: Chiron Publications).

Sacks, Oliver (2007) *Musicophilia: Tales of Music and the Brain* (London: Picador).

Samuels, Andrew (ed.) (1985) *The Father: Contemporary Jungian Perspectives* (London: Free Association Books).

Samuels, Andrew, Bani Shorter and Fred Plaut (1986) *A Critical Dictionary of Jungian Analysis* (London: Routledge & Kegan Paul).

Scarry, Elaine (1999) *On Beauty and Being Just* (Princeton: Princeton University Press).

Schabenbeck-Ebers, Yola (2006), Personal communication (6 June).

Skar, Patricia (2010) 'The Matrix of Music and Analysis,' in Ashton and Bloch, 77–92.

Sobchack, Vivian (2004) *Carnal Knowledge: Embodiment and Moving Image Culture* (Berkeley, CA: University of California Press).

'Sophiatown' entry in Wikipedia http://en.wikipedia.org/wiki/Sophiatown%2C_Gauteng accessed 29 April 2006.

Stein, Murray (1980) 'Liminality,' *San Francisco Jung Institute Library Journal*, (Autumn) cited in Joanna Dovalis (2003), 99.

—— (1983) *In MidLife* (Putnam, Connecticut: Spring Publications).

—— (1993) *Solar Conscience/Lunar Conscience: Essay on the Psychological Foundations of Morality, Lawfulness and the Sense of Justice* (Wilmette, Ill: Chiron).

Sussillo, Mary V. (2005) 'Beyond the Grave – Parental Loss: Letting Go and Holding On,' *Psychoanalytic Dialogues*, 15 (4), 499–527.

Tarnas, Richard (2006) 'Jung, Cosmology, and the Transformation of the Self,' Paper delivered at the Pacifica Institute, 2006.

Thomson, David (2011) 'Terrence Malick,' *The Guardian* (21 April) www.guardian.co.uk/film/2011/apr/21/terrence-malick-david-thomson accessed 9 March 2012.

Toh Hai Leong (1996) 'Krzysztof Kieslowski's 'Trois Couleurs' Trilogy: The Auteur's Preoccupation with (Missed) Chances and (Missed) Connections,' *Kinema* (Spring) www.kinema.uwaterloo.ca/tohgp961.htm accessed 30 October 2005.

Turan, Kenneth (2011) Review of *The Artist* in *The Los Angeles Times* (25 November) Calender D4.

Ulanov, Ann Belford and Barry Ulanov (1994) *Transforming Sexuality: The Archetypal World of Anima and Animus* (Boston: Shambhala).

Von Franz, Marie-Louise (1964) 'The Process of Individuation,' in C.G. Jung (ed.) *Man and His Symbols*, 157–254.

Von Franz, Marie-Louise (1980) *On Divination and Synchronicity: The Psychology of Meaningful Chance* (Toronto: Inner City Books).

—— (1992) *Psyche and Matter* (Boston: Shambhala).

—— (1999) *The Cat: A Tale of Feminine Redemption* (Toronto, Inner City Books).

Wetzler, Lawrence A. (2010) 'In You More Than You: The Lacanian Real, Music, and Bearing Witness,' in Ashton and Bloch, 143–59.

Wilson, Emma (2000) *Memory and Survival: The French Cinema of Krzysztof Kieslowski* (Oxford: Legenda).

Winnicott, D. W. (1960) 'Ego Distortion in Terms of True and False Self,' in *The Maturational Process and the Facilitating Environment* (New York: International Universities Press [1965]).

—— (1971) *Playing & Reality* (London and New York: Tavistock Publications).

Woodman, Marion (2004) 'Worshipping Illusions,' *Parabola* 29, 2 (Summer) 64.

Wrye, H. K. (2002) 'Borders, Boundaries and Thresholds: Establishing the Frame and Setting Fees,' Unpublished lecture.

Yeats, William Butler (1893) 'The Lake Isle of Innisfree,' in *Poems*. A. Norman Jeffares (ed.) (London: Macmillan [1962]).

Žižek, Slavoj (2001) *The Fright of Real Tears: Krzysztof Kieslowski between Theory and Post-Theory* (London: bfi).

INDEX